Donato Bramante,
Santa Maria presso San Satiro, Milan,
ca. 1480–1490, interior.

Donato Bramante,
Santa Maria presso San Satiro, Milan,
ca. 1480–1490, rear façade along via del Falcone.

Donato Bramante,
Cloister of Santa Maria della Pace, Rome,
ca. 1500–1504, lower order.

Donato Bramante,
Cloister of Santa Maria della Pace, Rome,
ca. 1500–1504, upper order.

Donato Bramante,
Cloister of Santa Maria della Pace, Rome,
ca. 1500–1504, corner of the lower order.

Donato Bramante,
Belvedere courtyard, Rome,
ca. 1504–08, corner of the upper courtyard.

Donato Bramante,
Belvedere courtyard, Rome,
ca. 1504–1508, corner of the upper courtyard.

Donato Bramante,
Canonica di S. Ambrogio, Milan,
ca. 1492–1499, porch.

Donato Bramante,
Canonica di S. Ambrogio, Milan,
ca. 1492–1499, detail of the tree-columns.

Donato Bramante,
Canonica di S. Ambrogio, Milan,
ca. 1492–1499, detail of the tree-columns.

Donato Bramante,
Parish Church, Roccaverano,
ca. 1509, minor apse.

Donato Bramante,
Parish Church, Roccaverano,
ca. 1509, main façade, Doric order.

Donato Bramante,
Nymphaeum, Genazzano,
ca. 1507–1511, detail.

Donato Bramante,
Nymphaeum, Genazzano,
ca. 1507–1511, detail.

Donato Bramante,
Nymphaeum, Genazzano,
ca. 1507–1511, detail.

Donato Bramante,
Santa Maria del Popolo, Rome,
ca. 1505–1509, choir.

The MIT Press
Cambridge, Massachusetts and London, England

Translated from the Italian by Huw Evans

Published with the support of the Graham Foundation
for Advanced Studies in the Fine Arts, Chicago, and
the Politecnico di Milano

PIER PAOLO TAMBURELLI
ON BRAMANTE

With photographs by Bas Princen

CONTENTS

INTRODUCTION

In 1934, in a provincial magazine, Giulio Carlo Argan published an essay entitled "Il problema del Bramante."[1] Argan asked himself what was the object of Bramante's work, what was at stake in his approach to architecture. His answer was that this work was devoted entirely to space: Bramante's architecture was a "spectacle of space."[2] The exploration of space had no need to look for technical or moral justifications; space was sufficient as the scope of a research that could be conducted without pretext and without prejudice; architecture did not have to take refuge in statics or in literature. Argan was right: Bramante's problem was space. But what is *space*? What does it mean to work on space? Why do we attach cultural value to it? In short, just what is *Bramante's problem*?

Bramante's problem is space, the *possibility of space*: the possibility of *producing space* and the possibilities that are then *laid down in space*. This is a problem of *logic* (if and how space can be limited) and of *politics* (what actions can be carried out in space thus delimited). There is nothing new about seeing Bramante's architecture in this way. *Logical work* and *political work* appear already with Vasari, who inserted two observations that highlight these aspects at the beginning of his "Life of Bramante." On the one hand, the political dimension of the opportunity that arose with Julius II's papacy:

> ... no less a part was played in all this by the election at that time of Julius II, an energetic pope anxious to make his mark on posterity. And it was both our and his good fortune, something which only happens rarely to men of great genius, to find such a prince at whose expense Bramante was able to show the extent of his talent and his ability to overcome difficulties in architecture.[3]

On the other hand, the derivative and highly formalized character of Bramante's work:

> For while the Greeks were the inventors of architecture and the Romans their imitators, Bramante not only taught us new things by imitating them, but added very great beauty and complexity to the art, an embellishment that is plain to us today.[4]

Despite this authoritative precedent, any interpretation that tries to see Bramante's work as *logical–political work*, discerning in it *a universal hypothesis* made accessible *through the experience of space*, has to reckon with an undeniable fact: neither "universal architecture" nor "space" were expressions used by Bramante and his contemporaries. It was 1615 before Scamozzi spoke of "universal architecture;"[5] while "space," after a mention by Leon Battista Alberti,[6] does not appear in the architectural debate until November 1893, with Schmarsow's inaugural lecture at the University of Leipzig.[7] In this sense to speak of Bramante in terms of "universalism" and "space," and thus to view his architecture as *logical work* and *political work* is, at least in part, anachronistic. This anachronism,[8] to which I shall return throughout the book, trying to justify it, is based simply on what I believe it is possible to see in Bramante's buildings, on the almost offensive clarity of the intellectual work that is still entirely discernible in those buildings.

For contemporary architects, stories about Bramante risk having the same effect as the chivalric tales had on Don Quixote. And in fact, comparing Bramante with our everyday reality, it would be easy to start grumbling: to look back with nostalgia on the *bella maniera degli antichi* and draw the conclusion that there can be no logical rigor and spatial richness in buildings that are asked solely to communicate rudimentary promotional messages and contain the maximum saleable floor area. Browse through the issues of any architectural magazine that has managed to survive from 1970 to the present day and you will see how space has been progressively wiped out, the void has dried up, double-height rooms have vanished, atriums have shrunk, staircases have been crippled, porticoes have perished. Neoliberal wisdom has concluded that space is something we can do without; even more pointless is an intellectual practice of space—far better to replace this overambitious kind of work with a craft industry specialized in luxury articles. This tendency has been associated, at least in Europe and North America, with a growing inability to assign public value to the realization of spaces and buildings. Thus the more general *dearth of space* has been accompanied by a *decline in public space*, whose care is now considered a pastime for well-meaning but not very bright souls, the kind who dabble in building shacks and painting walls in order to receive subsidies and entertain children, apparently the only users of such space. This progressive reduction and infantilization of an ever more residual public sphere seem to lay waste to any possible *common place*,[9] leaving architecture more or less without purpose. Architecture in fact is *public art*. And in the absence of a public dimension, it becomes a meaningless activity, like music in a country of the deaf.

Today this rather unpromising condition goes hand in hand with the most dramatic growth that the cities of this planet have ever seen. There is less and less space, but more and more buildings. So contemporary architecture finds itself in a curious situation, in which bulimia (ever more buildings, ever bigger cities, an increasingly artificial planet) seems to coincide with depression (less sharing of common goals, less acceptance of responsibility, less and less desire to leave memories to the human beings who will come after us). The curious consequence of all this is that architecture, understood as art, as intellectual production, today finds its survival under threat and, at one and the same time, in a particularly propitious state for new experiments. In fact, in a context in which no other activity seems to be interested in anything that is not limited to the present or the immediate future, and in which it no longer appears necessary for anything to be shared, architecture has ended up being the only art that still exhibits an *extended* temporal horizon and a *common* destiny. Thus architecture acquires, in spite of its traditional (and never abandoned) penchant for the richer and the stronger, an unsuspected power of criticism, almost as if the loss of an explicit mission assigned to it by society had made it strangely freer than in the past and even surprisingly freer than other forms of art. In the face of these singular conditions, it is worth taking a look back at what was the most glorious (and ruinous) effort in the history of Western architecture and asking ourselves if it still concerns us, if we are still able to grasp its glory, and if we are still embarrassed by its failure. From this point of view, a comparison—even a rather clumsy one—with Bramante and his cultural project is useful in order both to redefine the sense of this hypothesis (what could, roughly speaking, be called "classicism") and to assess whether it is worth persevering with under such different conditions. A book on Bramante is therefore a book on architecture as *public art*, on the possibility that common experiences and emotions exist (as well as experiences and emotions *of the community*),[10] on the possibility of laying down these common experiences and emotions in space and basing a possible form of art on them. And it is also, perhaps, a modest attempt to evoke the external conditions that this form of art would need—the political conditions of a world slightly less hostile to what we all share.

This book contains no new research in the archives, no new surveys. There are no discoveries, not even any new attributions. There is no mention of watermarks and no one has gone rifling through the parish registers or notarial records. The arguments of this book are based solely on firsthand knowledge of the works[11] and on the literature already published on the subject, which has been freely utilized to construct a discourse focused predominantly on contemporary architecture. The account of Bramante's exploits is not even presented in chronological order but starts in Rome, at a time when the architect was already quite old, and then proceeds through the various episodes of his career. I believe in fact that in his Roman period Bramante's architecture attained a clarity that permits a better understanding of the earlier Milanese period too. For anyone interested in approaching Bramante's work, there is Arnaldo Bruschi's excellent introduction, the so-called "little Bruschi," the synthesis of his mammoth monograph of 1969 rewritten for the English translation of 1977.[12]

In the extensive literature on Bramante there are several works I consider decisive: the beautiful "life" written by Giorgio Vasari (1550, then marginally expanded in 1568); Heinrich von Geymüller's studies on the drawings in the Uffizi collection, later included in his book on *Les projets primitifs pour la basilique de Saint Pierre de Rome* (1875); Giulio Carlo Argan's "Il problema del Bramante" (1934), Renato Bonelli's penetrating—and incredibly hostile—*Da Bramante a Michelangelo* (1960); Arnaldo Bruschi's monumental research (1969), which turns Bonelli's judgment on its head while taking up many of his insights; the studies collected in the volume of *Studi bramanteschi* published to coincide with the celebrations of 1969;[13] and finally the essays written by Christof Thoenes since the 1980s. To these writings we must add the collection of drawings assembled with infallibly Bramantesque taste by Paul Letarouilly in his *Édifices de Rome moderne* (1855). In relation to these publications, which for me clearly uncover the meaning of Bramante's work, this book could even be said to be somewhat superfluous, in the sense that it contains nothing that a combined (and a bit extreme) reading of these contributions does not already provide. What distinguishes this latest attempt from its venerable forerunners is its viewpoint. This is a book written by an architect, not a historian, ("I write, then, as an architect who employs criticism rather than a critic who chooses architecture..."),[14] and it is guided by the thought that anyone who has had the inconsiderate idea of practicing the same profession ought to tackle the work of an artist like Bramante in the most direct way, *judging* it and perhaps *siding* with it, even—in a way—*sharing responsibility* for it, however ridiculous that may sound.

Starting out from this indisputably unrefined premise, Bramante's work is used as a pretext to present arguments that should not be attributed to him but are, rather, the logical conclusions to be drawn from his work with respect to the problems faced by architecture today. Thus, along with Vasari, Bruschi, and Thoenes, the terms of reference of this book on Bramante are Giorgio Grassi, Rem Koolhaas, Aldo Rossi, and James Stirling. These names—not so many after all, and always the same ones—pop up unannounced throughout the book (a bit like Inspector Clouseau's belligerent sidekick, hiding in the refrigerator or the washing machine to attack him), keeping us alert by pointing out the contemporary problems to which Bramante's work can be related. While this highly interpretative hypothesis might seem inappropriate or even incorrect,[15] I would like to stress that the title of this book is *"On"* Bramante, not *"About"* Bramante. This book, which does not "always want to give the impression of being very clever,"[16] is not a *history book*, but a *book on architecture* and (like all books of architecture that are not just pointless) it serves the purpose of producing, or getting people to produce, slightly less ugly buildings than would otherwise have been the case.

Finally, however obstinately this may be a *book on architecture*, there are no practical proposals to be found here. Bramante ended his career by persuading the pope to demolish St. Peter's and then died without having been able to rebuild it, leaving behind the most ideologically lethal heap of ruins in European history.[17] On such a case one cannot hope to base any manual, nor to found any school—and I am certainly not going to be the one to try.

The same attitude defines the use of the images that accompany the text and the photographs by Bas Princen that are presented alongside them. Images and photographs do not illustrate the subject. They simply present a parallel account, one that does not pretend either to document Bramante's work exhaustively or to adhere fully to the arguments presented in the book. Just as the book sets out to keep the void apart from the walls that define it, it maintains a separation between text and image. At the same time, it makes clear that it is not possible to think of the text in isolation, without the images, without their richness and blessing, and neither is it possible to use the images without the text, without the discipline it imposes. In this sense the book chooses to be somewhat difficult, at least in comparison with those so easy-to-read *catalogues of things we really like* which plague contemporary architectural literature.

I have written this book over the last fifteen years, with long breaks, while I taught at the Berlage Institute in Rotterdam, the University of Illinois in Chicago, the Graduate School of Design of Harvard University, the Technische Universität in Vienna and, above all, the Politecnico di Milano. During this period I published several things on Bramante: a text that was in a way a work program for what was to come after ("Space, or Bramante's Problem," which appeared in *San Rocco* in 2014) and a long digression, presented again here as an intermezzo ("Dante, Giotto, Piero, Bramante," from *Log* in 2019). In addition, over the last five years I have been preparing, together with Kersten Geers and Vittorio Pizzigoni, a voluminous anthology of writings on Bramante that have not been very accessible in English up to now. This work, which we hope to conclude and publish soon, has provided a fundamental opportunity for an exchange and discussion of ideas and has contributed a great deal to clarifying my arguments.

This book was written in parallel with projects and texts produced for baukuh and editorials and articles written for *San Rocco*.[18]

There are certainly similarities between those writings and this book on Bramante, but there is also a fundamental difference of responsibility and tone. Unlike the collective texts, this book has not been subjected to an "internal negotiation," and does not assume the responsibility of speaking for an entire group of people. I don't believe that this feature makes the book any more sincere; on the contrary it just makes it more irresponsible—and perhaps slightly more enjoyable as a result. Another important aspect that distinguishes this book from my previous writings is the difference in breadth, pace, and precision that corresponds to the choice of a different language—Italian, whereas the articles for *San Rocco* were all written in English. There are several reasons for this scarily counterproductive choice. One is that Bramante never left Italy and the sources (primary and secondary) are almost all in Italian. But the fundamental reason is that I would not have been able to write a book so full of pretensions directly in English. For once I wanted to be precise, and I needed a means I could trust completely. The choice was between a language I could wield to its full potential and one I am only able to use on condition of sticking to a syntax that is little more than primitive. Writing in Italian, in this case, has signified not accepting the brutal simplifications that would have been imposed by the elementary level at which I express myself in English. This is not going to be the most glaring naivety in this book, and at least the choice of language corresponds to the naivety and the ambition and the desire for complexity of all the rest. This complexity, this *difficulty*, is something I do not wish to renounce. And it is also a reason for this book on Bramante, which when all is said and done is a defense of architecture and, in a certain sense, of Italy, a defense of its unjustifiable excess of architecture, so evident to anyone who looks at it with a bit of attention:

> In Italy nothing is commoner than to find an architectural display wholly disproportionate, and even unrelated, to the social purpose it ostensibly fulfills, and to the importance or prosperity of the individuals or communities responsible for its existence. Princely gates, more imposing than those of a great mansion, lift up their heads in the loneliest places of the Campagna, but nothing glorious goes in. They lead, and have always led, to unpeopled pastures or humble farmsteads.[19]

Bramante did not *choose* Roman architecture; Roman architecture was already there, enormous and unavoidable. In the same way, it would never occur to anyone to *choose* Bramante. Bramante is already here, equally enormous and equally unavoidable. The only personal thing that I feel I can say about Bramante is that I didn't go looking for him.

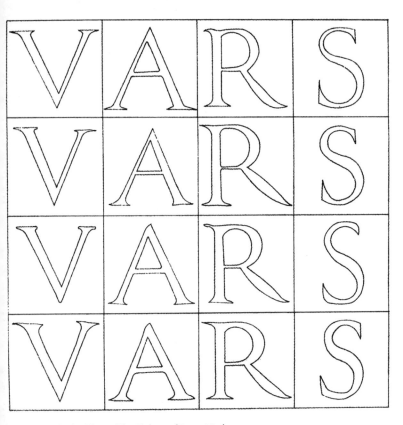

Lettertypes in the frieze of the Cloister of Santa Maria
della Pace, Rome, ca. 1500–1504, drawing P. Basso,
E. Cappella, from T. Carunchio, *Il Chiostro di S. Maria
della Pace: Note e considerazioni alla luce del recente
rilievo critico di precisione*, in "Quaderni dell'Istituto
di Storia dell'Architettura," n.s., 1-10, 1987.

Italiam non sponte sequor
(Aeneis, IV, 361)

PART I
LOGICAL WORK

INDIFFERENCE

1   Rome, *wie ich sie vorfand*

According to Vasari, Bramante left Milan with some cash and, by being very careful with it, was able not to work and to devote himself instead to exploring the Roman Campagna and surveying the ruins of the ancient city:

> Bramante had brought some money with him from Lombardy and earned some more by doing certain things in Rome. He managed this with extreme economy, as he wanted to remain independent and at the same time not to have to work, so that he would be able to measure with ease all the ancient buildings in Rome. And setting about this task, he wandered solitary and absorbed around the city; and in a short space of time he had measured all the buildings in Rome and in the surrounding countryside. He did the same as far as Naples, and everywhere he knew that there were relics of antiquity. He measured everything at Tivoli and Hadrian's Villa, and as will be related in the proper place, made great use of what he found.[1]

Bramante had been forced to flee the city where he had spent the previous twenty years to avoid being caught up in an invasion.[2] He was fairly old for the period (fifty-five when he moved to Rome—all that walking around the ruins must have been exhausting). What was he looking for?

Bramante had not chosen to go to Rome to study the classical world. The wanderings through the ruins were not to occupy his time because he was short of work.[3] They did not stem from any personal need. They were a *reaction* to something unexpected that Bramante found. And what he found was the city itself. Rome was so different from all the cities he had known up to then that he at once felt the need for a period of study. Faced with the remains of a city that was far bigger than any of his own day, he was obliged to take a step back and reconsider his work.[4] This immense carcass of a city, of which traces could be seen everywhere in the countryside surrounding the small area that was still inhabited in the fifteenth century, immediately presented itself as a challenge (and a model) for Bramante.

Pier Paolo Pasolini, *Mamma Roma*, 1962.

The atmosphere in Rome in 1499 was hardly cheerful.[5] The ruins that Bramante encountered as he wandered *solitary and absorbed* were more like the ones ensnared in Pasolini's hostile and archaic lands than the austere but predictable ones of Poussin or the ones tamed by centuries of nostalgia that Goethe was going to find. Bramante's ruins were immense in comparison with the city embedded in their midst and, rather than melancholy, seemed to be steeped in bitter sadness. The unknown and not very refined author of the *Antiquarie prospetiche romane*[6] says that the remains of the ancient city make even the stones weep. In Rome the landscape was filled with:

> ... *templi sacri picti e di scultura*
> *che ne son parte impié e guasti in toto,*
> *facendo per piatà piangier le mura*[7]

Bramante tried to understand the city he had found—and that he was in no way looking for—precisely on the basis of its immediate presence. Ancient Rome was simply a fact of contemporary Rome, a part of the city "as found,"[8] a piece of the world, *wie ich sie vorfand.*[9]

Bramante eliminated nothing from the ruins *a priori*, not the metropolitan energy of a city that he sensed was far bigger than the biggest city he had ever seen,[10] not the traces of the terrifying catastrophe that must have destroyed it. In the ruins, Bramante recognized a wealth of formal solutions to be decoded and presented in the purity of their gleaming grammar, and he also recognized the mute and intractable energy that a past impossible to tame seemed to have left behind in the contemporary city. The architecture of antiquity was at once clarity and fright: a limpid catalogue of architectural knowledge and a deposit of desires that were no longer identifiable, but none the less violent for this.

In referring to the architecture of the Romans, Bramante was not particularly original: the whole of Renaissance architecture was based on an enthusiasm for the ancients. But if awe at the glory of Rome was something shared by all the architects of the Renaissance, Bramante was the only one who did not want to soften the city that he had found, who preferred the reality of the ruins to the myth of classical antiquity, who was willing to see in the ruins not just the magnificence of the buildings of the past but also the barbarous richness of their present state, to observe not just the walls but also the enormous distances that separated them.[11] And this attitude may simply have been due to the fact that Bramante took an interest in the ruins only *after* actually encountering them. If Mantegna was a classicist whose enthusiasm was all the greater the further he was from the world that he venerated (when compelled by Innocent VIII to come to Rome to paint the chapel of the Belvedere, he wrote "I'd feel better at home"[12]), for Bramante the ruins were just one piece of the world of the present—a piece the same as all the others. They were a problem and a resource for *now* and for *this city*.

The *solitary and absorbed* wanderings had an immediate effect. Among the ruins of ancient Rome Bramante found the pieces he needed to assemble a much more rigorous system of forms than the one he had employed in Milan. His repertoire changed, the solutions of the Lombard period were abandoned. This change of style, perhaps the most striking aspect of Bramante's production, has not failed to attract the attention of art historians. To understand his work it is necessary to start from this very point, from this glaring fact—and a fairly unusual one with regard to the kind of behavior that we tend to expect from an artist. The abrupt change that takes place between the cloisters of Sant'Ambrogio[13] and the cloister of Santa Maria della Pace[14] (and then again between that cloister and the Tempietto di San Pietro in Montorio[15]) seems to challenge our romantic preconceptions. And in fact many historians have been unable to forgive Bramante for not having imparted sufficient "unity" to his "artistic personality," going so far as to consign his extremely clear formal choices to the realm of the impossible. Bonelli has written:

> ... an artist cannot, in general, pursue in the same short period a figurative ideal like that of the Tempietto and at the same time negate it in his methods and results, as happened in the cloister of Santa Maria della Pace.[16]

And yet these choices were quite deliberate, as is evident from an unequivocal passage in a letter from Guglielmo della Porta to Bartolomeo Ammannati (circa 1560):

> Bramante asserted that anyone who came to Rome to practice as an architect had to strip himself, as a snake sheds its skin, of everything he had learned elsewhere, and he proved this himself with his own example, saying that before he saw this city he used to think himself an excellent painter and architect, but that after practicing for many years he became aware of his error, and this was the reason that, after having drawn a great number of the buildings of ancient Rome, of Tivoli, of

Praeneste, and many other places, studying, noting and learning something new every day, he opened the way to the good and regulated architecture of antiquity.[17]

It is precisely this *shedding of skin* in the move from Milan to Rome that we need to take as the starting point in our observation of Bramante's work. Just what changed? And what did not change?

The abrupt shift in style that characterizes Bramante's work stemmed entirely from the circumstances in which he found himself. The "Milanese Period" and the "Roman Period" are as different as can be imagined from a "Blue Period" and a "Rose Period"; the adoption of the new repertoire was not accompanied by a new season of the soul nor even by a new ideology; architecture in the style of antiquity did not become an ideal of life. In Rome, just as in Milan, Bramante worked within an "accepted tradition, yet one he had explored and made his own."[18] He did not choose a repertoire but limited himself to *using* what was already there: the artisan tradition in Milan, and the example of the ruins in Rome. When in Milan he did as the Milanese, when in Rome he did as the Romans. But in Rome Bramante was able to rely on his previous experience, and could therefore recognize that—under different conditions—he was doing the same work.

Between Milan and Rome, the shift of paradigm was unavoidable, but this difference could be exploited *critically*. Through the process of first combining the elements of one set of forms and then moving on to combine the elements of another set of forms, Bramante realized that the most interesting aspect of his work did not lie in the forms themselves, but in the procedures by which they were put together. Thus, the repetition of the same operations with different repertoires and the comparison of the respective results revealed the identity of the operations and the essential indifference of the repertoires with respect to the relationships established within them. The specific characteristics of the elements lost their importance and the regularity of their relations emerged instead. The symbolic and allusive aspects moved to the background and "the speculative, intellectual character of the operation of composition" became even clearer.[19] In Rome, and due to the evident difference in working conditions between Milan and Rome, Bramante recognized that his problem was still the same: how to impart order to a given set of forms. And he saw that this operation could always be repeated on the basis of the results of the previous operation. Each time the work on the forms could be the subject of further work; the logic that combined the forms could always be turned back on itself. It became evident that operations on architectural forms are recursive.[20]

In a passage that, at first sight, seems to be nothing but a rather banal introductory panegyric, Vasari sets Bramante's work against the background of a historical series stretching into the distant past:

> For while the Greeks were the inventors of architecture and the Romans their imitators, Bramante not only taught us new things by imitating them with new inventions, but added extreme beauty and difficulty to the art, the extent of whose embellishment we can now see today.[21]

Not only does Vasari acknowledge the derivative and recursive character of the operation that Bramante performed on the basis of the architecture of the Romans, he also notices that the operation the Romans had already carried out on the architecture of the Greeks was of the same kind.[22] Thus Vasari sees Bramante's cultural project as part of a much broader historical process, recognizing his work not only for itself, but also in all its long-term implications. In their imitation of the architecture of the Greeks, the Romans gave it a systematic tone unknown to the original. In his turn Bramante—*by imitating them with new inventions*—ascribes to the architecture of the Romans a precision that it never had. Each time the forms become more clearly defined, their relations more constant and regular. On each successive reinterpretation the repertoire becomes more measured; each new round is conducted with more rigor, each time the subjects of his study come out distilled and further rationalized.

3   *La bella maniera degli antichi*

Bramante and his contemporaries—all of them—set themselves the goal of the revival of classical antiquity.[23] This is perhaps the most conspicuous aspect not just of the architecture and art, but of the entire culture of the Italian Renaissance. For the whole of this culture, architecture came to be seen as the discipline best suited to the reconquest of classical measure—a measure that could then be extended to the other arts and to society in general. This special role assigned to architecture was based on a simple fact: in architecture the Roman models were evident and therefore much easier to imitate than those of the other arts. Few works of classical sculpture had survived, and hardly any paintings, whereas the Campagna was full of ruined buildings. Nothing else was so plentiful in Rome. Thus architects ended up forming the vanguard of the Italian Renaissance's *plan for the reconquest of the classical.*

Some went along with this plan out of conviction and others out of expediency. For Mantegna and Alberti, the forms of ancient Roman architecture implied a moral choice and carried a message for contemporary society. For them the antiquity of Rome was the embodiment of a completeness of meaning to be contrasted with an inexorably disappointing present.[24] The enthusiasm for these values knew no bounds: Palladio called his children Leonida, Marcantonio, Orazio, Zenobia, and Silla.[25] For Bramante, however, *la bella maniera degli antichi*[26] was just a repertoire of forms, devoid of any intrinsic moral value. Bramante was not interested in any revival: he accepted the classicizing fashion as a fact of his time, as a matter of taste on which everyone seemed to agree and that was not therefore worth questioning. This repertoire was simply accessible and workable, and provided an orderly and efficient system of forms, as well as one that was incredibly popular among the ruling classes of the day. For Bramante that was more than enough. The world around him was classicist and so he was classicist too ("Cause we are living in a material world/And I am a material girl").

Bramante did not ask himself about the ideals that led him to measure the ruins with so much dedication. He did not wonder where the ancients had gone, or why they had abandoned us. *Ubi sunt?* is a question he did not raise. The ancients may not have been there any longer, but their remains still were. And a sufficient reason for investigating them was the fact that they were enormous, and impossible to avoid.[27] There was no need for ideal motives, eternal values were not required. There were columns, friezes, bases, and pedestals and it was necessary to find a way to put them together. Nothing more. The ruins had to be taken at face value: they could be understood architecturally, *as walls, as vaults, as rooms*; if they also represented something, it was a secondary matter.

There was nothing sentimental about Bramante's *solitary and absorbed* wanderings. The theory that he derived from his excursions into the Roman Campagna was a theory of how to learn from ruins, of how to look at buildings that already existed (whether intact or ruined) and of how to use them to make new buildings. It was a theory of how to assemble the pieces he found, a theory of *composition*, of *montage*.

Bramante's wanderings are reminiscent of the ones that Aldo Rossi claims to have undertaken in order to write *The Architecture of the City*:

> I read books on urban geography, topography, and history, like a general who wishes to know every possible battlefield—the high grounds, the passages, the woods. I walked the cities of Europe to understand their plans and classify them according to types.[28]

The walks were hurried and exhausting, but also fairly untroubled. Bramante moved through this landscape with a degree of confidence. The pieces he came across seemed ready to be reconfigured in many different ways; the ruins proved unexpectedly upbeat:

> *dicono con faccia lieta che mille facce*
> *ha la storia, e che spesso chi è indietro*
> *è primo ...*[29]

Bramante constructed for himself the viewpoint that would allow him to observe these things in the most effective manner. He chose the most favorable starting conditions: he postulated the strict superficiality and complete accessibility of the forms, presupposing a total absence of mystery. The most important difference between him and his contemporaries lies in his refusal to look for secrets. For Bramante the essential is right in front of his eyes; *the riddle does not exist*. The ruins are free from any enchantment; the architecture of the Romans is in plain sight. There is nothing to seek beyond form: it is necessary to fasten onto the surface, sacrificing if anything the depths. Hold onto the hose[30] and let the heart go without qualms. The operation conducted by Bramante is the same as those of Ludovico Ariosto and Sergio Leone: knights and cowboys are fine precisely because no one believes in them any longer. While Giuliano da Sangallo[31] agonized over trying to balance the books between nature (a rudimentary tectonics), codified theory (Vitruvius), and reality (the ruins) without ever managing to free himself from his terribly convoluted initial hypothesis,[32] Bramante avoided making life unnecessarily complicated. For Bramante the only thing that counted out of everything that Giuliano tried to reconcile was the ruins (that is, reality). The rest was superstition. In Bramante's eyes the buildings of ancient Rome could be understood only if they were not unnecessarily steeped in a bath of nostalgia that inevitably ended up obscuring their formal logic. Like Machiavelli, who analyzed the history of Rome without worrying too much about the political theory of the Romans (commenting on Livy in great detail and drawing on Cicero only occasionally and somewhat reluctantly), Bramante studied the remains of Roman architecture in the belief that a theory of it could be deduced entirely from those ruins, without the need for anything else. Bramante reduced to a *means* what for all of his contemporaries was an *end*: he used the ruins with the pragmatism of someone repairing a tractor with parts from an old Ferrari.

Bramante seems to have been endowed with the unenviable talent of not believing in his work and yet doing it much better than anyone else. So, once in Rome, he did what he found to do there: give substance to the classical ideal that everyone was trying to revive, finally going beyond declarations of principle. Quite simply, Bramante did *the architecture that everyone would have liked to do*, with just this one difference: he actually knew how to do it.

Unknown author, illustration for
F. Colonna, *Hypnerotomachia Poliphili*,
Venice: Aldo Manuzio, 1499.

The moves with which Bramante made his entry onto the architectural scene of sixteenth-century Rome were of an unparalleled realism. His cultural approach was certainly *loftier* (more ambitious, more general, riskier), but at the same time *humbler* (blunter, rougher, more practical) than that of his contemporaries.[33] What would end up being seen as the foundation of the architecture of the High Renaissance was in the first place a work that demolished the moralistic premises of the very revival that it was accomplishing. Bramante freed the ruins from the ideological trappings heaped on top of them and set out to use the resources obtained in this way in the most direct and brutal manner. Bramante went straight to the point. The models that attracted his attention were the most obvious ones (the Basilica of Maxentius, the Pantheon, the sanctuary of Fortuna Primigenia, the Palatine hippodrome). He took possession of the "mine of references"[34] provided by the Roman Campagna in the same way that Derek Walcott commandeered the most spectacular elements of Homeric poetry (the names of the heroes, for instance) to speak of the fishermen and taxi drivers of the Caribbean. In *Omeros*, Walcott repeatedly declared that he had never read Homer's poetry in its entirety:

... "I never read it"
... "Not all the way through."[35]

Further on, to the objection

"The gods and the demi-gods aren't much use to us"

he responds:

"Forget the gods" ... "and read the rest"[36]

and

... "I have always heard
your voice in that sea, master, it was the same song
of the desert shaman, and when I was a boy

your name was as wide as a bay, as I walked along
the curled brow of the surf, the word 'Homer' meant joy,
joy in battle, in work, in death, then the numbered peace

of the surf's benedictions, it rose in the cedars,
in the laurier-cannelles, pages of rustling trees.
Master, I was the freshest of all your readers."[37]

For Bramante too there was no need for the courtesies of philology: the act of appropriation did not require a perfect knowledge of the thing that was being taken over: all that mattered was the need not to let such an evidently rich heritage go to waste and the urgency of the immediate aims to which it could be applied. The forms of the past did not serve to resuscitate the spirit of an age; they were simply resources that could be expropriated and immediately put to work.

4 No style

For Bramante the different families of forms could all be treated with the same attention and the same refinement. Not only was there no hierarchy between the different families, there was not even a hierarchy within each family. The forms were *logically equivalent*.[38] All of Bramante's architecture was placed on a single level: the Doric was as plausible as the Ionic or the Corinthian. Whatever Vitruvius might have had to say about it,[39] the Doric had not been rendered obsolete by more advanced forms. Paolo Portoghesi has rightly pointed out that

> Bramante's reinstatement of the Doric, with metopes and triglyphs, in the Tempietto di San Pietro in Montorio is a mark of his refusal to make preferential choices of taste between the orders and his recognition of a whole range of correct solutions.[40]

In Bramante's buildings the forms are always all on the same level. There are never any elements placed there as testimonies of another world—fragments of an accomplished classical universe displayed as models, like the pediment on columns that Giuliano da Sangallo stuck onto the front of the villa of Poggio a Caiano. Bramante avoided making a distinction between fully classical forms and vernacular ones. While in the architecture of Giuliano (and later Palladio) the elevated and the picturesque elements divide up their spheres of competence in the same way as Latin and the vernacular in contemporary literature,[41] for Bramante there could be no distinctions of level between forms. The only distinction was between the forms, all of them, and the world in which they are located. His stubborn multilingualism excluded the variety of genres, postulating a single, gargantuan genre that comprised not only forms derived from the Romans but all other possible forms. For Bramante, just as for Dante, the "mingling of styles" meant the "violation of all style."[42]

Bramante declares his indifference to style in the only one of his writings on architecture to have come down to us: his report on the lantern of Milan Cathedral known as the *Opinio*.[43] In his suggestions of how to complete the construction of the cathedral, Bramante goes into detailed morphological and spatial considerations, but makes not even the slightest reference to the question of style. As far as ornaments are concerned, the best thing is to copy what is already there:

> As for the ornaments, such as stairs, corridors, windows, masonries, pillars, and spires, what has been done above the sacristy allows us to understand a great deal, and even more from some drawings that were made at the time that this Cathedral was built. ...[44]

Gothic ornaments are fine. The Gothic cannot be treated as an ideological problem. It cannot be condemned morally. Since the Gothic is *already part* of the city, it has to be accepted: the Gothic should be understood through a formal analysis identical to the one applied to other families of forms. The Gothic is not a global alternative to classical antiquity, it is just another province of the empire of forms and thus can be treated with the same impeccable detachment, just like the Doric or the Ionic.[45] On the one hand, Bramante sets to work on the forms with great humility, without any futile arguments; on the other he is perfectly aware of the complexity and ambition of this work. He knows that the procedure of analysis and assemblage that he is proposing has immediate practical advantages (which he stresses in his report), but he is also aware that this operation is not as easy as he seems to be claiming. He knows that such an avowedly opportunistic method of working cannot be applied without a sophisticated theoretical basis and without specific expertise: "not without great ingenuity."[46]

Bramante's attitude toward the ornaments of Milan Cathedral is the same as the one he takes roughly twenty years later with regard to the ornaments of St. Peter's. When the workers ask him for designs for the capitals of the pilasters in the nave, Bramante tells them to go and copy the ones in the Pantheon and to scale them up from five to twelve palms, so that they would be "as well carved and with the same projection of the leaves and with the same amount of details as have those."[47]

Bramante does not try to eliminate the arbitrary nature of the choice of any repertoire of forms; he does not conduct a crusade to

Antonio da Sangallo the Younger for Bramante,
drawing of Corinthian capital for St. Peter's,
UA 6770r, Galleria degli Uffizi, Florence.

liberate architecture from style (efforts that, without exception, have led to the replacement of one style by another[48]). He simply strips the choice of style of any expressive intent. It is precisely the fact that style conveys no meaning that makes it possible to use it. Only the *use* of style has meaning, not the *choice*. If the question is: "In what style should we build?"[49] Bramante's answer is: "In whichever you prefer." And this is simply because the question "In what style should we build?" is for him completely nonsensical, as there is only *one* architecture and the most important thing about it is that is valid *for everyone*.

Classicism is nothing but the commitment to use any style and therefore to accept *all styles*: a radical *stylism*, rooted in the conviction that all styles have equal value, and any convention is fine so long as it is recognized as a convention and nothing "authentic" is required on which to found an artistic practice. Thus the *choice* of repertoire and the *content* of forms—things that have obsessed architecture from eclecticism to modernism to postmodernism and right up to the present day—can once more recede into the background and allow the questions of form to reemerge in all their complexity and richness. If there is only *one* repertoire, then it can't help but be universal.[50] And as *there is no choice* the only obligation with respect to this repertoire is to make good use of it, remembering above all that it is common currency. In this sense learning from Bramante means trying to imagine a work that *can be valid for everyone* and that immediately puts itself in a position where it *has to learn from everyone*.

5 Architecture implies the city

In Rome, at the beginning of the sixteenth century, the architecture of the ancient Romans was accessible to all. Its ruins were scattered around the landscape: everyone could see, measure, and understand them. Bramante's architecture was derived from these ruins, but for Bramante the fact that it was *derived* was much more important than the fact that it was derived *from the Romans*. The nature of the operation was much more important than the set of objects that made it possible.[51] It is precisely because the starting point of this work has not been chosen that it assumes a general value. Architecture is in fact a form of reflection on the city that is already there, and it establishes a connection with the people for whom it is intended precisely because it adopts as its specific material a world of forms that already belongs to them. So the *derivative* character of this architecture coincides with its *public* commitment, with its fidelity to cities that already exist and to people who already live in them.

Bramante's work always began *in medias res*. His operations were all carried out on pieces that were already available in the city. His position with respect to this set of given things was the same—banal and disconcerting—one that Dante took in the *Convivio* with respect to the vernacular, which was the thing that brought his parents together, "for they conversed in it."[52] Language is part of the poet's life from the start, and it is only on the basis of this already given language that poetry can be produced. In the same way, for Bramante, forms are already given *prior* to any possible work on architecture, and are given, very simply, in the form of the city: "architecture implies the city."[53]

In the city the different architectural cases are all given without distinction, accessible to all. The forms are all already there, *common* purely and simply as a result of their being there, ready to be encountered and observed and used by everyone, just like a lamppost on a street or a parking lot in front of a supermarket.

Once the city is recognized as the precondition of architecture, it becomes the objective of architecture as well. Thus the city is at one

Vitruvius, *De Architectura. Translato, commentato et affigurato da Cesare Cesariano*, 1521, Book II, XXXII.

and the same time the set of precedents that contribute to the solution of every new case (the toolbox that makes reflection on the city and transformation of the city possible) and the objective of any work of architecture (the totality to which any transformation of it makes reference). The city lays the foundations of architecture as its *material cause*, the set of all possible cases which architecture can deal with, as its *formal cause*, the set of all possible solutions to all possible new cases, and as its *final cause*, the objective of a work that can have no other purpose than to serve as the material infrastructure of human coexistence. It is no coincidence that the great transformation of architecture in the Renaissance was made manifest in the first place as the representation of an already existing piece of city. The drawing with which Brunelleschi "demonstrated" artificial perspective was not a new design proposal but an urban view: the baptistery of San Giovanni viewed from the door of Florence Cathedral.[54]

The consequence of a work that sees the city as both the precondition and the objective of architecture is *formalism*, the investigation of forms starting out from the awareness that they cannot be invented—because, very simply, they are already there. So the job of a *formalist* architecture is to understand and clarify the forms already given in the city, to select the forms best suited to desires and actions that already exist in the world, and so demonstrate that every architectural problem can be solved on the basis of the fundamental idea that all forms belong to everyone. *Formalism*, as adhesion to an already given repertoire, is therefore a commitment to observing the world, to recognizing the complexity of reality and working from there. Formalism implies the maximum of openness to all the situations which architecture has to deal with, the immediate expansion of the scope of its research.

An architecture founded on the city knows only two terms: the concrete datum with all its circumstances (the piece of land on which the building is to be sited, the desires of the clients, the financial and technological limitations, the legal requirements), i.e. the *particular*, and then the rule that brings the concrete case in line with a general law (all the knowledge deposited in the architecture of the past, the whole range of people to whom architecture is addressed), i.e. the *universal*. For Bramante, there was nothing between these two extremes: no *kinds*, no *characters*, no *types*. These expressions were mere *flatus vocis*. Bramante did not go along with the social determinism of *De re aedificatoria*[55] and did not venture along the path that would lead Serlio to devise his odious tables of correspondence, where houses resemble their owners like dogs do the old ladies who take them for walks.[56] Even when he worked on projects with clear functional and symbolic connotations, as in the case of the Palazzo dei Tribunali,[57] which was supposed to unite all the judicial offices of the papal state in a single enormous complex, Bramante avoided producing an unequivocal, transparent object whose function could be grasped without any prior experience of it. The mass of the Tribunali is deliberately opaque, its appearance intentionally hybrid and reticent. The *types* (*castle* and *palazzo*) seem to be the starting point for a demonstration of their nonexistence: since they coincide here, they cannot be independent and recognizable entities. In the immense bulk of the Tribunali, the distinctive features of the *castle* and the *palazzo* are canceled out: the *castle* is swallowed up in the urban discipline of the *palazzo* while the *palazzo* is intoxicated with the rustic arrogance of the *castle*, a bit like what would later happen at Caprarola and in Piacenza and in Bernini's marvelous third project for the Louvre.

In architecture the objectives and the preconditions are always already given, and these objectives and preconditions are at one and the same time the city. So the analogy is fixed and inevitable: every building refers to the city, not to nature, not to paradise, not to history, not to science.[58] Buildings prefigure only the city: "that wholly human and wholly artificial thing that is the city."[59]

This idea of architecture has a paradoxical consequence. If we go along with this hypothesis, it becomes necessary to admit that what is given—what is particular and accidental—is the city and what is universal and rational is architecture. It follows that if the city is the precondition for architecture, the ambition of architecture is always greater than the ambition of the city in which it is placed. The city in fact cannot be anything but itself; its complexity is that of reality.

Architecture on the contrary, as *project*, as an idea of the world realized in a concrete case but always implicitly extendible to innumerable other cases, implies a possible city and as such its ambition and responsibility are always greater than those of the city onto which it is grafted. This dual plane on which architecture acts also implies that architecture sometimes *has to ignore* the immediate problems of the city, that architecture cannot be extended to the whole of the city. Precisely because it is intrinsically a model, architecture cannot be entirely a solution; precisely because it is always analogy, it cannot allow itself to be metaphor.

6   Pantheon + Basilica of Maxentius

According to a tradition that is recounted by all the authors who have dealt with the question, Bramante pictured the new church of St. Peter's as the dome of the Pantheon mounted on the nave of the Basilica of Maxentius. Even Metternich and Thoenes, in their fundamental study of the early designs for St. Peter's, admit that they do not know where this *vox populi*, sometimes erroneously attributed to Vasari or Michelangelo, came from.[60] But even they were unable to resist the persuasive power of this explanation, which appears at once so convincing and so typical of Bramante's bent for sarcasm. And in fact it really does seem to have been his idea: to pile the most obviously monumental building of all those known to him on top of the second most obviously monumental building of all those known to him. The idea for the greatest church of Christianity was—very simply—*not to have ideas.* Even in the face of the immense pressure to come up with a symbolic response,[61] Bramante excluded all metaphor and treated St. Peter's as if it were just any church, as a problem of space, of the organization and experience of space. Thus Bramante had no compunction about using as a model for the design of the most important church in Christendom the Basilica of Maxentius, a building that, according to the *Golden Legend*, had collapsed (!) at the moment of Jesus Christ's birth.[62]

Once the hypothesis Pantheon + Basilica of Maxentius had been accepted and thus all the symbolic requirements associated with the project set aside, the problem of St. Peter's was confined to its architectural aspect. From this point on Bramante would have to solve an extremely complicated problem—but one that had the advantage of having already been *turned into a question of architecture.* In his designs for St. Peter's, Bramante limited himself to investigating this alone: how was it possible to get the dome (Pantheon) to fit onto the nave (Basilica of Maxentius). The problem was reduced to the design of a single formal device: the pier of the dome, which was given the

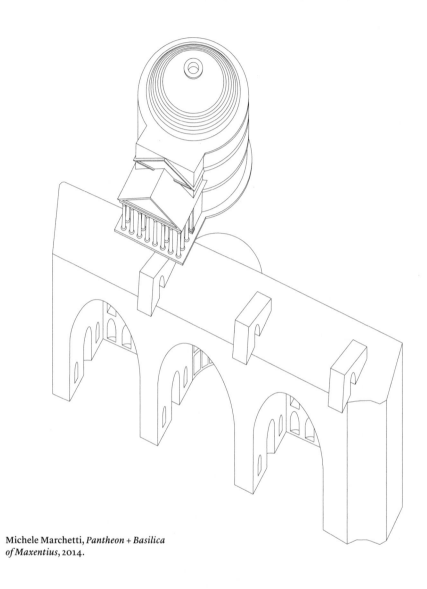

Michele Marchetti, *Pantheon + Basilica of Maxentius*, 2014.

task of ensuring the coexistence of the two basic models. All of Bramante's drawings for St. Peter's that have come down to us are devoted to the design of the pier and to a thorough examination of all its consequences for the surrounding space, of all its multiple echoes in the ambulatories and the aisles. In addition, as if the definition of the problem were not yet sufficiently abstract, the pier is studied *only in plan*. The problem of St. Peter's, for Bramante, was not only reducible to the *problem of the dome's pier*; it could be reduced even further, to the *problem of the plan of the dome's pier*. Slowly, in the series of these extraordinary plans of piers (studied in such persuasive fashion by Christof Thoenes), Bramante was able to reconcile the different pieces that made up his initial hypothesis. The Basilica of Maxentius and the dome of the Pantheon were adapted to one another, stripped of their original identities, and reassembled in a new configuration that made it possible for them both to be in the same place at the same time.

By proposing to construct the new basilica of St. Peter's as a sum of the dome of the Pantheon and the vault of the Basilica of Maxentius, Bramante reduced the Pantheon to a dome and the Basilica of Maxentius to a nave. Entire buildings became *parts* of a composition in which their original organization was chipped away in order to extract (in what was truly a technique of despoliation) semantically neutral pieces that could be used for new assemblages. The brutality with which Bramante treated antiquity seems susceptible to the same criticism that Pietro Bembo leveled at Giovan Francesco Pico. Significantly, Bembo resorted to architecture to make his position clearer:

> What could in fact be more absurd than wanting to take a multitude of diverse forms, differing even from one another, that have already been used by many others and trying to put them all together in a single form? As if when building a single temple you were to think you could take something from each of the many examples of different temples, built in a variety of images and styles. ... This could instead be called a sort of cobbling together or, if I may go so far, of begging. It is in fact what men used to do in times of famine, taking what they needed not from one but from many.[63]

Bramante would undoubtedly have felt sympathy for the plebeian urgency and brusque methods of *men in times of famine*—men whom he probably would have recognized as not so different from himself. Bramante seems to have felt the same sympathy for the elderly and the disabled, for whom, according to the *Simia*, a satirical dialogue published in 1517, the spiral ramp would be built to connect Earth to Heaven, allowing everyone to ascend it on horseback: "*per quam seniorum et debilium animae equestres possint scandere.*"[64]

UNIVERSALISM

7   Universal language

The work of systematizing the repertoire of forms derived from the architecture of ancient Rome, on which Bramante embarked at the beginning of the sixteenth century, has often been seen as a perfect case for the study of the origin of a true "architectural language." Not only does the architecture of the Italian Renaissance, with its regular application of the classical orders, seem to offer an example of such a "language" but, out of all the architects of the time, none appears to embody the systemic spirit and cult of grammar better than Bramante. In a slim and highly popular volume entitled *The Classical Language of Architecture*, John Summerson wrote:

> The reason I go straight for Bramante is this. It was he, more than anybody else, who reestablished the grammar of ancient Rome in buildings of pre-eminent consequence. [I]t was Bramante who set the seal on all this, who stated firmly and finally: "this is the Roman language—this and no other is the way to use it."[1]

Many other examples could be found: Bonelli speaks of "universal language,"[2] Bruschi of "architectural language of supposed 'universal' validity,"[3] Portoghesi again of "universal language,"[4] Lotz of "classical language."[5] These expressions take on somewhat different meanings in the various passages cited and are used with varying degrees of confidence.[6] Bonelli and Lotz utilize the expression frequently and assuredly; Bruschi seems more uncertain; Portoghesi is decidedly circumstantial.[7]

However confused this terminology might be, it is nevertheless incredibly insistent. So, it is worth asking if Bramante really saw buildings as vehicles of meaning. Did he want to use "a set of well-characterized forms" to address "a public already accustomed to them"?[8] Did he view architecture as "language"?[9] Did he want to *say* something with his buildings? Or, is it possible to understand his work even without resorting to such markedly (and somewhat unwittingly) interpretative terminology?[10] Finally, if it is not possible to treat architecture *as language*, is it still possible to assign it a *universal* ambition?

Perhaps a more appropriate terminology for the study of Bramante would be the old one. Instead of "language," the set of elements derived from the architecture of the ancient Romans could in fact be called an "order," as Bramante and his contemporaries did, although without much rigor. The term "order" can in fact be used to refer to the "system" and the "problems related to the coherence of the system," that undoubtedly characterized his work, without introducing any unnecessary hypotheses. Indeed, while "order" is just one of many words used by the architects of the Renaissance to refer to the coordinated system of forms that could be deduced from Roman architecture,[11] adopting it here at least leaves the question in its original terms, without proposing a relationship of the signified/signifier type to justify the use of the elements of classical architecture. All that "order" implies is a logical operation, one that *orders* a set of conventionally defined architectural elements.[12] In this sense the terminology of the time may be less naive than it at first appears: in the architectural theory of the Renaissance, "order" can denote the series of architectural elements that can be deduced from classical architecture (the so-called "five orders," such as the Ionic), the "order" of a building, or the particular combination of "orders" employed in a certain work (for example the combination of Doric, Ionic, and Corinthian in the Theater of Marcellus), or, finally, the set of all the "orders." This usage may not seem very clear, but it is not particularly different from that of concepts like "set" or "class," and shows how the notion of "order" is never separated from a multiplicity of "orders": in fact the construction of an "order" generates exactly the same complications as any other recursive operation.

Looking at the elements of architecture as parts of an "order" rather than a "language" allows us to conjecture that they are linked by regular relations without considering them as parts of a "code to transmit a message."[13] This does not mean denying the existence of ties between architecture and language. In fact, language is the principal means of production of architecture ("*pas de géométrie sans la parole*"[14]) and architecture remains steeped in the words that have produced it. However, this intimate connection of architecture with linguistic exchange is not sufficient to attribute messages to buildings. Buildings do not speak, and yet they are not completely mute either[15]—and it is always fairly easy to pretend that they can tell the tales that are most in fashion. By the way, architecture would be a decidedly less significant activity if buildings had nothing to do with language. But, once again, this is not the case: even though buildings do not speak, buildings are made for somebody to talk about them. Architecture cannot be elevated to the status of a language, but neither is it possible to remove it from the context of language. Architecture is a non-linguistic activity that is possible only in a linguistic context. Whether the statues of women that support the entablature of the Erechtheion really represent the women of Karyai and stage their imprisonment, architecture cannot say. Nor can it say whether the punishment of these women was just or unjust. Nor can it dispose of this question. It can only establish how much room the statues take up, what distance they are from one another, how long a shadow they cast at three in the afternoon.

In Bramante's buildings the choice of the orders can always be explained in terms of space, dimensions, pictorial effects. It's no good looking for symbols, there are no hidden meanings.

The cloister of Santa Maria della Pace, while it contains all the orders, is Ionic. Indeed the elements in the foreground are Ionic: the pilasters on pedestals and the entablature with the dedicatory inscription in Roman square capitals. This screen is applied in front of the Doric arches, from which it is only very slightly detached, and extends the fragility of the Ionic to the whole of the courtyard. The choice of the Ionic for a cloister dedicated to the Virgin Mary could be explained by the association between the Ionic and the female, which can be traced back to Vitruvius.[16] But if we really want to follow this theory, the order of the cloister ought to have been the Corinthian, which Vitruvius associates with the character of a virgin.[17] The Ionic order of the cloister of Santa Maria della Pace is more easily explained in formal terms: the Ionic has been chosen because it is flat, because it articulates the space without intruding on it and because it presents to the light a perfectly smooth face, wiping out any sculptural effect. Bramante does not wish to impinge on the volume of empty space, and so dresses the arches in the order that encroaches least on the courtyard. Besides, the Ionic order is the one that most accentuates the difference between the brightly lit slabs of the pilasters—stuck to the prism of void like fingertips on a misted-over pane of glass—and the shadows of the arches that separate them. The pilasters and to an even greater extent the pedestals are drawn into the space of the courtyard,[18] making the wall behind recede further back. Having defined the rule of this ground floor perfectly separated into a succession of fragile and brightly lit zones and areas of dense and deep shadow, the floor above is developed in a completely different way, with the frantic succession of the brackets and with the crude and still Lombard, deliberately provincial, Corinthian capitals, which distort the figure and make the uncertain and peremptory purity of the lower order stand out.

The Tempietto di San Pietro in Montorio is Doric. Its image is defined entirely by its sixteen Doric columns and the frieze with metopes and triglyphs. In this case too the choice of the order could be put down to Vitruvius's association of the order with virile heroism, a characteristic that could be attributed to the Christian martyr.[19] But there is no need to look for hidden messages here either. Once again, the choice of the Doric can be more easily explained on the basis of formal criteria. The Doric was chosen for the plasticity of its columns and for the regular rhythm of the frieze—both requirements that excluded not only the excessively pictorial Ionic, but also the not sufficiently axiomatic Corinthian. The implacable metrics of the Doric, with its correspondence of all the components of the order, assigns to the Tempietto a mathematical rigor that would not have been so evident if the architect had adopted the other—more indulgent—orders. In fact, Ionic and Corinthian friezes run continuously and indifferently above the columns. Bramante on the contrary wanted to stress the coordination of all the elements of the Tempietto, to expose its studied "difficulty," literally to proclaim that any problem of classical architecture could be resolved.

If it is not possible to explain Bramante's architecture by discovering messages within it, it is not because of a more general attitude of his toward the world. Bramante was in fact a decidedly loquacious man. His poems (which in the end are not even bad) are the proof of a keen desire for expression. So it was not a paradoxical authorial choice that led to his refusal to entrust messages to his buildings. Rather, it seems that it was his own experiments with poetry that led him to conclude there was not a lot that architecture could communicate. In his sonnet XVIII, Bramante used Milan Cathedral as a figure to describe the state of his hose. The holes in them were as big as the windows of the cathedral:

> *Immaginate un fico ben maturo,*
> *e tuta la lor forma intenderete,*
> *e gli ochi delle stringhe aguagliarete*
> *a una merlata rosa intorno a un muro.*
> *A chi volesse dir de le calcagna,*

de' varchi e de' pedugi e de' gegnocchi,
convería de scritura una campagna.
E le costure èn piene di pedochi,
e pareno un vestito de la Magna,
o ver del Domo le fenestre o gli ochi.[20]

Buildings can provide images to be used in poems. But Bramante never tries to do the reverse. The relations between architecture and language are not symmetrical: while architecture can be contained in language, language cannot be contained in architecture. Architecture's means are inevitably more limited.[21] Here it is worth considering an episode in which Bramante seems to try to get architecture to speak. The story is quite an amusing one. Vasari wrote:

> On a whim Bramante decided to have a frieze carved on the external façade of the Belvedere with some letters in the style of ancient hieroglyphs, to make a better show of his ingenuity and place there his name and that of the pope. He began it with "Julius II Pont. Maximus," and then made a portrait in profile of Julius Caesar, along with a bridge with two arches that stood for "Julius II Pont." and an obelisk from the Circus Maximus to represent "Max." The pope laughed at this and had him make the letters one ell in height and in the antique manner that we see today, saying that he had copied this silliness from Viterbo, where an architect called Francesco had put his name on a lintel above a door, carving a figure of St. Francis, an arch, a roof and a tower so that it said, in a manner of speaking: "Francesco master architect."[22]

As well as demonstrating once again Julius II's infallible judgment in matters of the figurative arts, this episode shows the clear limits that Bramante assigned to his experiment with hieroglyphs: just an inscription. Bramante's "silliness" did not stand out from the plane, did not modify the structure of the building, did not become architecture. The Belvedere hieroglyph was not a "duck."[23] Bramante did not try to make *architecture parlante.*[24]

An architecture that speaks would immediately render the work on space useless. If the relationship between architecture and human life could be linear, if architecture could speak directly about life, it would no longer make sense to work on the indirect relationship that memory

Long Island Duckling, from P. Blake, *God's Own
Junkyard: The Planned Deterioration of America's
Landscape*, New York: Rinehart and Winston, 1964.

establishes between spaces and the actions that occur in space. Only *if it is not language* can architecture be an understanding of past experiences, a memory of places to which we have reacted emotionally, a science of dimensions, of distances, of quantities of light.

In the history of Western architecture there have been many attempts to use buildings as signs, seeking to establish an unambiguous relationship between them and the "concepts" they are supposed to explain. Examples abound: doors in the shape of a mouth, libraries in the shape of open books, stores in the shape of a duck, shrines in the shape of a phallus. And yet the cock-shaped temple will never remind you of the experience of making love in the way that a room with the same closet and the same smell as a room in which you have already made love does, and the duck-shaped store will never evoke the taste of duck in the same way as the light that filters between the shutters of your grandmother's dining room. In architecture, the indirect link between spaces and experiences is always more convincing than the direct one between meanings and figures—which is not strictly impossible, but always too vague to communicate effectively and too weak to spark the imagination.

9   Text envy

If we examine the theories of Western architecture, we cannot fail to see that the royal road to affirming its intellectual value passes through the attribution to architecture of some characteristics of narration. Mere work on space does not seem to suffice and so architecture seeks a legitimation in the stories that it thinks it can tell. The premises for this age-old envy of the text can already be found in Vitruvius's encyclopedism:

> [The architect] should know a great deal of history because architects often include ornaments in their work, and ought to be able to supply anyone who asks with an explanation why they have introduced certain motifs.[25]

In this apparently inoffensive passage, an all too insecure author makes the sense of architectural choices depend entirely on a literary paradigm. Ever since, architects have been unable to forgo the intellectual prestige associated with narration. Rather than basing the authority of their discipline on a theory of space, they have preferred to rely for their legitimation on a much more facile analogy with literature—and this may also be the clearest proof of their lack of substance as intellectuals.

The fundamental step in this voluntary subjection of architecture to a rhetorical paradigm was taken by Leon Battista Alberti. Alberti, who had a legal and literary training and wrote about architecture (or at least started to write about it) before he had had any practical experience of it, was the first to treat the design of buildings as an explicit intellectual problem inserted in a precise cultural framework. He weighed up architectural choices in relation to their *pertinence*—that is, to the thematic coherence that was established between forms and meanings—thus laying down, as a measure of the suitability of those choices, a criterion based on content. The architectural "phrase" had to match its "content" and provide a rhetorically adequate expression of it. And since empty space could not be assigned any "content," this also meant that architecture could only be a discipline of the "full," of the solid, of the volume. Not coincidentally, its subject was defined, right at the beginning of *De re aedificatoria*, as *corpus quoddam*, "a form of body."[26] With these presuppositions, a theory of space—and therefore a theory of voids, a theory of what is not there—was immediately excluded.

10 Architecture as painting

The relationship between Bramante's work and that of Leon Battista Alberti has been the subject of very different interpretations. It will suffice to cite the extremes: for Bruschi it is a direct and fundamental relationship,[27] while for Metternich the chronology makes it hard to imagine an encounter between the two men and there are no real cultural ties between them.[28] In my opinion, the truth lies somewhere in between. Bramante certainly recognized in Alberti a model that, aside from class differences, allowed him to regard architecture as intellectual work; at the same time he saw clearly that he could not adopt his strategies.

Alberti's operation had been twofold. On the one hand, he had raised the status of architecture by associating it with humanist culture, and on the other he had brought the extraordinary production of the Tuscan artists of his time within the fold of humanism—with which, up until then, the art of Brunelleschi, Donatello, and Masaccio had had little to do.[29] The fundamental work for this operation was *De pictura*, which in this sense was a genuine "instant book," and one that was immediately translated into Italian (if indeed it had been written in Latin in the first place[30]). With *De pictura*, Alberti defined the artist (in this case the painter, but it would also hold for the architect) as:

> a sort of ideal rhetorician, a morally upright man learned in many things who acquires assured fame and fortune in society, parallel to Quintilian's model of the consummate orator-citizen.[31]

Bramante was no aristocrat. His education was that of a painter.[32] Cesariano, who had been one of his pupils and certainly thought highly of him, recognized his teacher's limits and wrote that Bramante was "*facundo ne li rimati versi de poeti vulgari, licet et fusse illiterato.*"[33] In terms of the prototype of the intellectual architect defined by Alberti, the *unlettered* Bramante was out of the running from the start. And this would not change even when Bramante was accepted into the literary circles of Sforza Milan, nor even when he would expound Dante for the pope. So Bramante had to bring into play an alternative hypothesis, one that could legitimate architecture as an intellectual activity on the basis of an almost exclusively visual culture, without any need for additional textual legitimation. Bramante was *unlettered*, and he knew it. As such, as an *unlettered* intellectual,[34] he founded his working hypothesis on the only culture of which he had a thorough command, that of a painter. Among Renaissance architects, Bramante was the one who most consciously evaded the paradigm established by Alberti, the one who made the most lucid attempt to put an end to the ostentation of labored metaphors and uncalled-for erudition that pollutes the history of European architecture. And he could do this precisely because of his highly unusual profile: it was because Bramante was *also* able to compose verse, was *also* able to expound Dante, that he could see architecture exclusively as an investigation of the experience of space.

Following Alberti's ideas, the majority of the architects of the Renaissance approached their work *from the viewpoint of the man of letters* (or—things that strangely coincided—*from the viewpoint of the sculptor or the woodworker*). From this perspective, buildings are agglomerations of elements combined according to a law of tectonic accumulation, i.e., aggregates of signs assembled in such a way as to convey a message. As such, buildings are fundamentally *solids* and it is not necessary to pay much attention to space in order to produce and understand them. Men of letters (like Alberti), sculptors (like Michelangelo, Sansovino, and Palladio) and woodworkers (like Giuliano and Antonio da Sangallo the Younger) were all agreed on proposing an architecture in which the solid (volumes, columns, statues) counted more than the void. This architecture aspired "to the beautiful architectural phrase, to that ornate sonority of the constructive word that is expressed in the beauty and above all in the pertinence of the decoration."[35] Buildings composed the scenes of a heroic history that was revealed in three-dimensional and didactic episodes. Columns and statues were the protagonists of this mute and yet declamatory theater, the showpiece of an architectural register that was always high, always noble, always dramatic. In the church of San Francesco in Rimini the semi-columns stand out proudly from the background against which they are set; the façade, as triumphal arch, expresses a glory that turns the church into a temple—the *Tempio Malatestiano*—and makes a classical hero out of a mercenary.

Bramante did not share this enthusiasm for statues, columns, and triumphal arches. He had no interest in "conveying literary humanistic and intellectually refined messages" through "the display of the architectural and sculptural symbols of antiquity, with the ostentation of materials and colors, with statues and with 'stories' in relief, 'in the manner of antiquity.'"[36] Bramante's classicism was not that of a collector, an antiquarian; Bramante had no passion for luxury, no passion for the unique piece, no passion for marble, no passion for alabaster, no passion for jasper, no passion for gold.[37] There is nothing to be touched in his architecture.[38] Christof Thoenes has summed up this aspect of his work perfectly. The buildings of Bramante are:

> materially unpretentious, frugal, even dry in sculptural decoration, they stand out through their wealth of ideas, sharpness of articulation, compositional daring, and formal wit. Their effectiveness is of an intellectual, nonsensual nature.[39]

Plastic elements are extremely rare in Bramante's architecture. There are few columns, few semi-columns, and very few sculptures. Bramante used columns only in the Tempietto di San Pietro in Montorio (and he would have wanted to use them in the exterior of the dome of St. Peter's). Otherwise he just used colonettes that introduced a variation of tone, as in the case of the Ponticella, of the second order of the cloister of Santa Maria della Pace, and of the *serliane* of the Nymphaeum at Genazzano. He used semi-columns in the courtyard of the Palazzo dei Tribunali (?), the Nymphaeum of Genazzano, Palazzo Caprini, in the *tegurio* of St. Peter's, and in the Santa Casa in Loreto. As far as we know, Bramante (a man somewhat inclined to experiment, even in a fairly casual manner) never tried to sculpt and did not include sculptures in his buildings, except in the sacristy of San Satiro, where he had to reach a compromise with the Lombard craftsmen, and in the late claddings of the Santa Casa and the *tegurio*.[40] Otherwise projections were slight and increased only when the distances became enormous, as in the upper courtyard of the Belvedere. Bramante used architectural forms "where chiaroscuro had less of a hold." The articulation of the mass was minimal, the limits of the space were only suggested, there was never any element in relief that stuck out into space, detaching itself from a backdrop. Bramante made use of the same catalogue of things that, according to Roberto Longhi, Giovanni Bellini took from Piero della Francesca:

> drawn-out strips of the architraves, ... cornices that do not jut out very far, vertical bands of flattened little pillars that Piero adapted to use in painting for the first time at Rimini, shiny slabs of marble, polychrome pools of flooring, light pilasters, medallions.[41]

For Bramante there should be no characters in architecture, given that real people were going to have to move around in it. So columns, which Alberti regarded as the highest form of ornament,[42] had to be avoided as far as possible, and it was always better if there were no sculptures. This ostentatious impatience with any form of plasticity (which can only have come from Piero della Francesca) stops the architectural elements from speaking, requiring them to confine themselves to measuring the relations that define space. The orders are systematically prevented from protruding beyond the plane in which they are embedded. By comparing the solution for the corner of the cloister of Santa Maria della Pace with the equally paradigmatic one of the vestibule of Michelangelo's Biblioteca Laurenziana, it is easy to see that in this last case the columns and the brackets move *perpendicular* to the walls, invading the space and clashing violently, while at the same time remaining motionless, holding each other back. Michelangelo's corner is closing, the brackets seem to smash into one another. Mark Rothko said that Michelangelo

> achieved just the kind of feeling I'm after—he makes the viewers feel that they are trapped in a room where all the doors and windows are bricked up, so that all they can do is butt their heads for ever against the wall.[43]

Bramante's corner on the other hand seems to be opening up: the Ionic volute at the corner sprouts in the place in which the oscillating orders that run *parallel* to the planes of the two façades overlap. Bramante's corner expands and contracts, as if it were swinging lazily in the heat of a summer afternoon. In the architecture of Bramante nothing comes close, no element is allowed to invade the scene. The volume is always negative, hollow, carved into the mass of the walls and at once left free to be occupied. Space remains *empty*, without drama, without exclusions, with no preestablished contents, *comic*. Space is for everyone: there is no special treatment for lofty spirits, there are no distinctions between repertoires, there are no traditions with which to identify, there are no refinements that allow the emergence of elective affinities, there is nothing tragic and nothing authentic. The pearls are—and cannot but be—for the swine as well.

11 Order of all the orders

The first building that Bramante designed on the basis of his direct experience of the Roman ruins was the cloister of Santa Maria della Pace. The cloister marks perhaps the sourest moment in his work. For Milizia it is not "a particularly beautiful thing" and in his view its success can only be explained by the fact "there were no better architects in Rome at the time."[44] In the cloister of Santa Maria della Pace the classical orders are deliberately utilized to make the space as abstract as possible. Here Bramante declares the instruments that allow architecture to deal with reality and shows how this acceptance of the real coincides with the possibility of moving away from it. The orders can in fact be used to measure the different contexts with which they come into contact, precisely because they make up a system of forms with no content, distinct from what it frames and operating on a separate plane. No one has singled out this characteristic of the orders better than Giorgio Grassi:

> Thus the orders bestowed on architecture a universality that it has not regained since. This universality derived precisely from the fact that the orders themselves were "universal" in the broadest sense, i.e. in the sense that no image was linked with them.[45]

The heroic fragility of the cloister of Santa Maria della Pace matches its desire to declare—more than any other building in the history of classicism—the fundamental distance separating the architectural orders from human actions. The cloister exposes the operation that submits buildings to these actions precisely through the radical removal of any direct connection between them. The abstraction of the architectural machinery is conceived to defend the possibilities of action encompassed within the prism of the void. To do this, Bramante marshals *all* the orders. With all the zeal of the soldiers in the service of the Queen of Hearts, these very flat guardians stretch along the four sides of the courtyard. Bramante establishes a very difficult

Michele Marchetti, *cloister of Santa Maria
della Pace*, worm's-eye axonometric, 2014.

initial hypothesis: the presence, in the same building, of *all* the classical orders, which in this case are four: Doric, Ionic, Corinthian, and Composite. (After Bramante, architectural theorists of the Renaissance would conclude that the orders are five, but the actual number doesn't make much difference here: what matters is that Bramante set out to build a courtyard that contained them *all*.[46]) Thus the orders were combined in such a way as to produce a further order, an *order of all the orders* that governed them all and guaranteed their coherence. Bramante was not interested in developing a "theory of the orders," a complete explanation of their origin and justification of their use.[47] He aimed solely to define a "system of the orders," a context in which the differences between them were enough to make distinctions and establish relations.

Bramante worked on the basis of a finite repertoire. With respect to this repertoire, his problem was to establish an equilibrium of forms that met the specific conditions of the context in which he was working while at the same time expounding a rule that could be extended to new cases as well. On each occasion, Bramante reworked the repertoire he employed entirely, proposing a definition of it that could hold good for all the previous cases *and* for that specific new one. So the rule that emerged from the treatment of the new case was clarified and expanded, and the repertoire was renewed with regard to both the future and the past. Bramante set out each time to show that there was a more refined and general rule, which *did not exclude* the particular condition to which it had to respond: the bay was repeated, adapting to the various conditions of the fronts of the Belvedere, the alternating niches carved out of the external wall made the cella of the Tempietto usable, the hybrid geometry of the pillar held together the dome, nave, aisles, and ambulatories of St. Peter's. What was at stake in this work was not the invention of new forms, but the confirmation that all forms are part of a common life. Architecture is *logical work,* immediately entailing a universal ambition (to which corresponds in turn an immediate political commitment). From this approach derives an inescapably tautological task: to make available to everyone what is everyone's, to lay down *for all* what belongs to all.

The forms found in the buildings of classical antiquity are every-one's—offered without distinction to all and prescribed indiscriminately for all. This radical universalism makes it possible to formulate a hypothesis of architecture that can be used to deal with any problem, any client, and any formal tradition, but only on condition that it—all architecture—is not asked to place itself solely at the service of that specific circumstance, that particular tradition, that individual client, that specific social group. The treasure belongs to everyone, and so "there will be no need of an arbitrator to parcel it out since ... the heritage is untransferable and cannot be split up."[48] For Bramante, on each occasion, it was a question of showing that *all forms* were valid *for everyone*, that the set of all forms coincided ideally with the set of all human actions. And this without any particular form corresponding to a particular action (only the *set of all forms* and the *set of all actions* coincide). Architecture, as work on already given repertoires of forms, took on the not limited aim of making all the forms that in some way already existed accessible to all. Here humility and ambition coincided: Bramante did not allow himself to choose anything from the architectural traditions he inherited. His forms were *those of all the others*, they were simply *all the forms*. Thus he accepted everything as it was, without being too fussy, without selecting privileged forms. He submitted without hesitation to the whole of his discipline. His purpose was the one that Eliot recognized in the work of Dante: "To pass on to posterity one's own language, more highly developed, more refined, and more precise than it was before one wrote it ..."[49] This is why Bramante had to maintain a "perfectly invariable equidistance"[50] from all possible families of forms, reasserting each time that forms could not belong to anyone, that the whole range of forms is "*omnibus commune nec proprium ulli*."[51]

12 Against Roman architecture

Bramante was familiar with a fairly small number of architectural traditions. He came into contact with Byzantine, Gothic, Roman, and Romanesque architecture and may have had a vague notion of the existence of Arab, Greek, and Ottoman architecture. The only differences between systems of forms to which he was directly exposed were those—all in all only slight—that distinguished Urbino (perhaps Padua and Venice), Milan, and Rome in the late fifteenth century, and that distinguished the various classicisms of the Quattrocento from the architecture of ancient Rome. Despite having to rely on such limited evidence, by redoing in Rome what he had already done in Milan, Bramante developed a method of working that was at least to some extent comparative. As a consequence, in Rome, the role of forms became clearer; the repertoires finally appeared *as repertoires*, the conventions could be systematized precisely because they were recognized as such. The different families of forms were finally understood as logically equivalent.

And if the Roman repertoire were *logically equivalent* to the Milanese one, if the operations to which the repertoires could be subjected were the same, then an infinite number of other repertoires would also be logically equivalent. A more rigorous analysis of classical forms had to conclude there was no reason to assert the moral superiority of those forms. The consequence of this disenchanted classicism was the extraordinary opening up of the world of forms brought about by Bramante. This munificence was discovered entirely *within* the repertoire of antiquity, and derived in a wholly *negative* way, by investigating the architecture of the Romans without any concession to antiquarian sentimentalism. The rigor with which the operation was conducted ended up turning against its own subject (universalism, from St. Paul onward, has to stand primarily *against* the law). And like any universalism, Bramante's implies a colossal *pars destruens*. Thus Bramante's architecture is not simply derived from the Romans. It is also explicitly anti-Roman. For Bramante the classical repertoire cannot be viewed as *tradition*. A tradition is in fact based on a distinction that defines it in contrast with something else, and as such implies an opposition between what is inside and what is outside that tradition. Bramante's classicism does not set out to evoke the values of a civilization of the past. It is not a sort of *nationalism of antiquity*. Bramante does not base his work on a *shared past*. The unity of forms is an objective, not a premise. Classical forms depend on a *shared future*.

13 Eclecticism and classicism

At the beginning of *Architectural Principles in the Age of Humanism* Rudolf Wittkower poses a fundamental question:

> [W]hat would be the essential difference between the eclecticism of the fifteenth and sixteenth centuries and that of the nineteenth century? If both are derivative styles—in the sense they derive from classical antiquity—is the difference between them only that nineteenth-century architecture, as far as it is classical and not Gothic, is twice removed from the ancient models?[52]

The famous "principles" are introduced precisely in order to make this distinction. For Wittkower, Renaissance architecture, unlike nineteenth-century eclecticism, was "based on a hierarchy of values culminating in the absolute values of sacred architecture."[53]

So for Wittkower "the difference between the eclecticism of the fifteenth and sixteenth centuries and that of the nineteenth century" is a difference of sincerity and ideological purity. This position has the curious consequence of throwing doubt on the integrity of figures obsessed with morality (can we really doubt Semper? Or Viollet-le-Duc?[54]) in order to celebrate instead those who worked for bloodthirsty criminals and serial traitors, like Sigismondo Malatesta or Ludovico il Moro. Not only does this "ethical" explanation of the architecture of the Italian Renaissance fail even the most cursory check on the moral stature of its heroes, it is also so generic and pompous that it does not even identify a recognizable stance toward forms.

But if Wittkower's thesis does not account for the difference between the eclecticism of the fifteenth and sixteenth centuries and that of the nineteenth century, it becomes necessary to compare once again the derivative and classicist architecture of the Renaissance with the derivative and classicist architecture of the nineteenth century and try to come up with another explanation. If the difference cannot be traced back to the *symbolical value of the forms of the Renaissance church*, then it is possible to make a *logical* distinction between the universalism of Renaissance architecture and the exoticism of nineteenth-century architecture. This difference could not be clearer: the architecture of the Renaissance (and above all that of Bramante) addresses the multiplicity of architectural traditions on the basis of a realist attitude and with universal goals, and thus *proceeds from multiplicity to unity*; eclectic architecture, starting out from a rigid technical rationality, goes instead in search of new forms,[55] and so *proceeds from unity to multiplicity*. The difference between eclecticism and classicism is not so much a difference between values that go beyond architecture, but a difference in the way of understanding work on architecture, a difference in the *direction* of the gaze that observes cities. For eclecticism the work has to move toward complexity (on the basis of an unjustifiably simplified idea of the city), for classicism the work has instead to move toward simplicity (on the basis of a realistic image of the complexity of the city). For eclecticism the complexity (of buildings) is an *objective*; for classicism the complexity (of the city) is a *premise*. For eclecticism the repertoires are different and these different repertoires can be used to refer to different themes and to address different groups of users.[56] For classicism all repertoires are *related to one another*[57] and coincide in a single universe of forms; classicism is precisely the feeling of their ideal unity.

14   Classicism, colonialism

Bramante was the founder of European classicism understood as *universal architecture*, that is to say of architecture conceived on the basis of a claim to validity that embraced every possible architectural problem and was addressed to everyone. This founding role was not assigned to him by others. It was Bramante himself who chose it, setting himself goals—and demanding resources—that no one would ever after dream of taking on.[58] Just as Dante and Plato did not stand out from other authors for their greater talent but for the immensity of the cultural project they proposed to (and imposed on) their contemporaries and successors, Bramante did not distinguish himself from other Renaissance architects by "the elegance of the capitals, bases, brackets, and corners"[59] but by the ambition of imagining an architecture that could apply to everyone and that could turn everything into beauty.

Bramante (1444–1514) lived in the age of the great geographical discoveries and thus at the dawn of colonialism. He was a contemporary of Christopher Columbus (1451–1506) and Amerigo Vespucci (1454–1512). His plan was also a plan of conquest, and the connection between the two was already clear at the time. In a moment of particular enthusiasm, when Manuel I of Portugal was reporting the successes of the Setima Armada da Índia and Julius II had returned from his triumphal campaign in Perugia and Bologna, Giles of Viterbo did his best to put together Perusia, Bononia, and Taprobane,[60] seeing the renewal of the basilica of St. Peter's and the conquest of new lands by the Portuguese and Spanish as signs of a new golden age.[61]

The treasure of forms *from another time* on which Bramante wanted to lay his hands is not unconnected with what, at the same time, Almeida and Albuquerque wanted to steal *from another place*.[62] Here the generosity of a beauty that can be good for all coincides with the ruthlessness of a scheme of global domination. And the architecture of European classicism was undoubtedly part of this plan of

Werner Herzog, *Aguirre: The Wrath of God*, 1972,
© Deutsche Kinemathek–Werner Herzog Film.

domination: one of the first things our ancestors did to secure the territories they had seized around the world was to fill them with Doric, Ionic, and Corinthian columns.

Now that there is nothing left to conquer, now that the whole of the world has been polluted with Western architecture (be it classical, modern, or postmodern), now that all the violence that produced the landscape through which we move has already been expended, now that victims are already everywhere, forgetting the promises that were mixed up with the conquest would just add insult to injury. Denying classicism's promise of beauty, in this sense, would mean admitting that it was just an excuse to plunder and destroy—and thus pave the way for even more certain looting and devastation in the future. If we are inescapably heirs to the violence of classicism, we are left with the choice of whether we also want to be heirs to the promise of freedom and equality which accompanied that violence.

ABSTRACTION

15 Distance

Auguste Choisy pointed out the dualism that characterized the architecture of the Romans, highlighting its divarication between the layout and the structure on the one hand and the ornamentation on the other.

> Analysis of construction among the Greeks would be so closely intertwined with that of architecture it would be difficult to consider it separately: but the difficulty vanishes as soon as we look at the monuments erected under Roman rule. Their architects cared very little for delicacies of form: the laying out of plans and the choice of means of execution were better suited to the very practical bent of their minds. As if they had felt incapable of embracing, as the Greeks had done, architecture as a whole and carrying out the various operations it entailed, they established a clear division between the structure, which they were able to handle in masterly fashion, and the decoration, for which they affected a disdainful indifference: they left the job of decorating their buildings to others, while themselves taking on the task of planning and building them, and they would approach the two aspects they had reserved for themselves in a truly Roman fashion.[1]

Choisy's analysis fails to recognize the consequences that this split had on the spatiality of Roman architecture. In fact the dualism did not concern solely the coexistence of layouts, structures, and ornaments that were not fully matched: in Roman architecture, space and the order that measured it also remained distinct. The columns, semi-columns, pilasters, and architraves that punctuated the walls did not correspond perfectly either to the walls or to the rooms that they delimited. A gap remained between the trilithic ornaments of Hellenic origin and the walls and ceilings, a gap between the order, the boundaries of space, and space. This was probably just the consequence of the adoption, for reasons of cultural prestige, of the Greek orders. The Romans might have preferred a more consistent and peremptory architecture, but they were unable to renounce the Greek orders, and the buildings they left us are all characterized by this split between orders and spaces.

Bramante recognized this splitting in the Roman ruins, but what Choisy would see as a defect was for Bramante the basis for a possible architecture.[2] In fact the disconnection discernible in those ruins allowed him to maintain a gap between space and order, to multiply space in a representation that did not correspond to it perfectly,[3] to slow down and expand the gestures performed in the rooms by distancing the pilasters from the walls onto which they were projected.

While all the other architects of the Renaissance were driven by the desire to *reduce the distance from the ancients*, Bramante wanted instead to *increase the distance from the present*. The *bella maniera degli antichi* was in the first place a guarantee of this distance, a way of stepping outside the flow of events and so securing a bit of room for maneuver, a way of moving away from reality without giving up its transformation. What Bramante got from the ruins was "a derived style that he used of his own initiative to express his thoughts in a language not his own."[4] The grammatical accuracy with which the classical orders were employed served to underscore this distance, to make the forms more detached, to strip them of any immediacy, to disconnect them as much as possible from the world.

Bramante took the side of the *ancients*. He used the past to suspend the present and defended the existence of some concrete Otherness against which the present could be measured.[5] This was the aim behind his deliberate quest for difficulty. The captious and paradoxical handling of the corners in the cloister of Santa Maria della Pace, the anti-virtuoso illusionism of San Satiro, the exaggerated purism of the choir of Santa Maria del Popolo, the suicidal intellectualism of the staircase in the Belvedere, and the smug stupidity of the new St. Peter's were all tricks that Bramante used to distance forms from actions and gain himself some "space" for his work on space.

16 *Difficultà grandissima*

Vasari grasped with great precision the consequences of Bramante's work for the architects that came after him. To go back to a passage that has already been quoted:

> For while the Greeks were the inventors of architecture and the Romans their imitators, Bramante not only taught us new things by imitating them, but added very great beauty and difficulty to the art, an embellishment that is plain to us today.[6]

For all the architects who came after Bramante, the work became *more difficult*. Not only more complex, more interesting, more refined, and richer in clever ideas (all meanings that can be assigned to the *difficulty* mentioned by Vasari), but *more difficult*, more regulated, more ambitious, more dangerous, more complicated to carry through. Bramante made sure that his work would be continued not so much by selecting a repertoire to be repeated as by identifying a way of using it, by imposing an intellectual style. Bramante did not train his successors in the manner of the founder of a school, as Raphael was to do after him. Rather he seems to have influenced his colleagues and competitors as a rival. Bramante perfected the rules of the game at the very moment he joined it, simply by acting as the most reckless of players.[7] Faced with his absolute insolence, all those who had had the not very good idea of sitting down at his table were obliged to up their game. Thus Bramante established, for the brief period of a generation, a climate of competition between gentlemen, in which everyone accepted the new level of difficulty and tried their hand at a game of intelligence so free and rigorous that the history of European architecture would never see its like again. The singular chivalrous ethic of this extremist game is the same as the one played by the writers described by Henry James (who must have known something about it) in "The Figure in the Carpet":

> literature was a game of skill, and skill meant courage, and courage meant honour, and honour meant passion, meant life.[8]

The formalism that Bramante imposed on the architecture of the sixteenth century created the conditions for a true *golden age*,[9] one in which the work on forms was carried out as a logical operation based on a common repertoire, in which architecture was recognized as the abstract and non-narrative art that it unquestionably is, in which no one thought of asking from architecture things that architecture is unable to offer, and in which there were no doubts about its *public* nature and its *extended* duration. Bramante ushered in this prodigious *golden age*, bequeathing to posterity nothing but problems:

> Bramante's strength lies in the brevity and incompleteness of his experience ... If Bramante's work had not had this character of an open and mixed legacy it would not have seen the exceptional flowering that came afterwards, in the work of the pupils who were to carry on with his research for another thirty years.[10]

Bramante's successors had to finish the enormous buildings that he left incomplete. They literally had to work *within his problems*, and their architecture was inescapably conditioned by this, as is evident to anyone looking at the extraordinary Bramantesque corpus to be found in Letarouilly's *Les édifices de Rome moderne*.[11] And yet none of the architects who came after him seem to have shared his attitudes. In fact, after Bramante had made available the abstract and nonreferential instruments of the new architecture in the style of antiquity, his successors did their utmost to reconnect this explicitly arbitrary repertoire to an improbable natural necessity, and to restore to the forms their presumed meanings—the same meanings that had long impeded a coherent use of those forms. Thus, for all his "pupils," Bramante's formal logic was both a solution (a practical solution that offered a concrete starting point for the design of buildings) and a hindrance (an ideological inaccuracy, an obstacle to the development of a more sophisticated cultural hypothesis). The architecture that came after Bramante, commencing with Raphael, was preoccupied with freeing itself from what was judged to be an excess of abstraction.[12] Bramante's logical and spatial advances were once again made to serve the original literary objectives; the city being a seemingly inadequate foundation for their work, architects went back to trying to base their discipline directly on nature.

Donato Bramante, cloister of Santa Maria
della Pace, Rome, 1500–1504, corner solution,
from A. Bruschi, *Bramante architetto*,
Rome-Bari: Laterza, 1969.

This became the specific problem faced by architecture under Leo X: readapting a set of forms that clearly did its job to suit the ideal premises that had shaped the expectations which accompanied its emergence but had been completely ignored in its actual production; rediscovering necessity and reinserting values into the skeptical and nominalist foundations of the empire of forms conquered by Bramante. All the options put forward (from Serlio's odious search for "character," to Palladio's playing dumb with his villas, to Michelangelo's expressive furor, or Borromini's conspiracy theories) challenged Bramante's hypothesis of architecture. Despite its apparent success, Bramante's *logical work* remained fairly isolated. If Bramante's formalism defined the *letter* of the architectural orthodoxy of the High Renaissance, in the last analysis almost no one showed an interest in the detached and paradoxical *spirit* of this cultural product—and Bramante was to prove even less popular later on, when everyone would prefer to see the Italian Renaissance in the terms of Palladio's agreeable and enthusiastic version than in those of Bramante's bitter and paradoxical one. Over the far from brief history of classicism, only a very few would be loyal to Bramante, perhaps just Peruzzi, Vignola, and McKim, Mead, & White. And yet, at least until the time of Bernini's ill-fated journey to France, the context in which this research was conducted was still the one defined by Bramante. No one, not even Michelangelo and Palladio, thought of questioning Bramante's paradigm in its entirety and the architecture of the sixteenth century maintained that characteristic combination of distance and proximity (or rather *proximity through distance*) between spaces and life that was the wonder which Bramante had made accessible to those who carried on his work.

17 Remote future

Wandering amidst the remains in the Campagna, Bramante was fascinated not only by the clarity of these models for a fully rational architecture, but also by the obscurity of these deposits of an unknown past, by their incompleteness, by the way their silence was able to prompt associations. Of these enormous and splendid objects, Bramante grasped the clear and incorruptible (as well as immediately reusable) logic, but he also sensed their violence, and deluded himself into thinking he could arouse their brute and implacable force. In the ruins intentions were lost: the Romans had certainly done something in those enormous buildings, but what, Bramante did not know. The ruins had certainly had an initial purpose, but they had outlived it, and now that purpose was no longer recognizable in the dumb pile of bricks that had been meant to meet it. Whatever the emotional investment that had produced them may have been, it could no longer be discerned. To some extent the intensity of those feelings remained, but without a specific theme, without a direction, without an objective. Love lingered, but without a loved one. The ruins, like Don Quixote's madness, *had no reason* and displayed all the metropolitan potential that could emanate from them "if there were cause."[13] This potential was evident in what was the ruin par excellence of Renaissance Rome: the Basilica of Maxentius, which, split in half, its gaping mouths filled with a shadow deeper than its constructors could ever have imagined, cried out to the city the love call of a three-throated monster, as if it yearned to find its missing half in some other Godzilla built of brick, who could heal its loneliness. Bramante heard this raucous and indomitable lament, recognized the foolish navigation through time—neither entirely calculated, nor entirely unplanned—of these heaps of stones, left to drift like space capsules after the end of the mission for which they had been planned. Standing in front of the huge "deposits of labors"[14] abandoned in the Roman campagna, Bramante wondered if it would be possible to rouse these sleeping giants, "to ignite the explosive materials that are latent

Etienne Du Pérac, *Basilica of Maxentius*, 1575.

in what has been,"[15] tapping their energy, channeling the "revolutionary force of the past"[16] into a network of dams and canals that could turn it into the city of the present.

The architecture of the Renaissance, which in other ways anticipates and prefigures a modern subject and a modern condition, is also something undeniably *non-modern*, something that deliberately refuses to belong entirely to just one time.[17] The architects of the Renaissance in fact produced the architecture of their present through the architecture of the ancient Romans: they created buildings for obviously contemporary uses out of the remains of a very distant past. This operation was based on some implicit hypotheses that were obvious at the time, but which are worth spelling out, since they are not so obvious anymore. First, the architecture of the Renaissance postulated the continuity of some human conditions, for instance, that people are many and succeed one another in time, are always more or less the same size, and perceive light in the same way. To these fairly rudimentary ideas corresponded another rudimentary idea, and one which was self-evident in that context, but less so for us today: that buildings have a lifespan which stretches for decades, if not centuries, much longer than the lifespan of human beings. It follows that buildings can house many generations, and connect with situations entirely unforeseen at the moment of their creation.[18] Buildings are things deliberately left to others in a time to come to modify their (entirely unknown) lives. Buildings are heavy and cumbersome things, thrust into a time not planned for, ramparts deliberately rolled into the future to keep it attached to the past. Buildings do not count solely at the moment in which they are constructed, when they are fleetingly impregnated by the zeitgeist; buildings also remain in place afterwards. And it is with this unforeseen time, this remote future, that architecture is concerned. What is specific to it, more than any other form of art, is precisely this duration, and it may be for this reason that, notwithstanding its blatant attempts, architecture has never succeeded in being fully "modern."[19]

The extent of their duration in time makes buildings products that are hard to control, and strangely coy, in some ways even innocent with regard to their always dreadful conditions of production. Buildings open onto a timeframe so broad that it is fundamentally unforeseeable, facing onto a future that the predictions of the architect (as well as those of the client, the bureaucracy, and the users) are unable to embrace, but that is nevertheless already present at the moment of their construction. Design is therefore a twofold exercise in anticipation and non-anticipation, in predetermination and liberation.[20] In this respect architecture is the place where the *maximum precision* (of distances, of relations between the body and the bounds of space) coincides with the *maximum indeterminacy* (of content, of the actions possible in space). Architecture is therefore something fundamentally unpredictable and even strangely irresponsible. For men and women accustomed to constantly having to update and never thinking in timeframes longer than a few years, but also to always being *insured*, to carefully avoiding any unforeseen event, architecture comes as something of a surprise. And this is also where contemporary architecture finds its greatest value, as evidence that the world did not begin yesterday and hopefully is not going to finish tomorrow, that different ways of measuring time coexist in our lives, that not everything is exhausted in the interval between the appearance of a model of phone and the announcement of the one that will replace it. Architecture seems to suggest a longer timeframe, seems to grasp the pulse of a *longue durée* inscribed in a history that is first of all *natural history*. This is where its greatest responsibility, an *ecological*, i.e. *political* responsibility, lies today. And this ecological responsibility is not going to be met by an ostentatious morality backed by questionable carbon footprint certifications, but through allegiance to an unknown and, at least in part, unpredictable time. Thus the yardstick of judgment of this highly responsible irresponsibility is provided, in first approximation, by the *remote past*, which is still the thing least different from the *remote future*.

18 The object is simple

Near the beginning of the *Tractatus logico-philosophicus* Wittgenstein defines form. This is his proposition 2.0141:

> *Die Möglichkeit seines Vorkommens in Sachverhalten ist die Form des Gegenstandes.*[21]

In the proposition that follows immediately after, which in the numbering system of the *Tractatus* is 2.02, he adds:

> *Der Gegenstand ist einfach.*[22]

For Wittgenstein, form is the coincidence of a set of possible relations enveloping the object, the rule of all the actions that occur around it. The form of the object seems to imply a development: form is the archive inside the object of the object's possible future. This is a surprisingly architectural definition: the object appears to be something immobile and at the same time capable of developing in time. The form is what the object is going to do, considered at the moment in which it is still doing nothing. At the same time the form is not a prophecy, it is a reserve of future, but one that *doesn't know the future*. Wittgenstein seems to be looking at the form not so much from the viewpoint of events, of history, of the people who imagine, produce and utilize the form, but, in so far as this is possible, from the perspective of the object itself, watching the evolution of the world through its fixity. Form seems to keep in reserve a stock of unforeseen possibilities that pertain to it precisely as form, quite apart from the conditions that determine it. Form registers its conditions but does not immediately turn them into the object. Rather it consumes them in the process of becoming form, sublimating the conditions that in this way will be passed down in the object. And in fact the multiplicity of the conditions is not lost in the simplicity of the object; on the contrary, it persists in it like the store of food in which the yolk of the form is wrapped. *The object is simple.* It will be left to time to reveal its richness.

Everything that architects can do is done through form (unless they are going to arm their workers and seize power by force, as Phalaris is said to have done[23]—lucky man). Architects can only act on the form of buildings, on the amount of space assigned to performing actions, on the light that falls on those actions, on the size of the openings that are made in the walls and that frame the landscape. They can act on balancing the desires of the people who initiate and fund the buildings only once these have already been understood as spaces, only when the actions have already turned into rooms for carrying out actions. The form of the buildings is in fact the compromise between the fears and the hopes placed in buildings, *once understood as spaces*. Form corresponds to a temporary balance, not necessarily the best one, just the last of a series that concludes with a building. Thus the form fixes the last of the different possible agreements that are reached in the process of design, and the final form, the configuration that the buildings eventually assume, is no less accidental than all the alternative forms that have been possible at various stages of this process. Despite architects' particular fondness for the platitude, beauty has nothing to do with necessity.[24] The sturdiness that is assigned to the architectural object at the end of the construction process does not imply any higher necessity for that particular form. The necessity of the form is always something recognized from the outside; for whoever has created it, the form could always have been different. And yet the absence of necessity in the process that produces it does not prevent the object from behaving like something complete, which has included or excluded some possibilities forever. From this point of view the *history of the form* (the history of the intentions, the feelings, the passions that accompanied the emergence of the form, *le temps que tu as perdu pour ta rose*) is fairly irrelevant. All that matters is what is left at the end, the *logic of the form,* for the way it remains lodged in the object, at the disposal of anyone who encounters it.

19 Form follows function

Modern architecture has done everything it could to eliminate the distance that separates rooms from the people who live in them. The history of modern architecture can in fact be seen as the history of the attempt to establish a bi-univocal relationship between space and actions carried out inside it. This desire to permanently connect activities and spaces has produced "functionalism," an attitude that, even more than insisting excessively on the more prosaic aspects of architecture, claims to identify a *function* (in the mathematical sense) capable of linking acts indissolubly to spaces, as for instance in the *function* "form follows function."

Functionalism is nothing but an attempt (and a substantially successful one) to reduce form to content.[25] In fact functionalism seeks to close the gap between order and space and the corresponding gap between space and the activities that inhabit it, linking actions, spaces, and architectural elements in a single chain of correspondences, thereby removing any complexity of spatial experience and any possibility of representation, any difference between the object and the image of the object—and with them any possibility of understanding architecture as intellectual work. In fact, if spaces were to correspond perfectly to acts, not only would the spaces be reduced to *signs*, but the signs would not be able to say anything except what we already know: that the pool is the place where we go swimming and the cemetery is where we are buried.

In reality, the set of actions and the set of forms are incommensurable: to an extensive but finite range of architectural forms corresponds an infinite range of actions. While all suspended ceilings made of mineral fiber panels on a square grid of 60 x 60 cm are the same, the movements from desk to coffee machine and the conversations on all Monday mornings at all insurance agencies are different. Form does not "follow" function for the simple reason that a single form relates to a very large number of functions—or actions, or activities, or whatever you want to call them. Architecture therefore makes sense only if there is a relationship between order and void but, equally, it makes sense only if this relationship is not entirely predefined, if form *does not follow function*.

In the transition from the reality of action as it is carried out in time to the fixity of the spatial configuration that defines the conditions of its performance a stiffening takes place, a removal of the subjects involved in the action, and with this stiffening and this depersonalization comes an unexpected opening. Space eludes the intentions of its producers and users. This reserve is what gives architecture its peculiar capacity to store up and register the activities for which it will be used over time, its ability to harbor possible futures. This precious opacity is also the reason why it is advisable to limit as far as possible the quantity of forms. The fewer the forms, the more spaces remain indefinite, opaque, rarefied, ambiguous, multiple. The ideal tone of this work that deals with all forms, and at the same time is committed to using as few of them as possible, is therefore the "colored monochrome"[26] that Bruschi recognized in Bramante's architecture. The only "choice" necessary for this work on space is the choice of an explicitly finite, rigidly formalized repertoire, one that makes no claim to lay its hands immediately on life, that cuts off any direct link between form and content, keeping solid and void separate, leaving a gap between the measure of the order and the experience of the void and thereby preserving the greatest number of possibilities within space.

20 Abstract architecture is public

Architecture is *protection of empty space*. What makes it necessary is a need for form that perhaps has never been put so well as in the lines of Ingeborg Bachmann:

Wenn alle Krüge zerspringen
Was bleibt von den Tränen im Krug?[27]

It is the *form* of the pitchers that prevents the tears from being lost. And the form of the pitchers was not meant for tears. Pitchers were made to hold water or milk, certainly not tears. And the pitchers tell us nothing about tears. They just collect them.

Architecture matches the complexity of the human motivations that bring it into existence, or subsequently invade it, only if it accommodates those motivations without attempting to express them. If it tries to do so, it simply chokes them. From this perspective, if there is one thing that is always right in architecture, it is breadth, distance, space in the sense of width, separation, abundance, the willingness to let others say what architecture has neither the means nor the motive to say. In architecture "the only sure thing is the void."[28] If it remains empty, if it limits itself to constructing the frame that lets things appear, if it simply *contains* anything that ends up in it, just defining its borders, then architecture works its specific wonder of creating space for human actions, and recognizing them as human. If the order and the void remain distinct, if the scene is left bare, without content, then the room welcomes countless unknown guests and becomes the proof of a possible life in common. Abstraction makes space available; distance makes appropriation possible, lays the foundations of proximity. It is because it is abstract that architecture is public.

A theory that could be of some use to contemporary architecture is a theory of abstraction, a theory of the non-correspondence of spaces and functions, of inside and outside. This theory would make it possible to

Donato Bramante, choir of Santa Maria del Popolo,
ca. 1505–1509, Gabinetto Fotografico Nazionale.

put back at the heart of the architect's work the gap between gestures and space and thus the gap between space and the order that measures it, without accepting preestablished couplings. It would allow us to imagine an architecture without needs (in contrast to modernism) and without desires (in contrast to postmodernism—of whatever kind it may be); an architecture constructed around activities that are neither anticipated nor explained, nor controlled, nor psychoanalyzed but just accommodated—and accommodated in such a way as to be remembered. Thus architecture could be seen purely as the production of rooms to contain the desires of others, a technology able to lend precision to actions without predetermining their nature, able to augment the definition of the memory *of others*, and to anchor those memories to places. A good theory for contemporary architecture would be a theory independent of the notion of *function* and thus independent of the notion of *meaning*, a theory that would clearly explain that in architecture there is nothing to explain, a theory on how to make buildings *that serve no purpose* and *that do not have anything to say.*

INTERMEZZO

DANTE
GIOTTO
PIERO
BRAMANTE

I

Bramante spent the cold evenings of December 1510, during the preparations for the siege of Mirandola,[1] which Pope Julius had the pleasure of conducting personally, commenting on Dante. Withdrawing into his quarters, the aging pope, "with a beard that looked like a bear,"[2] had his equally elderly architect read the *Comedy* to him. An entry in Isabella d'Este's chancellery reads:

> Our Lord is feeling better and it seems he wishes to become learned in Dante, as every evening he has Dante read and explained to him by Bramante, architect and most erudite mason.[3]

This is not the only testimony to Bramante's literary preferences: Gaspare Visconti noted that one of his particularly Petrarchesque sonnets had been written to provoke Bramante, "ardent champion of Dante."[4]

In Rome and in Milan, decades apart, in peacetime and in war, someone took the trouble to note Bramante's devotion to Dante and his expertise on the subject. This apparently irrelevant information (the literary tastes of an "illiterate") must have been of some significance if authors from such different times and contexts thought it worth mentioning. The side Bramante took in this literary debate involved the whole of his work and can be explained only by recognizing the cultural project to which he had decided, *ardently*, to adhere.

II

The first intellectual hypothesis that Bramante met in his formation was the one to be found in the painting of Piero della Francesca, which he had already gotten to know as an apprentice of Fra Carnevale, if not of Piero himself.[5] Bramante was a fairly poor painter,[6] but he was also too refined a critic not to recognize all the cultural implications of this work.

Piero della Francesca painted what happens between people and between people and things: the distance of a hand from a face, the alignment of a nose and a hat, the way an item of clothing stands out against the background of a mountain. His working hypothesis envisaged the reduction of Masaccio's art to pure painting, to the pure laying on of areas of color, eliminating any trace of sculpture. Faces had no contrast, perspectives were only very slightly foreshortened, always *almost* frontal. Depth was not suggested by long flanks extended according to receding lines, but left to the intervals between planes that are almost always flat, parallel to the plane of the painting, in the manner of the late, archaizing photomontages of Mies van der Rohe.[7] Space was rendered through a series of suspensions. All the successive layers of depth were painted in a flat, uniform way, in incredibly clear and powdery tones. Piero went back to the specific nature of the discipline: painting represents an instant through fields of color distributed on a plane: "*la pictura non è se non dimostrationi de superficie.*"[8] Immobility is the starting point of this art. In Piero's pictures there is never a breath of wind: in the *Battle between Heraclius and Khosrow* the standards are as flat as if they were made of tin or hang limply like stockings left on the line for weeks. The immobility of the painted things defines the particular interpretation of time in these images. Piero painted scenes from sacred history and therefore painted the past, but he painted it at the moment in which it still had to happen. His images are suspended in a sort of anterior past in which the action has yet to take place: the Queen of Sheba stops to pray before the wood of the cross laid across the entrance to the palace where King Solomon awaits her, while the woman in the red dress holds her back and the woman in green signals her to wait; the man with a black beard leaning on the spade has stopped digging and is waiting for the crosses to emerge from the ground (in the meantime he has other concerns: perhaps his wife is cheating on him, perhaps he owes someone money); Emperor Constantine is still asleep, although the angel has already arrived at his tent; even in his depiction of "the wounded, the fallen, and the dead in scenes of almost incredible carnage,"[9] Heraclius and Khosrow's soldiers seem to have come to a halt, as if surprised by the blows they are inflicting on one another; Khosrow's son has been killed by a dagger plunged into his throat, but has not yet fallen—and it looks as if he is going to tumble backward like a sack, as actors do in silent films, or like Krazy Kat when

Ignatz throws a brick at her (him). Piero painted the instant in which the action is still only possible and only the conditions for it as yet exist. He moved in time with supreme indifference (not so much against the tide like any *conservative*, but dispassionately, like the editor who runs the film of a football match backward and forward to find the moment prior to the decisive assist). In this way his images acquire that specifically architectural tone of detached contemplation of the flow of time and of opening up to a multitude of possibilities that are deliberately not expressed. Piero's figures wait before actions that they do not refuse to carry out but for which they do not want to take responsibility:

> For Piero della Francesca, perspective serves to construct a clearly articulated location in which to install figures, but not to clearly develop the drama of the story. In any case, this tendency is confirmed by the various panels in which the extreme modernism of the mathematical perspective is strangely accompanied by an almost "primitive" stasis of the figures.[10]

In Piero's frescoes there is no drama, no commentary, no anecdotes, no gossip.[11] The tragedy is immediately done away with, simply because *nothing has happened yet*. The comedy is viewed from afar, the fat man is still three steps away from the banana peel.

In the whole of the Renaissance, Piero della Francesca's art is perhaps the most deliberately impersonal,[12] the one most proudly subordinated to the collective ethics of mural painting.[13] This choice, combined with his absolute rejection of a hardness of line and the use of chiaroscuro to accentuate volume, places Piero in a special position with respect to the evolution of Italian painting. On the one hand he was an outsider, an arrogant provincial who did not care to adapt to the manner of the artistic capital of the time; on the other he was perhaps the most rigorous and consistent heir of the pictorial tradition initiated in Assisi by Giotto. The path from Giotto in fact branched off in two opposite directions: either toward tragedy, hardening the figures further and making them out of earth like Masaccio (or even marble like Mantegna), or toward comedy, emptying the skies, rarefying the air and imagining an art even more *spacious* and impersonal, as Maso di Banco started to do and then Piero did even better.

Piero della Francesca, *Finding of the Three Crosses and Proof of the True Cross, Stories of the True Cross,* S. Francesco, Arezzo, 1453-1464, detail, Nicolò Orsi Battaglini, Archivi Alinari, Florence.

It was through Piero's work that the young Bramante came into contact with the cultural project implicit in the whole of Italian painting from Giotto onward. Through Piero, Bramante reconstructed in its full extent the hypothesis that Giotto had proposed to the Italian painters who came after him, and also recognized the *alliance* that—at the basis of this tradition—had been made between Giotto and Dante.

III

Giotto painted gestures. He painted them in such a convincing manner as to give the impression that his figures had been caught mid-act:

> ... images formed by his brush agree so well with the lineaments of nature as to seem to the beholder to live and breathe; and his pictures appear to perform actions and movements so exactly as to seem from a little way off actually speaking, weeping, rejoicing, and doing other things ..."[14]

To let these gestures happen, Giotto had to construct a stage on which they could appear. So Giotto's paintings needed a device to make the actions evident, a "technology" able to transform actions into *gestures*, thereby ensuring that they could be *seen* and *remembered* by a whole community. This technology was architecture.[15] The stage on which the gestures painted by Giotto appeared was the city: of the twenty-eight scenes of the *Legend of Saint Francis* in the Upper Basilica of Assisi, twenty-four have an urban setting. In the Scrovegni Chapel, twenty-five of the thirty-eight scenes are urban.[16]

Giotto's painting is devoted to investigating the position of human beings in space, and the space in which these human beings are placed is always public, constructed, enclosed, artificial: "the room, enclosed space, is the artistic achievement of the Italians."[17] For Giotto and for all his successors the position of the figure in space implied its relationship with the universe and with other human beings; space became the form of all possible relationships. Space became a way of investigating the nature of an entire *form of life*. Giotto set himself one of the most absurd (and well-accomplished) tasks in the history of art: using the plane to explore space, producing motionless images to sound out the possibility of action, showing the configuration of the city to present a plan to transform it. With Giotto, for the first time—and to some extent *against nature*—painting placed its subject on the other side of the wall on which it was set. Thus painting claimed for itself an intellectual significance that it had never had in classical antiquity, when it had never really gone beyond the stage of mural decoration. Once this somewhat paradoxical hypothesis of research—using two-dimensional space as a means for the comprehension of three-dimensional space—had been accepted, the Italian artists of the Renaissance developed the tools they needed to put this initial premise into effect. And these tools (the *perspectiva artificialis* in accordance with the technique defined in Brunelleschi's *tablets*) could not but confirm the "architectural" idea of painting they presupposed: "What else can be drawn in perspective except architecture, furniture, and a few other man-made objects?"[18] Thus painting became, throughout the Renaissance, the preferred place for experiments on space. The whole of Renaissance architecture would *first be painted* and then built.

In Giotto's painting the atmosphere is never intimate.[19] The gestures are always set in public space. The interiors are always outdoors. In the *Annunciation to St. Anne* in the Scrovegni Chapel, only the angel has to address the saint through the little window, everyone else can easily see the scene through the large opening facing viewers. This opening is not the result of a graphic convention that takes a wall away in order to show something we would otherwise not be able to see: St. Anne's "house" really is made as we see it, with an enormous hole on one side. The ends of the walls and the architrave that surround the opening are decorated with a frieze, which would not make sense if the wall had only been removed "virtually" to reveal what was going on inside. Giotto does not enter St. Anne's room in the way Jan van Eyck does in the *Arnolfini Portrait*. He stays outside. But, while he does not venture to invade the saint's private space, he has no problem about dragging her room into the public sphere. As an episode in the history of salvation, the *Annunciation* is of collective interest and the

Giotto di Bondone, *Annunciation to St. Anne*,
Scrovegni Chapel, Padua, ca. 1303–1305,
Archivi Alinari, Florence.

place in which it happens can only be public. And in fact for Giotto there is nothing personal in St. Anne's room, only things without an owner, without a story, without affection: a striped blanket, a chest, a drape, a shelf with a box on it, a pair of bellows. No mirrors, no combs, no jewelry, above all no fluffy little dogs.

Dante (1265–1321) and Giotto (1267–1337) lived roughly contemporaneous lives. Although there is no proof that the two knew each other, their "friendship" has been repeatedly claimed on the basis of the mention of Giotto in *Purgatorio*:

> Credette Cimabue ne la pittura
> tener lo campo, e ora ha Giotto il grido,
> sì che la fama di colui è scura[20]

and the presumed "portrait of Dante" in the Podestà Chapel. From a historical viewpoint, at least in the current state of our knowledge, it does not seem possible to answer the question.[21] What is certain in any case is that Florentine and then Italian culture after Dante and Giotto has never given up trying to establish a link between them. And yet, as has been pointed out many times,[22] Dante and Giotto came from very different worlds. The former was an aristocratic and conservative poet who became a refugee—and therefore a radical—after a ill-starred dalliance with politics, while the latter was an astute artisan who moved with the times and, notwithstanding his humble origins, was able to set up the most profitable artistic workshop of his day. Giotto was a self-made man of the Middle Ages, Dante died in exile.

But even if it is not possible to say anything about the personal relationship between the two, the fact remains that Dante refers explicitly to Giotto in the *Purgatorio*. This mention is important for the context in which it is made. In fact, in the very next lines (*Purgatorio*, XI, 97–99), Dante speaks of himself: "la gloria della lingua" (the glory of our tongue) is destined to share the same fate as the figurative arts.

In *Purgatorio*, XI, 94–96, Dante chooses Giotto as an ally, acknowledging contemporary painting as a means as decisive as poetry for the development of his cultural project. Even the military tone of the expression, "held the field," with which he describes Cimabue's brief reign implies that a similar role has now been entrusted to the new star of Florentine painting. Dante enrolls Giotto in his party and gives him a position to defend in a cultural battle. The appropriation is brutal, but accurate. Dante assigns the political tone of his art to contemporary painters, but does not prescribe a method that is not the specific one of painting; he does not impose a literary paradigm on painting. And it was perhaps partly for this reason that the painting of the Renaissance would never really take the turn suggested by the reflections of Guarino da Verona or the *murales* of Cola di Rienzo and would not even become that sort of didactic comic strip that it ought to have been if artists had really chosen to follow the indications in *De Pictura*.[23] For Dante, painting ought not to become poetry, it was no *poema tacitum*. However unilaterally imposed, the alliance between Dante and Giotto is a pact between equals, founded on a common quest for a glory that can only be fleeting, on a work that knows it will have to face oblivion. And it is precisely on the basis of the transitory and broadly unsuccessful character of human work, reflected in the melancholic parade of the prideful penitents bowed down with immense stones in *Purgatorio*, XI, that the alliance is established. Since the glory of painting and the glory of the tongue will pass, the work of the painter and of the poet need to submit to a political and religious program, to contribute to a transformation of society that finds its ultimate purpose in the service of God.

Gianfranco Contini has written that "Dante is a man of themes rather than theses."[24] Dante did not really expound theories and did not really propose solutions (on the few occasions he tried to do so, he got it quite wrong). Rather, he identified the questions and chose the words with which solutions were to be sought, fixing them for the whole of Italian culture to come. The same thing happens with Giotto: Giotto too was an *author of themes*, rather than an *author of theses*. And Giotto's themes were the same as Dante's, only couched in the specific terms of the painter's work: the appearance of gesture in the urban setting, the memory of gesture, gesture as evidence of a supernatural order, space as condition of action, the city as the stage of events that change the life of the community, the city as hypothesis of coexistence, painting as collective responsibility.

This agreement on the nature of the themes on which poetry and painting are called to reflect is of much more importance for Dante and Giotto than their—moreover not even so clear—"political positions." Dante and Giotto are *political authors* without *political positions*. Their *political art* is not accompanied by a *political message*—Dante is not Bertolt Brecht and Giotto is not Diego Rivera—but by a *political mode*. Whatever their "positions" may have been, Dante and Giotto are agreed that the city is not just the place but also the means and the representation of any political project. Only through the city is it possible to obtain justice. Only through the city is it possible to represent the city in which justice will be reestablished. Thus city and political projects coincide completely: the city is the objective correlative of a common destiny, "*la chose humaine par excellence*."[25] Art is therefore entirely at the service of the city; it is by definition ideological, inexorably *made for others*. It is no coincidence that Dante reserves his greatest contempt for the angels of the *wicked chorus* who were unable to take sides and were *for themselves*.[26]

IV

One of the most conspicuous oddities of Dante's poem is its title: *Commedia, or Comedy*.[27] *Comedy* seems like the title added with a marker to an abandoned bundle of paper: as if a lazy but fairly well-educated employee of some lost-and-found office had come across the manuscript, read a few lines and thought the best way to avoid trouble was to classify the thing according to a cautious bureaucratic Aristotelianism: *Comedy*. And *Comedy* is in fact a title that has often appeared a mistake, an understatement that is not really in keeping with the overall tone of the poem. Saverio Bettinelli had already expressed great doubts about the title of the book:

> [E]veryone found it a strange title, as we are persuaded that it ought to be an epic poem, such as all Italy preached, like the *Iliad* and the *Aeneid*, nor could we understand why it was called a *Comedy*. And it seemed all the more so, when we found this *Divine Comedy* divided into three parts,

as if it were a scientific treatise, and these parts entitled Hell, Purgatory, Paradise. It came to everyone's mind that Dante wanted to play a joke and really stage a comedy.[28]

And yet the title of Dante's poem, entirely intentional and chosen at least as carefully as the verses of which it is made up, is *Comedy*.

Comedy is the most humble, most general of titles, one without specifications, one that does not allow any theme to be excluded, the only one possible for a poem that wants to speak of *everything*, and from a strictly realistic point of view. Thus the sheer size of the poem imposes the extreme humility of its language, whose only possible mode is the comic one, the *sermo humilis* or "low speech." The letter to Cangrande—whoever its author may have been[29]—leaves no doubts: the tone of the *Comedy* is deliberately the lowest, the most general possible: "*remissus est modus et humilis, quia locutio vulgaris, in qua et muliercule communicant.*"[30]

The *Comedy* places itself on the everyday linguistic plane, it sets its tone "at the lowest level."[31] Dante does not tire of putting himself at the disposal of the language, of showing how solutions are already there in contemporary Italian, remaining always "the servant of his language, rather than the master of it."[32] Once again it is Bettinelli's invaluable letter that throws light on the extent of the material, its programmatic immensity, its challenge to the classical theory of literary genres:

> Oh, how exhausting it was for us to drag ourselves, for a hundred cantos and fourteen thousand lines, through many circles and *bolge*, amongst a myriad abysses and precipices along with Dante, who fainted at every fear, slept at every stroke and woke up badly, and troubled me, his duke and commander, with the newest and strangest things that have ever been! ... Acheron, Minos, Charon, the Three-Headed Hound I knew well in the poetic Hell; but, together with them, Limbo and the Holy Fathers, and at a short distance Horace the satirist, Ovid, Lucan, then a little farther on a castle, where there are Camilla and Penthesilea with Hector and with Aeneas, Lucretia, Julia, Marcia, Cornelia, and Saladin soldier of Babylon with Brutus, finally Dioscorides with Orpheus, Tullius with Euclid, and with these people the two Arabs Averroes and Avicenna, ... And then all are talkative and garrulous in the midst of torments, or bliss, and never tire of recounting their strange adventures,

of resolving theological doubts or of asking tidings of a thousand Tuscan friends or enemies, and I know not what else.[33]

The economy of the *Comedy* is founded on this leveling universalism, where the whole enormous mass of poetry[34] is neatly laid out in the cells of a colossal spreadsheet in which all the dead are recorded, carefully divided up into different degrees of virtue. Dante brings together figures who have nothing to do with one another,[35] taken from different ages and places, and sets them one against the other in sequences that recognize no other category than that of (presumed) divine justice. Dante puts everyone on trial,[36] and in order to do so he has to bring them to life using the sole means at his disposal, language, and the only language that suits this universal trial is the comic one.

Starting out from an examination of the language of Dante and Petrarch, Contini has distinguished in the history of Italian culture a *multilingual* tendency and a *monolingual* tendency.[37] These two tendencies are not just the product of Contini's extraordinary historiographic construction, but cultural orientations already clear to their respective founders. Dante and Petrarch were well aware of the premises and consequences of their work and they fielded their "parties" in a wholly conscious way.

Dante's *multilingual* project envisaged a plurality of styles, a mixture of literary genres, the use of technical or foreign or dialectal terms and an *incessant experimentalism*. This project also reflected an explicit theoretical interest in the problems of language, one that did not entail a philological approach but retained an essentially linguistic and logical tone. Petrarch on the contrary constructed his revival of the classical in explicit opposition to the logicians (the "modern sophists" of Oxford and Paris) and threw discredit on logic as a form of knowledge, mocking its formalism and abstruse terminology.[38] Petrarch's project was authentic and aristocratic, cautious and modern, learned and romantic, polished and introspective.[39] Dante's was intellectualistic and plebeian, experimental and archaic, naive and classicistic, colossal and impersonal.[40] These were all characteristics that attracted the plebeian Bramante to the *party* that was willing to let him speak.

V

In an extremely ugly fresco painted for the house of Gaspare Visconti (long thought to be the property of Gottardo Panigarola, with the result that the frescoes are still known by that name[41]), Bramante depicted Heraclitus and Democritus, the "laughing" philosopher contrasted with the "weeping" one.[42] In the eighteenth century, Giuseppe Allegranza suggested that Democritus might be a self-portrait of Bramante. What particularly aroused the suspicions of the learned Dominican father was Bramante's shiny pate: "whose baldness had almost made me believe that Bramante had painted himself with a youthful air, but with a wisp of hair in the Gelasinus and Democritus above the Borri fireplace."[43]

More recently Carlo Pedretti has again proposed Democritus as a self-portrait of Bramante.[44] Indeed, the figure does show a certain resemblance to other presumed portraits of Bramante, such as the Euclid in the *School of Athens* and the prophet Joel in the Sistine Chapel, but these identifications are not certain either.[45] All that can be said of this particular Democritus is that he is horrendous, and that only a man with Bramante's passion for self-deprecation could have painted such an ugly picture of himself (which is perhaps the most persuasive argument for seeing Bramante in this balding and overweight philosopher).

If indeed this lumpen Democritus is Bramante, this could be read as a genuine taking of sides. In Milan, at the age of forty, after two decades of a less than brilliant apprenticeship in the Lombard provinces, Bramante knew he enjoyed a certain amount of credit[46] and felt entitled to take a public stand and pick his party. Thus, in the dreadful Democritus in Casa Visconti, this very self-conscious non-wunderkind would bring his slow and very patchy education to a conclusion by laying explicit claim to the comic tone of his work, thereby joining up again, through the work of Piero and Giotto, with the party to which he *ardently* wished to belong, the *Party of Comedy*.

Contini has acknowledged "Dante's inspired responsibility for the immediate conversion of the problem of poetry into a question of language":

Donato Bramante, *Heraclitus and Democritus*,
ca. 1480–1482 © Pinacoteca di Brera, Milan.

Art historians are amazed that, in comparing the history of painting from Cimabue to Giotto ... with that of poetry from the two Guidos to himself, [Dante] redeemed figurative dignity from craftsmanship; but historians of poetry should be no less astonished that "the glory of the tongue" is invoked here, in whose artisanal operation Dante precludes himself no possibility. He is helped by his belief in the continuity from Latin to the vernacular, which allows him to take possession of any tradition at the moment in which it makes itself available to any innovation.[47]

Here Contini, in just a few incredibly dense lines, identifies some fundamental aspects that apply as much to Dante's project as to that of his "ardent champion." Dante's "immediate conversion of the problem of poetry" into a "question of language" corresponds to Bramante's conversion of the indirect work on space into a carefully monitored work on the architectural order. And in his case too we are looking at an "artisanal operation" which is based on an opportunistic and at the same time rigorous assertion of the "continuity from Latin to the vernacular" (from the architecture of the Romans to contemporary architecture), and which sustains a voracious and omnivorous classicism, uninhibitedly bent on taking "possession of any tradition at the moment in which it makes itself available to any innovation." Here we really are talking about the same project, with the same "irrepressible experimentalism" and the same "complete open-mindedness toward reality," with the same brazen tendency to exaggeration and the courage of someone who "precludes himself no possibility."

VI

The *Comedy* provides a crude premise for all this public artistic work and thus also establishes the specific, cruel generosity of the party that coincides with it. All this work is in fact driven by love; love is the root of all public activity, the fundamental and highly impersonal feeling on which all coexistence is based:

amor sementa in voi d'ogne virtute
e d'ogne operazion che merta pene.[48]

... amore, a cui reduci
ogne buono operare e 'l suo contraro.[49]

This public love (which is *love*, not *duty*, and which therefore does not exist without a clear predilection for an object outside oneself) is expressed in form: in language, in painting, in architecture. And as love, it is anything but peaceful, and perhaps today appears incredibly violent, but this is exactly what it is: public love, which Dante would—if only he could—have made triumph with the sword.

PART II
POLITICAL WORK

REALISM

21 After seeing the cathedral

According to Vasari, Bramante became an architect somewhat by accident. While there is certainly not much truth in this part of the *Life*,[1] it does point to an aspect that is worth looking at. The story begins in the manner of a fairytale:

> He was born at Castel Durante in the state of Urbino, to a father who was poor but of good quality.[2]

Then the hero leaves home and immediately finds the going hard:

> ... he left Castel Durante and made his way to Lombardy, where he went from one city to another, working as best he could. Not on things of great cost or that brought him much credit, however, as he had as yet no renown or reputation.[3]

In the dispiriting calm of provincial Lombardy, Bramante did his best to while away the time:

> So that, determined to at least see something notable, he went to Milan to see the cathedral.[4]

This passage is followed by a brief digression on the artistic milieu of Milan,[5] before Vasari returns to our hero:

> But to go back to Bramante, after seeing this building and meeting these engineers, he took heart and resolved to devote himself fully to architecture. So he left Milan and came to Rome ...[6]

For Vasari Bramante was a *ligéra*,[7] still mooching around at the age of fifty, unsure what to do with himself, when he was blown away by a Sunday outing to the cathedral. As a result he left for Rome, where—once again having nothing better to do—he rediscovered the architecture of antiquity, so that:

> ... the same eternal gratitude shown to the ancients by those who study their efforts should also be felt for the labors of Bramante.[8]

Vitruvius, *De Architectura. Translato, commentato et affigurato da Cesare Cesariano*, 1521, Book I, XVI.

This clumsy and quite prosaic *Bildungsroman* does throw light on two aspects: in the first place Bramante was much prone to boredom, and secondly he became interested in architecture only after observing buildings that already existed. Bramante needed to "see the cathedral" to develop an interest in architecture. His work emerged as a reaction, as analysis and criticism of prior forms. His intelligence kicked into action only "after seeing this building."

It was to Milan Cathedral that he devoted the *Opinio*, the advisory report entered in the minutes of the Vestry Board at the meeting held on June 27, 1490.[9] In the *Opinio*, Bramante lists four criteria to be followed in the completion of the church: "strength," "congruence with the rest of the building," "lightness" and "beauty." The most important of these is the second, "*conformità cum el resto del edificio*" in the original. Even the fairly awkward manner in which the concept is introduced shows that we are not dealing here with a formula adopted in accordance with a preestablished professional etiquette.[10] For Bramante "congruence with the rest of the building" is truly the most important criterion in finding the best solution for the completion of the cathedral. Over a third of the text is devoted to this theme.[11] In order to draw his conclusions with regard to "congruence," Bramante briefly describes the building. It is a very unusual description: the author sets out to show how the cathedral is organized and breaks down its machinery into elements that are neither structural nor geometric nor symbolic. The analysis does not divide the building up into pillars, buttresses, and vaults, nor into squares and circles, nor even into orders or figures, but into basic spatial units (solid volumes and empty volumes) that are then combined in accordance with a mathematical rule. The description is orderly, objective, and realistic, and at the same time maintains an extremely abstract tone without ever being distracted by questions that do not concern space, apart from a few inevitable references to structural aspects. The *Opinio* presents a singular picture of the cathedral: the church is stripped of its Gothic atmosphere and turned into a limpid grouping of volumes,[12] from which Bramante deduces the form of the missing piece (the lantern on a square base):

... I say that this building is divided into four volumes of different heights, some of the same width and some not; and as you can well understand, the nave in the middle is the main volume that guides the whole building. At the sides descend two wings, making the two minor volumes, which are equal in width but different in height, as we said above, because the one that comes closer to the walls is lower. So that this first wing is about forty ells high; the second fifty-two, and the one in the middle eighty; and because the second volume is higher than the first, as is necessary for the strength of the building, buttresses run from the pillars of the first volume, which correspond to the pillars of the second, so from the pillars of the second run buttresses that correspond to the pillars of the third, which is the nave. And because this nave is roofed entirely with half-square cross vaults, nowhere is it possible to make a perfect square, except where the crossing intersects with it. In no other place can a volume of greater height than it be built except there. Therefore this is the square above which it will be possible to place the fourth volume, called the lantern, because it is square, and because all the rest of the church leads to it and is long; so it is necessary, in order to make this fourth volume fit with the other three underneath it that were referred to above, to have buttresses that correspond to this fourth volume run from the pillars of the third one, that is from the nave, and in that way the building will be regular, and otherwise it cannot look good ...[13]

By analyzing the relations between the forms given in the context, the architect can select, from within the stock of examples provided by the buildings of the past, the solutions best suited to solving the problem he has been assigned. At the end of the *Opinio* Bramante enunciates a cursory theory of montage:

... if these engineers wish, when we are assembled there before your Excellencies, in not even an hour, taking from this [model] one thing, and from that another, as I said above, we could make one from them, which would look good.[14]

Architecture is reduced to a realistic analysis and a choice made from a set of given cases,[15] that "in not even an hour, taking from this one thing, and from that another" leads to the production of the most rational assemblage of forms, "which would look good."

Bramante tackled the problems that were presented to him with extreme caution. He observed, de-coded and re-coded. His talent was for *criticism*.[16] His friends complained about it, however jokingly. Gaspare Visconti wrote: "*da l'altra parte il mio dottor Bramante / Mi morde quando il verso è grosso e umile.*"[17]

The attitude that Visconti recognized in Bramante's "literary criticism" can also be found in his architecture. No matter how unpredictable, and often paradoxical, were the expressions of Bramante's intelligence, they were never "original." They were always developments of something that was already there in the problem he was confronted with. Bramante never did away with the question from which he started out, never resolved anything by sheer ability. Indeed, in a certain sense, it is clear that Bramante was not particularly able, that he was not blessed with talent. It suffices to look at his pictures, for instance the horrible *Flagellation* attributed to him by Bellosi,[18] with its two perverts in underpants fumbling with ropes like small-town pensioners who have watched a few *kinbaku* lessons on YouTube. Bramante's skill was wholly defensive, made up entirely of suspicion and sarcasm. In a way we can see in his work the mark of a rustic intelligence,[19] a skeptical and mistrustful one, wary even of the fashions that it promoted. Bramante was not one of the elect and was not even disposed to pretend that he was (his was possibly the highest artistic career possible for someone unwilling to accept the ignominious title of genius). Even his elegance was *graceless* and Bramante was not always able to refrain from bad jokes or from pedantry. His buildings always follow rigid and explicit aesthetic codes, and these are also the source of their specific sweetness, one which invariably leaves a bitter, acrid aftertaste. His work is always visible; Bramante was too provincial to permit himself any *sprezzatura*.[20] He could only "exhibit art" and so (from Castiglione's perspective) "destroy the grace in everything."

Bramante's critical tone was never directed at anything other than the operation of design itself. If the dropped triglyphs of the Palazzo del Te seem to allude to a more general crisis, and are therefore to be understood as a comment on the instability of the universe or the disorder of the times, the frame of the door that cuts the pilasters on the exterior of the cella of San Pietro in Montorio, or the gigantic cornice set on top of the tiny octagonal lantern of the sacellum of San Satiro, do nothing but demonstrate the flimsiness of the hypotheses on which those very designs are based. The volumes of the two buildings are very small, but the corresponding architectural elements cannot help but maintain their dimensions: a door remains a door, a cornice remains a cornice, and so the ornament ends up deliberately abnormal, rigorously grotesque. These so purposefully ill-chosen forms expose the doubts that the designer of these buildings had about his own method of working. Bramante's sarcasm was in the first instance aimed at himself. His intelligence felt an obligation to reveal its failures, to declare bankruptcy at the very moment that everyone else was convinced of its complete success.

Bramante's nastiness proved even worse when directed at others. In this regard, the most disconcerting evidence is provided by drawing UA8 in the collection of the Uffizi, which has on the recto a proposal by Giuliano da Sangallo for St. Peter's and on the verso the brutal corrections made to it by Bramante. As far as I know, this is a drawing which has no equivalent in the history of architecture. The two most important architects of the day were not only at work on the same project, but working on the basis of the same repertoire and the same cultural hypothesis, and yet were in profound disagreement over the sense of this hypothesis and the formal objectives of this specific project (and one of them was also mean enough to expose all of the other's mistakes). On the back of the sheet on which Giuliano had drawn his plan, Bramante traced—*in nervösem Griff*[21] —his rapid corrections. With just a few lines, he broadened the niches in the piers, made the apses protrude on the outside, beyond the square block that defined Giuliano's church, reintroduced the ambulatories, making them correspond to the outward-facing niches of

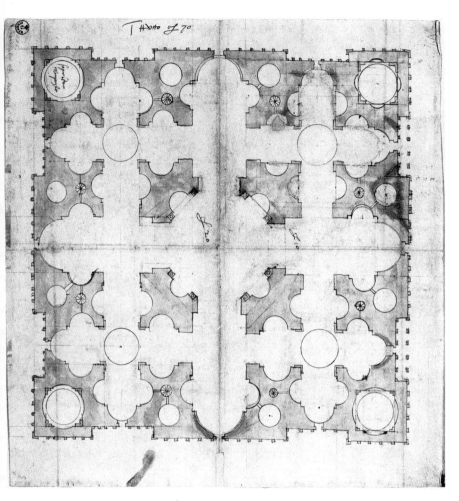

Giuliano da Sangallo, project for St. Peter's,
UA8r, ca. 1506, Gabinetto Disegni e Stampe,
Galleria degli Uffizi, Florence.

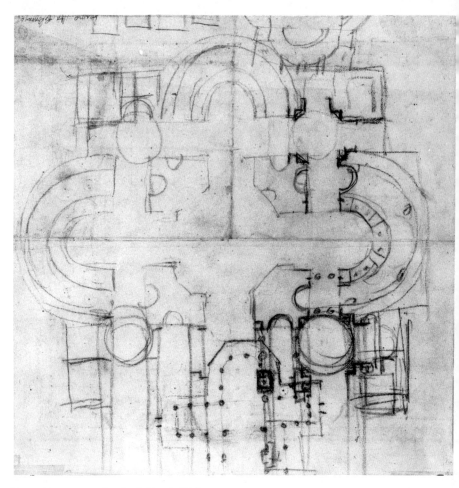

Donato Bramante, project for St. Peter's, UA8v,
ca. 1506, Gabinetto Disegni e Stampe,
Galleria degli Uffizi, Florence.

the central piers, multiplied the planes, inserted screens of columns and reconstructed a whole universe of smaller objects that served to underline the immense size of the church. For Bramante, Giuliano *had taken the solid for the void*, inverting the hierarchy between space and volume, and thus had squandered the richness contained in the initial hypothesis (Bramante's UA1 drawing, which established the starting point for all subsequent ideas for St. Peter's). Giuliano had clogged the church with dull and immense piers that had the sole merit of being structurally credible and had forgotten to hollow out niches in them that would be able to make the spaces between them vibrate, opening up a multitude of vistas. In Giuliano's drawing the dimensions of the building can no longer be discerned: the scale is lost and all that remains is a grotesque gigantism; St. Peter's looks like a parish church that has fallen into a cauldron of steroids, like Obelix as a baby. Bramante could not refrain from a rather unsavory sarcasm: the hasty citations of Milan Cathedral in the lower half and of San Lorenzo in the top right-hand corner seem to have been placed there solely to mock the authority of the Tuscan tradition so dear to Giuliano. We might ask under what circumstances this drawing was produced. Was it a private meeting? Did they exchange the drawings without even speaking to each other? Had Bramante resorted to some trick to get his hands on Giuliano's folio? Or did all this take place right in front of the pope? It is not hard to imagine Bramante taking his rival's drawing, turning the sheet over, heading to a window and, holding it up against the light, starting to scribble on the back while poking fun at Giuliano out loud, and being at once outdone by the pope in an outpouring of obscenity and malevolence.[22] In any case, this display of cruelty was not pointless, or at least it did not just serve to humiliate poor Giuliano. Bramante did not spare his own ideas: from a structural point of view Giuliano's much maligned proposal was more credible than Bramante's original proposition, and his "constructive" criticism was not ignored. In the passage from the first to the later stages of UA20, by way of UA1 and UA8v,[23] Bramante widened the pier that supported the dome and carved enormous niches out of it, decidedly larger than the ones devised at the beginning of the design process. The entire system was simplified and made more solid. The end product of this series—the drawing known as "Raphael's plan" and published by Serlio in his *terzo libro*[24]—is decidedly more robust than the hypothesis outlined in UA1. And yet, unlike in Giuliano's leaden solution, the spatial richness of the first proposal has not been lost. It is just better understood, precisely because of the laborious and ruthless reduction to which it has been subjected over the course of this long series of corrections.

23 *Prevedari Engraving*

Bramante's architectural work (at least that which we know of) begins with the drawing engraved by Bernardo Prevedari in Milan in 1481.[25] An explicitly avant-garde work, the engraving served to distinguish its author from his Milanese competitors and further his career at the court of Ludovico il Moro. What it depicts is the interior of a building in which there are around fifteen human figures. The building is partly in ruin and it is not clear whether it is a temple or a basilica or something else, nor, if it is a place of worship, what religion it belongs to. It is not even clear whether it is a building on a central or a basilica plan of which only the end part is represented.[26] The space is viewed from the inside (or perhaps it is a ruin without its façade, viewed from just outside?) and is defined by two piers and external walls that support four vaults, each different from the others. The aisle on the left concludes in an apse surmounted by a semidome decorated with a scallop shell. In front of the apse, at the end of the aisle, there may be a statue, but it is hidden by the candelabrum on an octagonal base a bit closer to the viewer. The various groups of figures in the building seem to share only the space in which they happen to be: the horsemen and the soldiers on the right do not seem to have anything to do with the two men apparently engaged in learned conversation on the left, or with the more prosaic figures in the background, beyond the candelabrum. The monk (?) kneeling in the foreground appears even more isolated.[27] The main order, which defines the impost of the vaults of the nave, is Corinthian. The order comprised within this principal framework is Doric. Both the orders are set on pedestals. The lunettes and vaults have round openings decorated with very different motifs (the ones that are not too foreshortened contain a wheel with eight balusters and a head with its face concealed[28]). The friezes are decorated with faces, putti, a procession of carts, oxen, and horses. The clipei contain more heads. The most obvious feature of the *Prevedari Engraving* is the amount of stuff that is crammed into it.

We could almost speak, if it did not sound so out of place in Bramante's case, of *horror vacui*. The engraving is filled with things.

Like all the painters of his generation, Bramante had to deal with the problem of Piero della Francesca's "grand form" ("the grand figures, the grand action, and the severe landscape"[29]). And like all the painters of his generation, Bramante tried to connect the monumental dimension of Piero's figures with the multiple manifestations of contemporary urban life, and sought to come up with a more versatile and varied art:

> Piero's style suggested a fondness for sturdy forms and space articulated by means of powerful figures standing out from an energetically cadenced background. But this influence, while strong, clashed with the opposite tendency, toward the singular, the minute, the tormented.[30]

This was the problem faced by the younger pupils in Francesco Squarcione's workshop,[31] and who knows if Bramante encountered it through direct contact with the "gangs of desperate vagabonds, sons of tailors, barbers, cobblers, and peasants who passed through Squarcione's workshop in those twenty years."[32] The *Prevedari Engraving* is just an architectural version of this problem. The drawing seems to reflect a theme that Bramante would continue to explore from that time on: given the amount of ambitions, interests, and discourses that produce space, how is it possible for the architect to control it? Is it possible to guarantee the survival in form of the multitude of desires that produce it? Is it possible to get the plurality of signs to coincide with the unity of space?

The response of the *Prevedari Engraving* is clear, even though fairly schematic. The space is structured in a unified manner; signs are accumulated without exclusions. There are sculptures, heads, clipei, friezes, putti, plaques, balusters, and keystones in every corner. Bramante accepts that the building should take in every message that wants a place in it. By renouncing full control of the final form, architecture seems to be able to define a tone capable of picking up an entire spectrum of whims, pretensions, and vanities, in a way allowing the form to oscillate within a field of existence without determining it fully. The building is thronged with a decidedly exaggerated and perhaps even

Bernardino Prevedari after Donato Bramante,
Interior of Temple with Figures (Prevedari Engraving),
1481, Milan, Castello Sforzesco, Civica Raccolta
di Stampe Achille Bertarelli.

intentionally grotesque amount of signs. Bramante makes it clear that nothing should be excluded from his architecture. He declares that his buildings are ready to say everything that the dukes and their courts want them to say. This ostentatious availability is not very reassuring: the signs are too many and too contradictory to permit an unambiguous interpretation.[33]

The *Prevedari Engraving* was a way for Bramante to showcase his skills. And yet, even in this case, where it would not have been difficult for him to demonstrate his adherence to the most advanced disciplinary paradigms and to give vent to his most unbridled fantasies, Bramante preferred to propose a construction without many pretensions and to refer to fairly unfamiliar precedents. The very peculiar combination of modesty and arrogance that distinguishes Bramante's work is already all here: the drawing that marks the beginning of the most ambitious career of an architect in the whole of European classicism presents a space as large as a tennis court[34] that is perhaps copied from some small churches in the province of Ancona (according to an interesting suggestion made by Wolff-Metternich,[35] the spatial scheme of the building represented in the engraving derives from some small Byzantine buildings in the Marche: San Vittore alle Chiuse, Santa Maria delle Moie and Santa Croce a Sassoferrato). When Bramante presented himself to his possible new patron (in what was the great *and up until that moment the only* chance of his life), he proposed a drawing based not on updated Florentine models but on the long-forgotten churches of his home region. This middle-aged painter, already a semi-failure, had so much confidence in his critical operations that he did not fear the cultural isolation to which the oddity of his sources would have appeared to condemn him. Here provincial skepticism matched metropolitan audacity, here consciousness of his own *unlettered* state coincided with supreme intellectual independence.

24 Opportunities and propaganda

For the architecture of the Renaissance two conditions applied: the range of *opportunities* for practicing architecture were given, and the range of forms to be used in architecture were equally given. The operations on forms carried out by Bramante should be viewed in this context of limited possibilities and gauged on the basis of the veritable *theory of opportunity* that was elaborated in the Renaissance. Here it suffices to quote a well-known passage from *The Prince*:

> And in examining their actions and lives one cannot see that they owed anything to fortune beyond opportunity, which brought them the material to mould into the form which seemed best to them. Without that opportunity their powers of mind would have been extinguished, and without those powers the opportunity would have come in vain. It was necessary, therefore, to Moses that he should find the people of Israel in Egypt enslaved and oppressed by the Egyptians, in order that they should be disposed to follow him so as to be delivered out of bondage. It was necessary that Romulus should not remain in Alba, and that he should be abandoned at his birth, in order that he should become King of Rome and founder of the fatherland. It was necessary that Cyrus should find the Persians discontented with the government of the Medes, and the Medes soft and effeminate through their long peace ...[36]

For Machiavelli opportunity is a moment of uncertainty in fate, a brief space of possibility that can be used to mold the desired form in the material on which the political subject has the opportunity to act. This scheme is repeated at the beginning of the "Life" of Bramante. Vasari introduces the situation that provides Bramante with his opportunity in exactly the same terms as Machiavelli presents those of Moses, Romulus, and Cyrus ("it was necessary, therefore"):

> But no less necessary than all this was the election at that time of Julius II, an energetic pope anxious to make his mark on posterity. And it was both our and his fortune ...[37]

The systematic pursuit of every possible opportunity led Bramante to accept any professional assignment he was offered. Bramante did a bit of everything: he traveled on behalf of the duke or the pope, inspected fortresses in Val d'Ossola and canals in Oltrepò Pavese, made a measured survey of the Ospedale Maggiore to be presented to the Venetian ambassador, copied astrological designs to decorate a room in Vigevano, organized the celebrations for the baptism of a prince of the House of Sforza, and may have designed the decorations for the wedding of Gian Galeazzo and Isabella of Aragon. In Milan and in Rome, he accepted jobs that were anything but exciting: the renovation of the rooms of the castle in Vigevano, the "little bridge" of the Castello Sforzesco, the parish church of Roccaverano. He did serious work on the Milanese rural repertoire and equally serious work on the Roman courtly repertoire: on the farmhouse porch of the church of Abbiategrasso as well as on the smug chic of the nymphaeum at Genazzano. Bramante seems always to have relished the complications that arose to disturb those situations. Costantino Baroni has rightly pointed out the "boldness of the improvised and makeshift solutions"[38] that characterize his work. As a true master of counterattack, Bramante derived his finest pieces from these impediments: the *false choir* of San Satiro where no choir could be built, the exedra that links up the divergent orientations of Innocent VIII's Belvedere and the upper courtyard, the other deliberately wrong exedra of the lower courtyard that frames the Apostolic Palace as if it were a rock formation, the hole carved in the bottom of the altar of the Tempietto di San Pietro in Montorio to make room for the stairs and illuminate the crypt. Bramante never opposed the existing city, never wished to remake the world from scratch. Even his purely theoretical contributions, such as the *Prevedari Engraving*, were not in any way fanciful. Bramante, *Architekt der irdischen Welt*, was completely indifferent to the utopian city, nothing could be of less interest to him than Filarete's "demented Babels."[39] Even his more implausible and reckless proposals (such as when he suggested turning the basilica of St. Peter's around to align its façade with the Vatican obelisk[40]) were always conceived with the intention of actually putting them into effect.

Leonardo Da Vinci (?), Sala delle asse after restoration
by Ernesto Rusca (1902), detail, Castello Sforzesco,
Milan © Civico Archivio Fotografico.

Bramante could not pick the opportunities which came his way, but he did try to forge a link between the different episodes of his career, orienting them toward the future and at the same time using them to redefine the past. Thus a critical tone and a promotional tone were intertwined in the series of his projects: the reflection on previous episodes coincided with the production of openings for possible follow-ups. Each new work criticized the conclusions drawn from the works that had preceded it in the series and promoted the possibility of new experiments in the ones that would follow. Criticism and promotion came to coincide in an activity that had to invent new opportunities each time by showcasing the earlier products, and was able to criticize the results achieved only by procuring new opportunities. It is this contradiction between Bramante's singularly reluctant muse and his desperate need for success that causes the imbalance which is so typical of his work. On the one hand his architecture is logical and in a way arid, on the other it is ready to make any compromise in order to obtain new opportunities for experimentation. The fact is that architecture, to a greater extent than all the other arts, is an *art on commission.*[41]

In architecture, success (and the strategy of promotion inevitably associated with it) comes *before* the possibility to experiment. Architecture has to win the trust of the client before it can put itself to the test: "it has to sell before it produces."[42] In this sense architecture is closer to politics than to the other arts. In politics, it is necessary to take power before exercising it, and it is necessary to represent the desired transformation of society in order take power. The same is true in architecture: you have to get your hands on the resources needed to construct buildings before you can do so, and in order to get these resources you have to represent what you want to build.[43] In Bramante's case the craving for opportunities to actually build—the real torment of any architect's career, and one that in his case is evident even from his nickname[44]—ended up conditioning the forms and altering the organization of the construction. The built form was adapted to the needs of his promotional strategies, becoming spectacle and publicity. It was held up, as soon as it was produced, as testimony and guarantee. Each building was the security for the next possibility to design. Each building was made in order to make a bigger one immediately afterward.

If buildings are episodes in an advertising campaign, then it is not just their quality that counts but also the speed with which they can be brought onto the market. Construction becomes the supreme rhetorical device at the architect's disposal. The need to obtain the building in time for it to appear in the advertising campaign for the next building prevails over the care needed to ensure its perfect execution. The haste of which Bramante has been accused on more than one occasion stems from this fundamental choice.[45] For Bramante, it was not particularly important to construct well. It was much more important to construct quickly, in order to be able to show results and secure new opportunities. The most important space was the one *seen* and *remembered*, the one able to stick in the memory and sway people's imagination. The entire organization of the building process was modified by decisions that pushed it toward an immediate, prodigious appearance of the figure. The most extreme and absurd example of this use of construction as a rhetorical device is the choir of St. Peter's, which was built at breakneck speed so that it could be put on show immediately,[46] even though Bramante knew that it would have to be demolished as it could not support the weight of the dome that he imagined on top of the pillars, on whose completion he was working at the same time. Bramante had to demonstrate to the pope—and perhaps to himself as well—that the church could actually be built. He had to show results as soon as possible, in order to encourage the pope and steady his (never certain) resolve to carry on with the initiative. The choir, which would immediately fill with cracks and have to be demolished in 1585, was literally a *paper tiger*, a preview of the triumph of space that would be presented in the church, if only it were to be constructed according to Bramante's plans.[47] The image entrusted to the choir prefigured the church that it anticipated, but the real material of which it was made did not. The piers and the choir were incompatible. The choir in fact could not have withstood the thrust of the dome that was to be built on top of the piers.[48] In Bramante's plans, the image he had temporarily presented would then have to succumb, so as to rise perfectly from its ashes in an even more majestic and triumphal form.[49]

Bramante *renounced linguistic invention*,[50] but this does not mean that he tried to shelter his work from language. On the contrary, he designed deliberately sticky buildings, able to let themselves be covered with words, to become figures, to celebrate and advertise—it didn't matter what. Bramante was willing to pretend that buildings could speak, if that was a condition of making them. Nothing was precluded: Bramante saw "meanings" as essentially uncontrollable and transitory and therefore endlessly negotiable and adaptable to the requirements of the client. His lack of confidence in the possibility of communicating through architecture ended up justifying the most extreme opportunism. His buildings were immediately at the disposal of everyone, the bad as well as the good. In Tafuri's customary high-flown words: "... in Bramante's work, the autonomy of the formal research and the observance of an external ideological dictate were combined with one another in a hermetic and ambiguous synthesis."[51] In a way it seems that Bramante bet on the narrative inefficacy of his buildings, on the frailty of their magniloquence, as if this premeditated failure to communicate could legitimize any alliance, authorize any ambiguity, as if architectural forms could evade responsibility for the monsters they brought into the world solely by dint of their insurmountable silence.

25 Tempietto

Bramante's career combines episodes of extreme rarefaction, buried in a disciplinary discourse that does not seem to have been at all concerned about the reactions of those outside it, with moments of shameless vulgarity, in which the architect seems to have brought onto the market precisely the product that the public was anticipating.[52] Bramante consciously alternated—and deliberately muddled—his *prêt-à-porter* and his *haute couture* lines. The most disconcerting example of this two-faced program is the Tempietto di San Pietro in Montorio.

The problem presented by the Tempietto was how to provide a culture with the image it was expecting, how to produce a recognizable and consumable object, perfectly fixed at the center of the contemporary imagination. When it appeared in early sixteenth-century Rome, the Tempietto did not trigger an "explosive moment"[53] in the way that Brunelleschi's *tablets* or Mies van der Rohe's Barcelona Pavilion did. Rather it acted as a confirmation, underscoring a body of knowledge that was substantially already available. The Tempietto is one of those rare cases in which an expected and hoped-for event occurred right in front of all the people who were waiting for it, a bit like so-called *cold fusion*, if it had ever worked.[54] The Tempietto responded to these expectations in an extremely literal and cursory manner: all the ingredients of the most obvious and unbridled classicism were lumped together. The catalogue of stereotypes was complete. Nothing was lacking: the absolute geometry, the symmetry, the circle, the freestanding columns, the Doric order, the metopes, the triglyphs, the dome, the literal adherence to some of Vitruvius's prescriptions.[55] Bramante assembled all these classical components with the nonchalance and cynicism of a Hollywood director.[56] He solved in a marvelous way the trivial (but not easy) problem he had assigned himself. In the Tempietto, the extremely refined solutions all sprang directly from the classicistic bulimia of the initial hypothesis. The circular geometry, the Doric columns, the triglyphs, and the dome are *givens of*

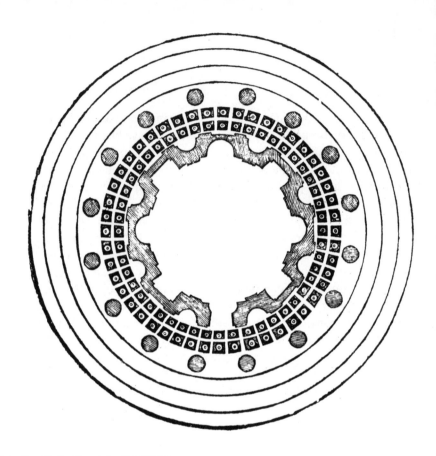

Sebastiano Serlio, Tempietto di San Pietro
in Montorio, *On Antiquities*, Venice, 1544,
Book III, XLII.

Donato Bramante, Tempietto di San Pietro
in Montorio, ca. 1502–1508, exterior from
P. Portoghesi, *Roma del Rinascimento*,
Rome: Electa, 1971.

the problem, while the rhythm of the walls of the cella, the insertion of the door, and the articulation of the interior space with four apses along the diagonals are on the contrary *solutions*.[57] And even though the Tempietto was primarily an image to be deployed as part of a marketing strategy, Bramante did not fail to treat it as a space as well. Even in this case the work was carried out with great attention and a sense of practicality. The result is astonishing: the room inside the tiny church, which has an internal diameter of just 4.56 m, is surprisingly airy. Bramante made some fairly counterintuitive decisions: despite the reduced size, the wall is thick (around 75 cm), making it possible to set niches in it, alternately on the inside and the outside. The windows in the drum are rotated through 45 degrees with respect to the ones on the lower level. Thus the small space inside expands into tiny secondary spaces that alter the perception of the room, enlarging its scale to a much greater extent than would have been possible through a uniform expansion of the cella by the small amount that could have been gained with an outer wall of constant section.

With the Tempietto, Bramante showed to everyone that what he was doing could produce results, that the splendor of the classical world could be regained, that any technical difficulties could be resolved, indeed to a great extent were *already solved*. The Tempietto demonstrated that everything that was desired from architecture in the late fifteenth century was possible—and not even all that complicated. Its success was immediate; the credit he earned immense. Thus Bramante was able to lay hands on new resources and move on to a new scale of problems.

26 *Kolossal*[58]

What most struck Bramante about the Roman ruins was the impression of a past grandeur, the glory implicit in the immense scale of the remains scattered around the landscape of Latium. This grandeur was perceived literally, as a matter of size. More than the architectural motifs, Bramante chose to copy the measurements of ancient Rome. Once again his vision of the classical heritage differed from that of his contemporaries. Bramante did not lose sight of the obvious: the ruins were *big*, and the architecture that was needed to transform the *whole* city had to be *big as well*. Bramante recognized the possibility of operating at a scale which had been forgotten since the time of the Romans.[59] He laid explicit claim to this *new dimension*. In UA20 the measurement of the dome's diameter is given with the compass and is exactly 200 palms, the same as the dome of the Pantheon.[60] Even more evident is the act of measurement with which the project of the Belvedere began: on the beautiful medal struck to mark the laying of the foundations[61] are set the large letters "M" and "LXX," which define the dimensions of the enclosure, 1,000 feet (ca. 298 m) long and 70 feet (ca. 21 m) high. The mathematical tone of the object is evident even in its organization: the medal is divided into two halves: the upper half is blank apart from the inscription with the measurements "VIA IVL(ia) III ADIT(uum) LON(gitudinis) M ALTI(tudinis) LXX P(edum)"; the lower half depicts a stretch of rocky ground on which is written "VATICANUS M(ons)." The composition is very simple. Along the diameter, halfway between heaven and earth, running all the way across the medal, is set the new courtyard, with Innocent VIII's villa on the left and the Vatican Palace on the right. The medal is very precise: there is an unequivocal topographic reference (the word "VATICANUS"), the context is given with care and above all there are the measurements of the new complex. Between the two preexisting buildings lies the courtyard, defined by its edges and three terraces. The angle from which the courtyards are viewed is slightly distorted,

Unknown, foundation medal for
the Belvedere, ca. 1504–1508.

as if the more distant edge had been tilted upward just enough to convey an idea of the internal spaces, which look like a system of artificial lakes sloping down toward the Apostolic Palace. The medal sets out the program of the Belvedere perfectly: the small valley between the palace and the villa is delimited by building two walls that frame it in a large rectangular enclosure and the ground is then divided up into a series of terraces; turning the valley into a room open to the sky. In this enormous rectangular room were arranged the exedra, the half-convex and half-concave circular flight of steps, the intersecting ramps with a central niche, the large basalt basin from the Baths of Titus, and the Pigna.[62] The frame was defined so clearly that the accidents and variations due to topography were all welcome: "... the courtyard was ennobled by that interruption, which together with the difference in levels did away with the unpleasantness caused by the length greatly exceeding the width ..."[63]

The sequence of flights and terraces followed the model of the Sanctuary of Fortuna at Palestrina.[64] As at Palestrina, in the Belvedere there are no signs announcing routes, there are no figures that help you get your bearings; the changes of direction are sudden and unpredictable, the enormous arches visible from a distance lead nowhere, the *objets trouvés* explain absolutely nothing. Bramante draws on all his skill in order *not to say anything about* the space, not to anticipate anything, not to insert signs that can be deciphered prior to their experience.

27 The conquest of Beauty

In the final years of Bramante's career the *dimension* of the buildings seems to have grown more and more important.[65] The Palazzo dei Tribunali was a heap of boulders piled up in the city in order to shift its balance with their mere weight, St. Peter's—at least as it appears on Caradosso's medal[66]—was an immense *Merzbau* of bricks in which the mass was meant as a self-sufficient rhetorical device. There was something terrible in these buildings, and Bramante did nothing to hide it. Indeed he appears to have gone in search of the most frightening cases, the most terrible walls, the darkest and deepest shadows.

The validity of the new formal order seems to have depended on its capacity to exercise control over the whole city. Too fragile to simply be *exposed*, beauty had to be *imposed*. Hence the enormous masses that counterbalanced the instability of beauty, allowing it to crash down onto the city and subdue it completely. The *conquest of beauty* was pursued through the construction of gigantic buildings, able to throw the entire city out of kilter.

Bramante always remained a realist. And knowing that he could not transform the whole of the city, he set out instead to control it by inserting dimensionally and formally dominant masses at its critical points. The plan of action was curt and ruthless and came down to just a few interventions, without connections, without axes, without networks (Via Giulia remained an episode, it did not imply a true *plan*). The logic of this urban design without illusions was wholly paratactic: all Bramante needed was a few points in strategic positions, as in the minimal metropolitan program of a young Rem Koolhaas: "A city is a plane of tarmac with some redhot spots of urban intensity."[67]

For all those involved in the story of the demolition and reconstruction of St. Peter's, for the pope, the curia, the architects, and the people of Rome, the new church would be "the greatest building that has ever been seen," as—with unexpected candor—Raphael wrote in a letter to his relatives in the Marche.[68] This shameless love of large buildings exposes an aspect that sounds awkward today,[69] but that nevertheless remains one of the irrepressible characteristics of architecture, to the point where Ugo Foscolo for example considered it to be the *only* significant feature of this "most unfortunate of the arts, precisely because it is the most confined and obliged to remain so: all its beauty depends on the size and the daring of its mass."[70]

The glory of buildings viewed as *masses*, piles heaped up with the sole purpose of proving their *daring*, has gone decidedly out of fashion. Nothing seems further from the ostentatious friendliness of contemporary architecture than buildings which intentionally inspire awe, though it is not possible to say anything significant about the monumental architecture of antiquity and the Renaissance without at least mentioning the menace that these buildings were intended to convey with their sheer presence. Classical architecture set out to intimidate its users: Alberti, despite being highly skeptical with regard to colossal undertakings, says clearly that he would like the temple to be designed in such a way that "anyone who entered it would start with awe ..."[71]

Even today, architecture deals with things that, in the vast majority of cases, are much bigger than people and will last much longer than they do. In addition, architecture requires the deployment of such huge resources that other possible uses of wealth have to be renounced. Beyond a certain scale, therefore, a building is always *public*, always *monumental*, even when it has no intention of being so, as is evident from all the silos, all the data centers, all the power plants, all the airport hangars. Architecture finds itself dealing with objects that tend to contain people and swallow them up, appearing to them as monsters and prodigies.[72] Architecture—simply on the basis of its dimensions in space and time—comes to establish a fundamentally intimidatory relationship with its users and to suggest a span of time in which its builders, clients, architects, and even inhabitants are all going to end up dead. For this great architecture is always, at least in part, funereal, and at the same time strangely optimistic. Architecture contemplates a time in which we will no longer exist, but it does it without sadness, in a way reducing our distance from this future and at least in part

Donato Bramante, Palazzo dei Tribunali,
ca. 1508–1512, photo Stanislaus von Moos, 1970.

determining it: architecture is a way of thinking about a time that we have decided is of interest to us even if we are going to be dead; it is a way of laying claim to a future in which we will not take part.

Bramante was not afraid of agreeing to the most questionable alliances in order to enact his *plan for the conquest of beauty*. If shared beauty can only be beauty *on the scale of the city*, and if the only buildings that can give form to the project of coexistence that is the city are *enormous* buildings, then architects have to lay their hands on the financial resources that will allow them to construct those enormous buildings and impose their presence on the city. But these resources can be accumulated—and then used—only *against* the rules of coexistence of which beauty expounds the law. Just like the rule of a new prince according to Machiavelli, beauty can only be established through an act of force, one that cannot be put into effect without ignoring the laws it proclaims. Like the prince, beauty can only count on the energy stored up by a form of accumulation whose detestable methods cannot be called into question. In order to cope with the absence of beauty already deposited in the city by ages of oppression and stupidity, beauty has to react with appropriate force, has to combat the violence already entrenched in the city with a greater and opposing violence. Thus architecture sees its loftiest and most generous political character immediately contradicted by the actual conditions of its production. All this ends up giving architecture its so characteristically dreadful aftertaste, which is in fact nothing but the dreadful aftertaste of civilization.[73] Architecture, grand monumental architecture, is in fact a theory (and a critique) of institutions (and therefore of violence) and this may be why it is so little loved today, in a society that clings to the childish belief that institutions can always be instantaneously revoked and that violence can always be avoided—and only for the simple reason that it can then go on ignoring the violence that recurs every day.

SPACE

Bramante's work developed out of a very narrow range of architectural elements and graphic instruments. The fundamental element is the wall, the fundamental drawing is the plan.[1]

The wall defines the conditions of spatial experience, what is included in or excluded from rooms, what is located behind a window and thus reduced to an image. The wall is the logical-political operator of an architecture understood as the technique separating the things that are inside a particular set from the things that are outside (and so producing a distinction between things, or people, or social groups). The wall is in the first place a negative element, it prevents you from passing or seeing through it. So, together with its local negations (doors, windows), which in their turn suspend its negation, the wall determines a whole choreography of flows and stases, of constraints and possibilities.

The plan, as the drawing of the walls, defines this geography of possible actions, marks the boundaries of rooms and enclosures, and prescribes the interruptions that allow the body, or at least the gaze, to pass through. The plan selects movements, as is clear from Raymond Hood's impeccable summation:

> the plan is of primary importance, because on the floor are performed all the activities of the human occupants.[2]

For Bramante, defining routes and limiting vision is more important than shielding from the natural elements; social, ritual, and political aspects are more important than those of technology, energy, and climate. Architecture is a discipline of gestures and memories, not just a technology of shelter. The wall is more important than the roof; the plan is more important than the section.[3]

The wall is the barrier that holds in the mass of air, the surface marking the beginning of the void. The wall is the primary means for defining

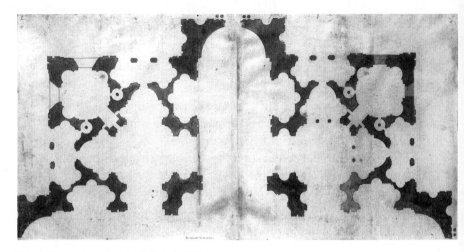

Donato Bramante, project for St. Peter's, UA1, ca.
1506, Gabinetto Disegni e Stampe, Gallerie degli
Uffizi, Florence.

the relationship between people and the setting that receives them, the fundamental tool for the *production of space*. Bramante bends and presses on this mold of the void; thus the wall curves, moving away and coming close and turning into apse, niche, projection, pilaster, vault, conch, dome:

> Bramante was not able to see the surface except dilated by the convexity of the apses, nor could he conceive the plane without taking it beyond the limits of a perspective vision ...[4]

The wall is the means used to build a space that is pictorially imagined. For Bramante:

> The mass is no longer imposed ... as a value of heightened solidity: what matters in this mass is its boundary with the atmospheric space surrounding it; it is the gentle linear vibration of the decoration, the subtle rippling or calm relaxation of the surface that suggests this boundary.[5]

Architecture is brought back entirely to Piero della Francesca's idea of painting, it is nothing "but a demonstration of surfaces."[6]

For Bramante the wall is nothing but the shell that defines the edge of the void. What is *inside* the wall, what remains *behind* its surface, is a matter of complete indifference to him. Materials are irrelevant, construction technology just a distraction. The material he builds with is always the same, a single opaque slime, able to flow into every corner, filling the mold that shapes the void and blocking the propagation of light.[7] All that matters is its radical difference with respect to the void and its ability to model it, give it substance, bestowing on it that hollow but firm appearance, that astounding "sense of solidified but not heavy mass, drowned in a bath of unreal boreal mistiness"[8] that Costantino Baroni recognized in his works. Bramante is not interested in what the wall *is*, he is interested only in what the wall *does*, the effect that the wall exerts on people through the delimitation of void and light.

Bramante never distinguishes the structure from the masonry that is used to plug it.[9] The elements marked on the outer surface of the wall have nothing to do with the material inside it. The substance of the wall is completely different from what it shows on either of its faces: a perfect example of this is the wall of the cella of the Tempietto di San Pietro in Montorio, where the pilasters on the internal and external faces are different in number, position, height, and impost level. The wall separates absolutely the spaces it divides. Defined in this way, the rooms determine wholly distinct moments of perception, which are reconnected only in the memory of their users, not in the substance of the building. Looking at the two sides of drawing UA8, we see that, while Giuliano da Sangallo always *adds* the pilasters and the columns in front of the wall, Bramante hints at them straightaway, already altering the line that defines the walls at the moment of the first draft. The pilasters are marked as small deviations of the perimeter or as thickenings of the line. So the orders are reduced to their mere positional value. The lines of the drawing do not specify whether they are Doric or Ionic or Corinthian pilasters. They just show their positions, their dimensions, and the relations they establish with the other architectural elements distributed in the surrounding areas. The pilasters are used as spatial accents, constrictions that mark and modulate the configuration of the space. This notation was born with the drawing, it was not added later on. Giuliano constructs, and then decorates; Bramante sees always just one problem, configuring space.

Bramante's work on the relationship between the wall and empty space arrived at an incredible conclusion (and one that is even more incredible if we consider his probable point of departure) in the case of the piers of St. Peter's. The solution of the piers came, in fact, through the transept of Pavia Cathedral, from Brunelleschi's Santo Spirito. Bramante saw what for Brunelleschi was just a makeshift solution (the fusion of the walling of the two somewhat squashed apses on the corner between nave and transept[10]) as a method that could be extended to all architecture: the wall, as simple mold of the void, could absorb all the organizational and structural requirements into its mass, thereby leaving space free of any visual irregularity. If form is an attribute *of the void*, then volumes become residues (*"des éléments en soi amorphes et sans individualité"*[11]). The resources for meeting all the practical needs and solving all the problems of construction can be found within the mass of the masonry. Thus, once

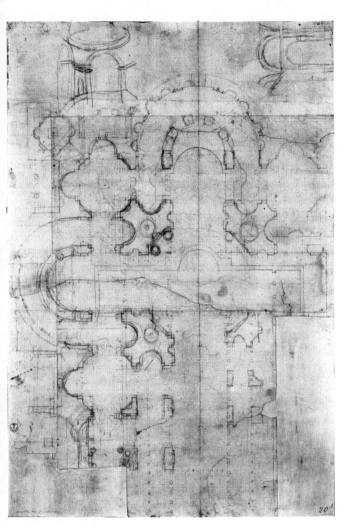

Donato Bramante, project for St. Peter's,
UA20, ca. 1506, Gabinetto Disegni e
Stampe, Galleria degli Uffizi, Florence.

viewed as a "reserve," the wall can be interpreted—in another inversion—as a further opportunity for space. Unsuspected cavities can be discovered *inside* the wall: at Santa Maria presso San Satiro the illusory space of the choir is found entirely within the width of the wall that concludes the church at the end of the nave, jutting out slightly into Via del Falcone and producing the beautiful motif of the rear façade; at San Pietro in Montorio, increasing the thickness of the wall (and thus reducing even more the already scant internal diameter of the cella) made it possible to carve tiny secondary spaces out of the body of the wall and expand the interior visually. At St. Peter's, the dimensions of the piers developed in the successive passages recorded in UA20 are sufficient to let a second order of empty space appear, a lesser void, comprised entirely within the mass of the supporting structure. Bramante carved niches with a width of forty palms in the pier[12] and in this way discovered a void *inside* the supports of the dome as well. The enormous cavities of the pier face in three directions: one inward (mirrored by the opposite niche beyond the dome) and two outward, generating the ambulatories and the small aisle contained within the pillars of the nave. The piers are not matched by equally massive counter-pillars,[13] and so the annular spaces of the ambulatories and the aisles that flank the nave conclude, on the other side of extremely broad arches cut in the counter-pillars, directly in the forty-palm niches. The enormous piers (which are supports and therefore obstacles, opaque elements, *volumes*) correspond to the ambulatories and the aisles (which are corridors and therefore spaces that can be traversed, *voids*). The incredible conclusion at which Bramante arrives through his formal reasoning is that an entire aisle can originate from a pier.[14] The solid and the void are of perfectly equal value and so can exchange roles:

> in Bramante's imagination a solid mass is equivalent to a hollow mass: both are equally unbounded, equally lacking in reality and rich in spatial suggestion.[15]

29 Spectacle of space

For Bramante the wall is never, as it was for Brunelleschi and would be again for Palladio, a screen that the gaze encounters at right angles and onto which the activity of the person moving in space is projected and measured.[16] His rooms never conclude in a flat surface that defines their limit, but twist around in cavities that catch the movement of the eyes and turn them back toward the viewer. The routes do not come to an end; there is always something that refers to somewhere else, mirroring, distorting, deviating. The conclusion is always deferred, there is always a way to escape. Perhaps this way of organizing space also reflects a psychological trait, a desire not to make a statement, to send any possible question back to the observer. At the territorial level, for example in the exedra that concluded the Belvedere, these semicircular elements function as mirrors that oblige viewers to look back toward the place from which they are coming, as in the case of the Sanctuary at Palestrina. In the interiors, in Santa Maria del Popolo for instance, the apses seem to act like bellows, first sucking people in and then puffing them out again, leaving them suspended in an intentionally undetermined position. The sequences of spaces imagined by Bramante leave only a reduced role for static elements like domes or crossings, which remain suspended at a higher level and are often hidden from the view of anyone moving around the buildings. This is the case in San Satiro, in Santa Maria del Popolo, and then in a majestic fashion in the *School of Athens*, and it would have been the same in St. Peter's. Barrel vaults, by contrast, play a fundamental role, arranged in series like channels through which the space flows, often narrowing progressively and thus exaggerating the perspective, stressing one direction, suggesting a movement. Depth is the explicit problem of this architecture,[17] which does not want to bring all the planes back to a single fundamental plane to be used as a measuring instrument of people and space, but lets this dimension oscillate, assigning to the people moving in the space the task of bringing into focus—on each

Raphael, *School of Athens*, ca. 1511,
Archivi Alinari, Florence.

occasion—the specific distance that separates them from the scene in which they are inserted. This work on depth, in which the planes seem to have been deliberately kept blurred,[18] is accentuated by the fact that Bramante often designed choirs for churches, i.e. terminal portions of buildings that already existed and that were strongly oriented toward the parts still to be added. In Santa Maria del Popolo, proceeding from the nave, Bramante inserted first a large arch that detached the choir from the rest of the church, framing the new sequence, and then—in a wholly counterintuitive manner—a cross vault, which broke up the flow of the perspective and suspended the effect of depth, and only after this, the great coffered arch with the main source of light of the whole system at bottom right and finally the apse surmounted by the conch. The choir is made entirely of a single material, uniformly plastered and with no properties, apart from an exaggeratedly light-sensitive whiteness. Bramante wasted most of the space at his disposal on inserting the cross vault that is imperceptible to the observer in the nave and essentially doesn't appear in the perspective series, acting solely as an interval, a particle of emptiness that separates the episodes of the sequence.[19] This architectural machinery absorbs the harsh light of Roman afternoons from the outside and distills it, making it ripple over the crests of the conch before returning it to the church almost tamed, slow and studied like the moves of an ornamental fish. The movement of the light toward the nave—the dazzling counter light of the white choir that must have looked so alien viewed from the nave before the insertion of the altar weakened the effect[20] — contrasts the movement of people through the church. The gaze and the light travel in opposite directions. The inverted movements are distributed on the two sides, animating the space with something like an *oblique function*.[21]

The *spectacles of space* staged by Bramante were always produced out of concrete cases, which were reconfigured without diminishing their complexity. Bramante did not embark on the radical operations of algebrization of the real that would characterize early modernity and that had already appeared in Brunelleschi's work. He did not see abstraction as reduction, made no attempt to simplify, nor to idealize the real. The geometries were always deduced from concrete circumstances; the proportions were established between elements that already existed.[22] In St. Peter's, Bramante immediately accepted reusing the foundations of Rossellino's choir and so accepted the measurements already given in the context. In doing so he renounced ideal geometry once and for all. No one has ever succeeded in deriving absolute mathematical ratios from an analysis of Bramante's drawings for St. Peter's.[23] The measurements of the various parts of the new church were all defined on the basis of the need to reuse the foundations of the choir and cover the whole of the consecrated area of the old basilica. This geometry is not unambiguous, it is not ideal. St. Peter's is not "the supreme example of that organic geometry, that kind of proportionally integrated 'spatial mathematics,'"[24] which Wittkower held to be the goal of the ecclesiastical architecture of the Italian Renaissance. Bramante's church does not attempt to demonstrate the harmony of macrocosm and microcosm, it is not proof of an ideal coincidence between the laws of nature and the values of classical civilization. Rather than a central-plan church, it is a *centralized* church,[25] a product of the combination of groups of spaces aggregated around a central element. This construction of artificial landscapes, in which the center is echoed in the multitude of elements that rotate around it, has nothing spontaneous or natural about it. Unity is introduced from the outside, the different pieces are always recognizable; the effort required to put them together is evident. The different elements remain distinct. The whole is made up of parts that are not fused. The unity is always "abstracted from plurality,"[26] it is dialectical, not organic. Order is not *found*; order is *produced* by means of work. The different parts do not descend from a uniform natural law, they have to negotiate a possible harmony, they must recognize one another. The problem of the central plan is political, not metaphysical. Rather than its conclusion, the immense dome in the middle is the condition for Bramante to imagine sequences of secondary spaces. The dome is the classicist pretext that allows Bramante to lay out the infinitely receding landscape of ambulatories and aisles that are generated from the forty-palm-wide niches. The visitor who entered the church of St. Peter's (if it had been built according to Bramante's plan) and raised his or her head, would have found there a universe with semidomes above the niches and coffered arches in the foreground, and then with large barrel vaults and semidomes concluding the aisles and beyond the minor domes rising progressively, ever more swollen and suspended in relation to their size, first the intermediate ones and finally, in the distance, the main one.[27] Above and beyond his negative judgment, Bonelli grasps Bramante's intentions perfectly:

> Bramante's plan is too complex, and the structure that results from it excessively varied: each bay of the great nave has a different background at the sides, intended to enliven and complicate the views and perspectives; the immense covered space is divided up into main and secondary areas and branches out into minor cross-shaped arms, each with its own apse, and into passageways and small and large niches. The number and dimensions of these secondary spaces diminish the importance of the great cross, and the architecture of the interior would have resulted, in its execution, exaggeratedly animated, intricate, and confused. The most telling criticism of this plan (and of the ones that followed it, retaining its characteristics) was made by Michelangelo, not just when he got rid of the ambulatories, towers, and external porticoes, but in particular when he eliminated the deep cul-de-sac spaces situated at the end of the aisles, which created minor crosses around the small domes, in order to reduce these spaces to a single square corridor running round the space of the main dome.[28]

Rather than Roman examples, the spatial configuration imagined by Bramante is reminiscent of late antique or Gothic and above all Byzantine buildings (his models, in addition to the explicit ones of the Pantheon and the Basilica of Maxentius, were San Lorenzo, Milan Cathedral, and Hagia Sophia[29]). Thus the decisive elements of this geography of spaces are the ambulatories, which multiply the space crowned by the great dome, making it deviate into an incalculable number of vistas and rendering the boundary of the complex unstable. For all his successors, the ambulatories remained the most incomprehensible and problematic aspect of Bramante's design. And so the ambulatories, along with the pedestals of the main order, would fall victim (even before the moralistic zeal of Michelangelo) to the brusque common sense of Antonio da Sangallo:

There were two measures that Sangallo used to oppose the concept of his former master. The first envisaged raising the floor by about 3.70 m, a solution that, conceived as a means of correcting the building's entire system of proportions, was put into effect around 1543 in the south tribune: while the pedestals of the large pilasters disappeared completely, the columns (whose height was fixed, as they were taken from the old St. Peter's) were raised on the new level. As a result, however, their capitals reached all the way to the top of the barrel vault that was to cover the ambulatory, instead of supporting its impost. This made a second, even more incisive measure inevitable: the free passages between the apse and the ambulatory had to be closed. Thus in Sangallo's final design (that of the wooden model) we find three niches with small doors instead of the gaps between the columns; the columns are used in three aedicules that frame these niches. It was with this operation that the ambulatories lost their function of enriching the image of the apses with a spatial backdrop, degenerating in fact into those isolated, narrow and dark spaces that aroused Buonarroti's sarcasm and whose destruction became nothing but a postulate of an economic nature.[30]

The corrections introduced by Antonio were such that, in the end, it was no longer possible to ambulate in these ambulatories—a development already foretold in Antonio's *memoriale*, in which he spoke of "hemicycles," or of a nave *pichola*, "small aisle."[31] Antonio misunderstood Bramante's concept of space and orchestration of light and complained about the configuration of the nave, which he deemed "very dark" and narrow as "an alley."[32] It was in fact Bramante's plan for the aisles and ambulatories to be more brightly illuminated than the nave, thereby contributing to the more general centrifugal energy of the church. The mutable backlighting of the ambulatories, through the calm and indirect illumination of the aisles, would have contrasted with the solemn half-light of the nave and the bright and immutable—but suspended and unattainable—light of the dome. Thus the building would have taken on the form of an ample landscape in which the light assumed different intensities at different times of the day and year, combining places where the light remained almost constant with places where it underwent rapid change, as if the immense interior possessed a meteorology of its own, able to capture and multiply in space the variations of the sky with the passing of the clouds and the seasons.

Heinrich von Geymüller, interior of St. Peter
according to Bramante's drawing UA1,
ca. 1881–1882, courtesy Geymüller-Nachlass,
Karl-Franzens-Universität Graz.

In every work, Bramante repeated the same move: he increased the perceived distance between the parts of the building, expanded the space, suggested scenes receding into an ever more remote distance. This dilation of space is produced by systematically detaching the architectural elements from one another. The most exemplary operation of this kind is the one by which Bramante inserted niches and apses through an intermediate element that remained to distinguish them from the walls in which they were set. This solution was to become so common after his time that it seems entirely obvious today, but it was not at all so at the moment Bramante started to adopt it, in part because its origins are not classical but Byzantine:

> the niches ... are never connected directly to the wall in which they are inserted, in order to avoid a continuity between flat surface and curved surface; instead they are connected through a joint formed by an order (Santa Maria delle Grazie), or an extension of the wall beyond the beginning of the curve (Belvedere), or, in the most usual case, by means of a recess created by interposition of an arch between the wall and the niche (sacristy of Santa Maria presso San Satiro). This solution does not appear in Roman examples, and only very rarely in those of more recent tradition, but is fairly common in Byzantine structures. It may be a matter of interest to point out that the solution of passage between wall and niche through the interposition of an arch is rather common in the Italian deutero-Byzantine Greek-cross plan, and is present without exception, although in a variety of ways, in the structures of this kind scattered around the Marche.[33]

The various solutions adopted prevent the niches and apses being left without a border, scooped directly out of the mass of the wall as in Roman precedents.[34] This systematic work of separation means that the relations are never direct, the elements are always distinct. Out of this come landscapes arranged in series, in which each episode is simply a step farther away than the previous one and this progressive distancing is underlined on each occasion. Bramante inserts countless pauses, suspending the space and separating it from the actions that would take place inside. Thus these spaces appear more ample than any other space of the same size and the movements within them grow slower, a bit like Beethoven's symphonies grow slower when conducted by Furtwängler. The result of this is buildings that are *emptier than others*. Space remains unpredictable; it is neither announced nor described by the architectural elements: the columns don't explain the rooms, the pavilions don't comment on the landscape, the doors don't beckon us to enter, the benches don't invite us to sit on them. Bramante doesn't want to convince us of anything. All he wants to do is seduce and—above all—abandon us.

30 Space and images of space

The spaces designed by Bramante tend to *suspend the participation of the observer*.[35] In his buildings there always seems to be something that wants not to be present, wants not to be reached, wants not to be convincing. Anyone entering the space is always excluded from it as well. The spectacle of space is always best observed from outside: the tribune of Santa Maria delle Grazie and the choir of Santa Maria del Popolo from the naves, the Tempietto from the lower level of the present portico (if not from behind the never built circular portico), the Cortile del Belvedere from the rooms of the Vatican Palace. Even when there was no exterior from which to observe, Bramante tried to distinguish usable spaces from represented spaces. He employed pedestals (*Prevedari Engraving*, cloister of Santa Maria della Pace, interior of the Tempietto di San Pietro in Montorio, interior of St. Peter's, at least until Antonio da Sangallo got rid of them) and rusticated basements (Palazzo Caprini, Palazzo dei Tribunali) that made the order start above people's heads and forced them to look at the architectural display from below, *di sotto in sù*.[36] These tricks end up producing a double space: a bare and negotiable space below and an ornate and inaccessible space above, an under-defined space in which to move freely and a hyper-defined space in which to wander with the eye. This distinction is already evident in the *Prevedari Engraving*. The multitude of things that throng the drawing are in fact distributed very clearly: the lower part of the drawing is empty, the upper part is full. In the middle, a strongly emphasized sequence of cornices and bases in perspective (a foreshortened view that seems to have been taken from Moretti's *Spazio* or Portoghesi and Zevi's *Michelangiolo architetto*) defines a plane parallel to the floor, running just above the heads of the people depicted in the drawing. This construction is declared by a soldier with a spear, immediately in front of the pedestal closest to the viewer, whose head exactly touches the lower edge of its cornice.[37] Above this level is laid out the whole *spectacle of space* that characterizes the drawing, with the walls, vaults and cornices filled with bas-reliefs, clipei, rosettes, and balusters. This spectacle is radically separated from the space in which the human figures move, which is defined by a perfectly isotropic squared grid.[38] At the level in which people act (the one, stretching from the floor to a height of around two and a half meters, where they are able to move, touch, do things) there is the least architecture possible. The space remains uncluttered, free from obstacles, while the inaccessible area above it is richly articulated and decorated, defining a series of *represented* spatial conditions that accompany the real ones. The column of air that rises above the usable space is treated as a landscape spread out above the movements of people. This space in the air—even though no one will ever be able to occupy and make use of it—functions as an expansion of the space on the ground in which it is possible to move and act. Thus the place of action is multiplied on a series of stages where nothing can ever happen, but which echo and measure what occurs on the stage that can actually be occupied. This is not just a matter of spectacle, of set design: space is a deception that is more than real, and even if the nearby things are separated from the distant ones, the space between them is continuous, their perception is one and the represented space really does intervene to define the conditions that govern the actions carried out in it.

In the whole of the Italian Renaissance, the most striking example of an image of space used directly to modify real space is the *fake choir* of Santa Maria presso San Satiro. The *fake choir* serves to alter the perception of the whole building. The space represented opens on the same plane as the one on which people walk in the church and expands it—however illusionistically—in a direction in which it would be possible to move: "physical movement and the movement portrayed coincide."[39] The purpose of this operation is not to create the illusion of an impossible church, but to transform the real one. Many descriptions of Santa Maria presso San Satiro suggest that an arm of the building had been cut off by the opening of the street, making it necessary to compensate in some way, but in reality Via del Falcone has always been where it is now. Bramante decided the form of the

Andrea Mantegna, *Stories of St. James,*
Cappella Ovetari, Padua, ca. 1448–1457.

church precisely on the basis of the fact that the street was located in that position. In this sense the *fake choir* is not the vestige of the ghost of a central-plan church, but a piece of a real church with a T-shaped plan. And in fact the aisle that is missing from the transept on the side abutting Via del Falcone is not simulated along the same line as the one from which the *fake choir* originates, as would have been the case if Bramante had really wanted to pursue the aim of "completing" a centrally planned building. The transept is simply asymmetrical, with an aisle on one side of the nave and a series of apses on the other.[40] Bramante increased the visibility of the transept by first attracting visitors there by means of the fake choir and then exposing the deception and so pushing them back, leaving them suspended in the middle of the church. The revelation of the deception is as important as the impression of spatial depth. This character of a deliberately ineffective illusion has been described very well—once again—by Bonelli:

> ... the motif that most disturbs and impairs the formal integrity of the interior is the famous perspective: excessively squashed and flattened, it is located on the axis, in immediate and strident contrast with the heavily shaded spatial depth of the nave and aisles. The contrived insertion of this pictorial element, with its perspective compressed into such a small space, introduces values wholly extraneous to the architectural conception of the interior. This interruption in the formal continuity was intentional on the part of the architect, as is clear from the fact that the light entering from the lantern of the dome illuminates the entire surface of the fake vault, thereby annulling the impression of depth produced by the receding lines and the illusion that the space of the nave continues beyond the transept; otherwise in fact, we would have to say that Bramante was not able to overcome the difficulty of keeping the fake vault in shadow.[41]

Bramante chose the irksome tone of the solution. The *fake choir* was made to function, and thus to expand the space, but it was also made in order *not to function* and thus to push visitors back. Bramante used the choir as a flat and reflective bas-relief, not as a stage set. In San Satiro, *you experience* the unreality of the choir. The illusion is not a substitute for reality, but a component of it. Bramante's illusionism is not of the all too prodigious kind sought by Borromini or Andrea Pozzo. He does not want to attribute reality to the unreal, what he wants to do is to take reality away from the real. At San Satiro no one keeps up the part of the poor *fake choir*.

This way of using *perspective illusion* to deceive and not deceive at one and the same time has only one model in Italian art prior to Bramante:[42] the two *cubicles* that Giotto painted halfway up the wall in which the altar of the Scrovegni Chapel is set.[43] Longhi's description of these paintings is so fine that there is no point in trying to compete with it. Giotto painted:

> ... two Gothic spaces of which, closed off as they are by a rectangular parapet, we do not see anything but the upper part of the walls clad with square slabs of veined marble, the vault with Gothic ribs from whose keystone hangs an iron lamp in the shape of a cage with its phials of oil and the long and narrow two-light window open onto the sky. No figures ...[44]

> The effect of a convincing illusion is bolstered by the two Gothic vaults converging on a single center that lies on the axis of the church and thus in the "real," existential depth of the apse; by the internal light that, starting from the center, illuminates the two spaces in a different way, even playing on the newels and jambs of the two-light windows; by the external light of the sky that fills the opening of the windows not with an "abstract" ultramarine but with a pale blue that matches the (real) one outside the windows of the apse; to the point where we expect to see the same swallows pass by as streak from the eaves of the Eremitani, not far off ...[45]

Giotto uses his "optical illusions" to alter the experience of anyone entering the chapel. He works on the "real" depth, intervenes in the perception, in the "existential" (!) dimension of the space. "The two false spaces 'pierce' the wall, in an attempt to intervene in the architecture of the chapel itself." But not only do the *cubicles* suggest a space in which to move, they also at once set out to declare it impossible. Both the *cubicles* in Padua and the *fake choir* in Milan are immediately in contradiction with the elements closest to them. In the Scrovegni Chapel, the frescoes that surround the *cubicles* have nothing to do with their perspective construction. Just above them are the *Visitation* and *Judas's Betrayal* which, out of all the frescoes in the chapel, are

Giotto di Bondone, Scrovegni Chapel, Padua,
a. 1303–1305, interior with the two *cubicles*
flanking the choir.

the ones that show the least interest in architecture, and have backgrounds filled with flat and uniform blue. Farther up still, there are the two halves of the *Annunciation*, deliberately inserted to break down the perspective effect of depth that the *cubicles* had created:

> To understand this it suffices, on the same wall, to raise your eyes from the coordinated perspective of the two secret little chapels to the Annunciation where the figures in profile are in full opposition to the two aedicules in "anti-perspective," almost in a space that lies at the back of our actual vision and imprints itself the other way round in the *dulcis memoria* of the holy scripture represented.[46]

In San Satiro, the structure of the coffers is based on two deliberately different geometries; in the vaults of the nave there is a panel in the center, while in the fake choir there is a rib. Butting right up against the fake choir, the nineteenth-century block of the altar fits wonderfully into this sequence, as if caught by surprise that its movement toward the promised depth should have come to such an abrupt halt.[47]

31 Evidence of space

For Wittkower, the mathematical relations that govern a building are not apparent to people moving inside it:

> ... It is obvious that such mathematical relations between plan and section cannot be correctly perceived when one walks about in a building. Alberti knew that, of course, quite as well as we do. We must therefore conclude that the harmonic perfection of the geometrical scheme represents an absolute value, independent of our subjective and transitory perception.[48]

Since the geometric relations that define spaces cannot be "correctly perceived," it becomes necessary to give them meaning by invoking "an absolute value, independent of our subjective and transitory perception." Wittkower's argument brings in a *deus ex machina* capable of solving any problem, but perhaps there is no need. It is in fact possible to argue that the proportional relationships between the parts of the buildings can be perceived, if we are willing to renounce any expectation that they will be perceived "correctly."[49] According to this decidedly more modest hypothesis, figures can be separated from the background against which they are set without being immediately associated with a meaning or an interpretation, just as the apes in *2001: A Space Odyssey* recognize the singularity of the monolith without any need for an aesthetic theory and without making reference to any preceding symbolism. Arnold Gehlen came up with a similar hypothesis, attributing the evidence of the regular geometric form to its improbability in nature. For Gehlen, forms like the sphere and the cube, quite apart from any rhetoric about "divine proportion," would be imprinted on the memory of human beings (and then recognized, named, recalled, and associated or contrasted with other forms) only because they are statistically unlikely:

> The preference in our perception for precise forms may well have very deep roots and extend to the instinctive level. Lorenz had the brilliant

Otto Förster, reconstruction of the interior of
Pavia Cathedral according to Bramante's design,
drawing Hermann von Berg from O. Förster,
Bramante, Vienna-Munich: Anton Schroll, 1956.

insight that the universal characteristic of the releasing signal is its *improbability*. This holds true for the chemical signals of smell as well as for acoustical (such as the cock's crowing) and visual ones, in which regular, symmetrical figures, rhythmic patterns of movement, and colors play a crucial role. All of these precise signals are improbable in the sense that they stand out from the confusion of the background of total perception as being *conspicuous*. By the same token, the protective coloring of many animals, by means of which they render themselves inconspicuous, means that they relegate themselves to an average status or zero level in their surroundings; pale or spotted patterns along with grey, brownish, and muted tones predominate while colors of the spectrum are avoided. One can ultimately explain the preference for symmetrical figures only by their improbability.[50]

Bramante's architecture was made on the basis of his faith in the immediate evidence of forms.[51] His premises were visual; the experience of forms had no need either of direct contact (of the immediate confirmation of the presence of the world that we expect from touch), nor of a metaphysical construction to support it. The geometric figures that govern buildings were not chosen because they had an intrinsic symbolic or metaphysical value, but for their capacity to stand out from the background as conspicuous elements, for the possibility of their being recognized, for their ability to arouse an expectation and leave a trace in the memory. Bramante thought that rooms on a square plan, hemispherical domes, courtyards of elementary proportions, and pillars repeated at regular intervals were immediately registered by the people who experienced them. He assumed that the rule governing these spaces could be recognized, at least approximately, that it was evident to bodies at the very moment they moved in space. He was confident that the sequences could be stored in memory. Architectural forms based on elementary geometric figures in fact appear as the *product of human labor*, things deliberately made by human beings to measure the experiences of other human beings. So they establish a mute, artificial, material exchange among humans who make buildings and humans who use them. And this is also the reason to go on constructing buildings based on elementary geometric shapes, even when technology would allow buildings to be optimized with respect to other criteria (environmental, structural).

Those buildings would in fact appear as unknowable things, arcane and obscure precisely because they have been stubbornly designed according to pseudo-scientific principles, thereby repeating the perverse wonder worked by Gothic architecture of uniting an esoteric conception of science with a pretense of natural spontaneity.

If the forms of buildings are immediately recognizable without reference to any further meaning, then it is possible to see architecture as the technique that produces and measures the experience of space, a phenomenology developed room by room, for which no further justifications are needed. The architect:

> ... first senses the effect that he intends to realize and sees the rooms he wants to create in his mind's eye. He senses the effect that he wishes to exert upon the spectator: fear and horror if it is a dungeon, reverence if a church, respect for the power of the state if a government palace, piety if a tomb, homeyness if a residence, gaiety if a tavern.[52]

At first sight this seems like any theory of *architecture parlante*, in which each building is required to declare its "contents," to reveal its "character." But, to recognize that it is not, it suffices to compare this passage by Adolf Loos with a canonical exposition of the principles of *architecture parlante*, such as the opening passage of Boullée's *Essay on Art*:

> Our buildings—and our public buildings in particular—should be to some extent poems. The impression they make on us should arouse in us sensations that correspond to the function of the buildings in question.[53]

Loos speaks of "effect" (*wirkung*) induced by the "rooms" (*räume*); Boullée speaks of the "sensations" (*sentiments*) aroused by the "impression" (*images*). Loos equates the aim of the designer with the "effect that he wishes to exert upon the spectator," not an object but an experience, not a message that is delivered, but a gesture that is elicited. And this experience is not announced beforehand, the corresponding gesture simply occurs. If we accept this point of view, architecture no longer appears as an activity aimed at the production of objects, but one that suggests an action, that guides—indirectly at least—behavior. The aim of this activity is not the work but the effect of the work, the experience of the work: not the "church" but "reverence," not the "tavern" but "gaiety"—and "reverence" and "gaiety" not as concepts, as images, as messages, but as experiences that occur in space. Architecture is the production of these experiences and the reaction to these experiences, but it is not the description of these experiences, as it would otherwise be a communicative, semiotic, literary act—and therefore not an experience.[54]

As an experience, architecture is always part of a chain of experiences that precede it and make it intelligible. In fact, we can't produce space without already being in it, we can't *produce space* without first *receiving space*. Design is precisely the memory of these experiences: space "is nothing but a set of physical experiences expressed by means of forms."[55] Architecture is a technique for framing movement and for accumulating memories, starting from the experiences of the human body. Architecture constructs the scene in which the body, "as the power of adopting certain forms of behaviour,"[56] finds itself acting. Architecture is nothing but the thought of all these forms of behavior—before they can take place and on the basis of other, older behaviors, that they silently recall. Architecture does not *say* things; architecture, in a way, *does* things, or at least *lets them be done*. And everything that it does, it does through its immobility and its silence. Buildings measure the events they host, and they measure them not just case by case, but in sequence: a sequence that unfolds precisely because buildings do not move, because they remain as fixed scenery, with the rooms placed one next to the other, immobile and indifferent to the unfolding of the stories that play out in them. Architecture is immobility that produces action and memories, a non-narration that prepares the ground for memory and narration. Architecture is not a purely "productive" activity in the Aristotelian sense.[57] Its agency does not end with the making of the object but extends to the reaction to the object (to the gestures that space provokes). Architecture has action as its goal, even if it cannot pretend to carry it out, nor even to prescribe it. Architecture is a particularly slow and indirect kind of *action*—and *representation of action*.

33   A brief and not all that complicated theory of space

Space does not exist in nature. Space is *made*, like a pot, not *discovered*, like a planet. And space is made out of a context that is already given, imperfect, crowded and impure: space is a *social product*.[58] What exists in nature (seas, deserts, forests, caves, herds of gnus and the leopards chasing them) is not space. Space is always *taken from nature*, always *artificial*, always *measurable*, always *produced*. And as a *product* space also makes available its experience, which is always experience of something *recognizably made by human beings*:

> The spatial construct is a human creation and cannot confront the creative or appreciative subject as if it were a cold, crystallized form.[59]

Leibniz defined space as:

> *ordo coexistendi seu ordo existendi inter ea quae sunt simul.*[60]

Space, *as the rule of coexistence among things that are present at the same time*, implies an originally plural condition, and therefore a *political one*. In space the *things which are there at the same time* have in fact to reckon with one another, they have to choose between possible alternative configurations of their coexistence. Thus the experience of space is *common experience*, in the twofold sense of plain, everyday, immediate experience and plural, public, collective experience. Finally, space is an order of representation: things that are next to one another also come on the scene—in space—for one another.

34 Form of the void

Spatial relationships are relationships between *spaces filled with matter*, or *volumes* (or, to adopt a vaguely phenomenological terminology, *obstacles*), and *empty spaces*, or *voids*. The difference between volumes and voids (between the walls and the air comprised between the walls) is not a physical, material difference. Rather, it is a *practical* difference: voids are made of nothing, and so it is possible to act inside them. And voids have a form, one that is defined by the walls that protect them—otherwise the precious nothing produced by human beings would drain away down the indistinct shithole of nature. Work on space is all in defense of this nothing, and is therefore a fundamentally negative work, made up of a negative and a double negative, a *science of voids* that knows of two possible alternatives: voids as possibilities of action, and volumes as negations of the voids and thus as obstacles to action. In architecture form is a *negative* form, the cast of the true object of its interest, which is always absence, possibility, what is *not* there.

Undoubtedly, the hypothesis that *voids possess a form* is problematic, in that the void seems by definition to be indeterminate, and therefore formless. Even just the possibility of using the plural (*voids*) already means that they can be distinguished from a unique, indistinct *void*. So architecture has as its subject not a single *indefinite void*, but a multiplicity of *defined voids*. Here architecture poses what in a certain sense is its only real problem, obliging us to imagine the relationship between the void and its shell. And this relationship cannot help but establish a connection between something infinite and something finite.[61]

So we are left with the conclusion that even though walls and orders are finite and the void infinite, there is a relationship between them: *the form of the void*. The *form of the void* is therefore a *form of possibility*, the form of something that is not yet, and will not necessarily be,

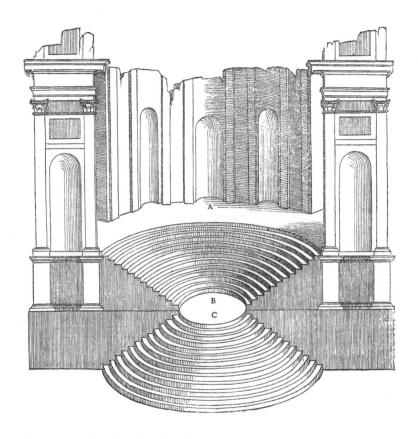

Sebastiano Serlio, exedra of Belvedere, Book III,
On Antiquities, Venice, 1544, CXLVII.

the rule of the innumerable gestures possible within it. The search for this *form of the void* is architecture, to the point where if the expressions "form of the void" and "defined void" made no sense, then neither would architecture make sense as an art with its own specific scope. The so-called *autonomy* of architecture is nothing but this: the idea that voids exist and that they can be distinguished from one another and that there is a specific form of knowledge of their relationship with human beings.

Once the relationship between the indeterminacy of voids and the determination of the walls that delimit them has been admitted, a specific and irreplaceable discipline becomes necessary to study this relationship, and this discipline made up of cases of walls and voids is architecture. There is no need to find (or invent) another science on which to base this work, submitting on each occasion to other forms of knowledge, from literature to physics, from sociology to psychology, from music to biology, as has been done—with unflagging enthusiasm—from Vitruvius to the present day. The form of knowledge which architecture requires is, very simply, architecture. Space is understood through measurements, through analogy with similar spaces that have already been experienced. The science of the emotions associated with spaces is the science of the dimensions and the lighting conditions of spaces we have already seen; a science based on acts of measurement and on drawings correctly executed in plan and section.

COMMUNITY

35 Public work

In an oration expounding his political and cultural agenda, Lorenzo Valla established a link between artistic production and the construction of the city:

> Now any of the arts is quite as difficult to perfect as a city is. Therefore just as no city, so also no art can be established by a single man, nor indeed by a few men; it needs many, very many men, and these men must not be unknown to each other—how otherwise could they vie with each other and contend for glory? But above all else they must be known and related to each other by virtue of communication in the same language. I have already taken a simile from the building of a city: do we not also learn from the Bible that the men who built the great tower of Babel stopped building it precisely because they did not fully understand each other's speech?[1]

The faith in the city that emerges from this passage is immense. In few places are the metropolitan character and public commitment of the Italian Renaissance asserted with so much conviction. Valla says that the work of producing art and city is a collaborative one, that it needs sophisticated linguistic tools, and that, for the political body that carries it out, this work is a way (the only way?) to know itself. The work of art, the expertise accumulated in an entire discipline and the city itself are all episodes in a community project: they can be developed only by a plural subjectivity, are valid only if they hold for all.

In Bramante's work the plurality of this politico-cultural hypothesis coincides with the concrete organization of production. In Milan, Bramante worked with the Lombard craftsmen and their teams, collaborated with Giovanni Antonio Amadeo, Giovanni Battagio, Agostino De Fondulis, Gian Giacomo Dolcebuono, and Cristoforo Solari and conferred with Leonardo and Francesco di Giorgio. In Rome, Bramante orchestrated the artistic world that gathered in the city at the beginning of the sixteenth century: Raphael, Antonio da Sangallo the Younger, Andrea Sansovino, Baldassarre Peruzzi, and to some extent Michelangelo and even Giuliano da Sangallo took part in his various

Fischli Weiss, *Mick Jagger and Brian Jones going home satisfied after composing I Can't Get No Satisfaction*. From "Plötzlich diese Übersicht," 1981–2012 © Peter Fischli David Weiss, Zurich 2020, courtesy Sprüth Magers, Matthew Marks Gallery New York and Los Angeles, Galerie Eva Presenhuber.

undertakings.[2] This teamwork does not mean that the collaboration was always desired, nor that there were no rivalries, disputes, or conflicts. Still Bramante's work was not carried out in an ideal space, free of any friction. His activity never lacked contributions from outside; it was always negotiated, never a solitary creation. And neither did he aspire to it being so; Bramante recognized that his work was carried out within a well-defined linguistic framework and given relations of production. His architecture was the result of a joint activity, done *by others* and *for others*. So, within certain limits, room was left for *other people's work*. *Other people's ideas* were okay too. Bramante accepted into his architecture both the desire of the workers to participate in the grand undertaking, the enthusiasm that caked the walls and ceilings with decorations that were not always of great elegance, and their understandable lapses, their very human lack of interest in subordinate work. Bramante did not fix the final result, he just defined the conditions that would make it possible, simply setting limits to the field where the figure is left free to swing. In Santa Maria delle Grazie he did not oppose the decorative frenzy of the Lombard craftsmen, limiting himself to setting it within a studied equilibrium of spaces and sources of light.[3] The elements of decoration covered all the internal surface of the domes and the semidomes. The swirl of astrological symbols was conspicuously imprecise; the lines were all shaky, the circles all dented. But the clumsiness of the product did not betray the clarity of the design; the sloppiness of the ornaments did not tarnish the thinking that organized them. The faltering execution took nothing away from the building's beauty, indeed it added to its attractiveness: uncertainty in fact is common, for the architect as well as for the masons. The workers were not excluded from the end product—and this was possible precisely because Bramante did not pretend that class conflicts did not exist, because he did not ask them to believe in the fairytale of the artisan's pious and heroic dedication, because he did not see "craft" as a mission to be carried through to the brink of martyrdom. And so he avoided requiring unnecessary heroism from them: Bramante never ordered the beating to death of a worker who ruined a slab of marble.[4] The masons who worked for him were not condemned to perfection and sacrifice; some of them may have been drunks and idlers who, at times, could make mistakes.

When Hollywood chose to portray Bramante, it treated him as an ass-hole. In *The Agony and the Ecstasy*,[5] Charlton Heston was Michelangelo, while Bramante was played by Harry Andrews, an actor who special-ized in villains (the Persian king Darius in Robert Rossen's *Alexander the Great*, the counselor Baltor in King Vidor's *Solomon and Sheba*) or ruthless officers (Sidney Lumet's *The Hill*, Andre DeToth's *Play Dirty*, Robert Aldrich's *Too Late the Hero*) and ended his career as one of the un-wise elders who refuse to evacuate Krypton in Richard Don-ner's *Superman*. For Hollywood, and for its self-serving romanticism, Bramante was a man consumed with envy who hatched plots behind the back of the genius Michelangelo, criminally presented as a sort of Howard Roark of the sixteenth century.[6]

The story told in *The Agony and the Ecstasy* is a fairly crude one, but there is a grain of truth in it: Bramante really was the enemy of romanti-cism and placed all the resources of his organizational intelligence at the service of an implacably anti-individualistic idea of art. This stance drove the whole of his cultural politics. In the "Life of Raphael" Vasari wrote:

> It happened at this time that Michelangelo caused the Pope so much upset and alarm in the chapel, of which I shall speak in his *Life*, whereby he was forced to fly to Florence. Bramante had the keys of the chapel, and, being friendly with Raphael, he showed him Michelangelo's meth-ods so that he might understand them.[7]

The anecdote—whether true or false—is intended to show Bramante's disloyalty to Michelangelo. But for Bramante Michelangelo's jealousy makes no sense: Raphael had to have access to the results achieved by him in the Sistine Chapel in order to be able make use of them as soon as possible (as he would in fact do, starting with the *Stanza di Eliodoro*). Setting any antipathy aside, research ought to be shared.

Bramante was fighting the battle that, in the *Querelle des Anciens et des Modernes*, would be fought by the *Ancients*. In an image originally proposed by Seneca and then reworked by Montaigne[8] and Swift, *bees* (the Ancients) are contrasted with *spiders* (the Moderns). Bees suck nectar from the different flowers on which they alight and then make honey from what they have absorbed. Spiders, on the other hand, weave their webs out of an inner slime that is all their own. Swift's spider sums up splendidly all the anthropological (and economic) implications of the question when it says to the bee:

> ... What art thou but a Vagabond without House or Home, without Stock or Inheritance; Born to no Possession of your own, but a Pair of Wings, and a Drone-Pipe. Your Livelihood is an universal Plunder upon Nature; a Freebooter over Fields and Gardens; and for the sake of Stealing, will rob a Nettle as readily as a Violet. Whereas I am a domestick Animal, furnisht with a Native Stock within my self. This large Castle (to shew my Improvements in the Mathematicks) is all built with my own Hands, and the Materials extracted altogether out of my own Person.[9]

The two positions, as well as implying two different opinions with regard to the authors and the sources of artistic production, propose two different conceptions of the public for which the work of art is produced. For the bees it is not really possible (and would not in any case be very interesting) to speak of themselves, while it is instead possible to speak of (and *to*, and *for*) a whole community. The spider on the contrary speaks only of itself, using viscerally private materials ("extracted altogether out of my own Person")—whose authenticity is always more important than their possible sharing.

For Bramante artistic work is collective, the knowledge on which this work is based is public, and the party to which it is addressed is a community. Through this uneven and uncertain work, all of it done *by others* and based on the desires *of others*, architecture is prepared for its plural destiny and placed at the disposal of the community. Such a radical attitude allowed Bramante to move on the artistic scene of early sixteenth-century Rome with great pragmatism. If we look at it from the perspective of this extremely clear cultural policy, the relationship between Bramante and Michelangelo becomes easier to understand. In fact Bramante had no desire to thwart Michelangelo's career, as Condivi and Vasari insinuate. He just wanted to make his work part of a wider project—and from this point of view Michelangelo's private goals were completely indifferent to him. As the main curator of the Roman art scene of the early sixteenth century, Bramante put Michelangelo in the place that he considered best suited to his own designs, without worrying all that much about the opinion of the Florentine artist. So Bramante was both the meddler who prevented Michelangelo from finishing Julius's tomb and the mediator who offered him the possibility of painting the ceiling of the Sistine Chapel.[10] A witness who can be assumed to be well informed (and in no way hostile to Michelangelo) like Benvenuto Cellini seems to confirm this version of the facts:

> Seeing how fond Pope Julius was of all kinds of beautiful work, and how he had a mind to have the inside of the Sistine Chapel painted, this Bramante introduced Michael Angelo, who was then living in Rome almost unknown & of little account.[11]

Why did Bramante on the one hand promote Michelangelo's career as a painter and on the other hinder his career as a sculptor? This may be explained without relying on gossip: Bramante wanted to use the financial resources allocated for Julius's tomb for St. Peter's and so he tried to dissuade the pope from the initiative of the tomb, saying "that it would be a bad omen to get Michelagnolo to go on with his tomb, as it would seem to be an invitation to death."[12] But if Michelangelo was not to be engaged on building the tomb, something had to be found for him to do. Bramante was a shrewd impresario and administered the talent at the pope's disposal with extreme care.[13] Michelangelo could be used as a painter rather than a sculptor, an activity that diverted far less money from the construction of St. Peter's,[14] and that for Bramante was indisputably more significant from a cultural perspective (and here this meager painter and very cynical man's love of painting is touching). Certainly the enormous effort of the Sistine Chapel was not proposed but demanded, and Michelangelo, who was to pay a heavy price (in physical terms as well), would complain about its consequences for the rest of his life—but from Bramante's point of view this was totally irrelevant. What mattered was to bring Michelangelo back to painting, to divert an artist of incredible talent from too expensive a project in order to entrust him with another that was both cheaper and more ambitious. Moreover, the discipline that Bramante imposed

C. Reed, *The Agony and the Ecstasy*, 1965, Harry
Andrews, Charlton Heston, 1965 © 20th Century
Fox Film Corp. All rights reserved. Courtesy
Everett Collection.

on Michelangelo was valid for him too. Condivi wrote that when work started on the ceiling of the Sistine Chapel, it was Bramante who was ordered to erect the scaffolding needed by Michelangelo. Bramante came up with a very clumsy solution to the problem, which Michelangelo then found another way to resolve. And yet, despite his personal failure, Bramante recognized the utility of the proposal made by his "rival." Condivi's account concludes with a further demonstration of his modesty and his willingness to learn: "This opened Bramante's eyes, and gave him a lesson in the building of a platform, which was very useful to him in the works of St. Peter's."[15]

It is likely that it was from this scaffolding of Michelangelo's that Bramante derived the technique of erecting arches of which Vasari speaks:

> He invented for this work a method of casting the vaults in wooden molds, carved with friezes and foliage in such a way that their impressions were left on the mixture of lime. And he showed how the arches in this building could be vaulted with hanging scaffolding ...[16]

Michelangelo would end up hating Bramante (much as anyone obliged to make a superhuman effort by someone else's ambition would do) but, despite the malicious remarks made by Condivi and Vasari, it is hard to imagine that there was really a personal rivalry between the two men, at least so long as Bramante was alive. Bramante was in fact thirty-one years older than Michelangelo: a huge difference—the same as between Orson Welles and David Lynch, between Beckenbauer and Ronaldo.[17] The "rivalry" would come later, when Michelangelo was old and Bramante dead for quite a while. There is nothing anecdotal about this *posthumous rivalry*. It is merely the result of the position that the elderly Michelangelo thought he had to assume with respect to Bramante in order to liberate himself from a cultural project that had been imposed on him in his youth and which he felt, at the end of his career, that he could not subscribe to entirely. This rivalry is not a matter of gossip, it is the consequence of Michelangelo's reflection on his own work. And it is something that arose in the forties and fifties, not in the early years of the sixteenth century.[18] And this reflection, at least in part, stemmed from the position of architect of

St. Peter's that was assigned to Michelangelo (at the age of seventy-one!) in 1546, and that obliged him to deal with Bramante once again. And Michelangelo at once paid Bramante back in his own coin. He proclaimed himself "the executor of Bramante's design,"[19] but completely distorted the approach he had taken, finding in the rough exterior of the choir with its giant order[20] the premise for reformulating in plastic terms an enterprise from which Bramante had radically excluded any trace of sculpture. And so, in the name of loyalty to the original, *clear* and *plain* and *luminous* design, Michelangelo arrived at the most anti-Bramantesque of theses possible:

> ... it is certain that the members of architecture depend on the members of man. Who has not been or is not a good master of figures, and expert on anatomy, cannot understand it.[21]

37   Work is exhausting

Among the medals struck to mark the founding of St. Peter's, there is one with a portrait of Bramante in the manner of antiquity, nude, with the words BRAMANTES ASDRVVALDINVS, or Bramante from Monte Asdrualdo, and, on the other side, a summary representation of the new St. Peter's along with a female figure in a fluttering dress. The woman is holding a pair of compasses and a straight edge, has her right foot set on a weight, and is accompanied by the inscription FIDELITAS LABOR, or fidelity (and) work.[22] According to Christoph Frommel, this figure resembles some classical representations of Fortuna.[23] The woman looks rather volatile. Her *fidelitas* unfolds precisely from this unpredictability, against which the tools of the trade do not seem to offer much protection. In contrast to this ambiguous figure of proclaimed fidelity and work (and evident fragility and unreliability), the architect on the other side of the medal is alone, and completely nude. Despite the classical pose, the portrait depicts a fat man with a receding hairline, anything but a hero. The man is very proud and determined, but also fairly tired and disillusioned; whatever his battle may have been, you couldn't say he was sure of winning it. This is undoubtedly a strange emblem, and not a very celebratory one, even though the occasion would seem to require it. It is hard to say what Bramante wanted to convey about himself by coupling these three images: a flighty woman, a tiny representation of a gigantic church, and a self-portrait in the guise of a naked and aging tub of lard—and stressing in this case too his origins in a small town in the Marche. The medal is a curious statement of pride and uncertainty. We can derive from it a succinct idea of the profession: architecture is work, and work is technical knowhow that has to deal with the twists of fate. And it is as work, as fallible and often unsuccessful work, that architecture should be understood: as a position in the division of labor, and as the only way to know this position. As such, architecture is a victim of circumstances, of chance; as such, architecture gets to know its specific weariness: "designing is hard work."[24]

Cristoforo Caradosso Foppa (?), medal, ca. 1506,
Museo del Castello Sforzesco.

38 Public space

Public space is perhaps the most obvious proof that, pace Margaret Thatcher, *there is such a thing as society*, that there are common projects which involve us all and precede us all. Public space exposes the collective dimension of our lives in an even more immediate manner than language, in which we are so immersed that it never appears to us *as something else in front of us* and at the same time *as something unequivocally common to us*, as for example Milan Cathedral does when we come out of the Metro station and see it there, enormous, with its façade on a scale that we are unable to get a hold on and drawing together the gazes of all the other people in the square, as heavy as the mountain from which it was quarried, transported, and reassembled piece by piece, and yet so orderly and regular, so clearly measurable and comprehensible. Public space makes possible *an experience of what is common* that does not present itself with such clarity in the other arts and that cannot find expression in a discourse or an argument.[25] In fact, public space is a condition in which we *happen to be*. Architecture—as reflection on the city immediately placed in the city—is therefore the public art par excellence, the proof of a project of coexistence that has been consciously formulated and then translated into reality, the plain, incontrovertible evidence that human beings have tried to imagine their future *as the future of a community*. Architecture gives visual presence to this hypothesis of coexistence *without communicating it*, outside of any symbolism, of any exchange of meanings, outside the hell of metaphors. This singular, mute connection that architecture establishes with the form of life to which it corresponds makes it completely different from any other artistic practice. This is why the thing most representative of a civilization is always its buildings, because they do not just represent a form of life, but belong to it—and belong to it not just as a matter of fact, but as a *project*, as a hypothesis of community that, at a certain point, has persuaded some groups of people to invest in it their own time, their own work, and their own material resources.[26]

Public space is not the spontaneous outcome of a set of individual operations of transformation of the territory and it is not a container that is automatically produced around a preexistent public sphere. Public space is made up of objects that have been deliberately constructed and intentionally arranged in such a way as to enclose and establish a public sphere. It is a piece of city that is more precise and clear than others, the place in which the city manifests itself with particular conviction as a project of coexistence (to the point of justifying a specific *art* and a specific *aesthetic experience* of this arrangement, otherwise known as architecture). The experience of public space is the experience of a law, the *law of a community* that one meets and recognizes as a *law of form*. This law does not require our assent: public space is given with the immediacy of a place in which we simply find ourselves sitting or where we stroll or chat. Even though its use can change, the form of public space is fixed, closed—and can only be modified with a *new investment* that redefines it. Public space is not the result of a contract; public space is *imposed*. And this imposition is foundational: public space *precedes* the people who end up in it. In this sense, public space comes before us, just as language and the city come before us. Even all the possible *transformations*[27] of public space that we can imagine and then bring about are always going to be located *prior* to the scenes and dialogues they will host. Public space is produced *for others* who will encounter it *as a given fact* and public space is produced on the basis of our *previous experience of public space as a given fact*. Perhaps the great and undeniable distrust that liberal democracy harbors for architecture derives precisely from this: that liberal democracy always wants to pretend there was a moment at which we were asked for our opinion, at which we agreed to sign a contract declaring that capitalism was acceptable. Architecture on the other hand (at least that of the classical tradition) makes no pretense of this. Architecture is not the product of an agreement with its users (in part because it would have had to know them all at once, even the ones who are not born yet); instead architecture is *imposed* and this undeniable violence is a constituent element not only of its horror but of its beauty too.

39 Public architecture is abstract

Architecture is something we have in common and that at the same time reveals the way we understand the common. In fact architecture, from the viewpoint of society, is in the first place an investment, a choice about the use to be made of economic resources, the macroscopic result of a process of institutionalization. Even its cultural significance, at least in the context of the European tradition, cannot be separated from the magnitude of the economic resources that architecture finds itself controlling. At the same time, architecture, as *intellectual work*, is a declaration of method, a representation of the rules, that might govern the use of those resources. This duality is evident in an extraordinary passage by Vilanova Artigas, which tackles, with incredible naivety and even more incredible profundity, the more general sense of architecture in the history of the West. Not coincidentally, Artigas goes back to Bramante:

> Bramante had already observed this dualism. In his design for St. Peter's in Rome he defined the principle as—four columns—the four Apostles, who supported a dome—heaven. The dome is the project of the community (which lives in heaven); it is supported, if you will allow me the image, not by columns but by Apostles. Thus, what comes to define architecture in history—at least the history of what we call Western civilization—is the project that society imposes on itself and which the builder represents in a building.[28]

Architecture, in the wide variety of cases with which it has to deal, is always the "project that society imposes on itself and which the builder represents in a building": an exemplary work which always refers to a more general project of transformation of society. As intellectual activity, architecture is precisely this: work on an assigned problem that serves to illustrate how, in general, problems can be solved and resources managed, giving substance to this abstract "problem solving," to this hypothetical "resource management," in the physicality

J. B. Vilanova Artigas, main hall, FAU São Paulo,
1961–1969, photo Raul Garcês.

of the built object and the immediacy of the experience of space. As Giorgio Grassi has written, buildings are "at once subject to and a representation of the rules that govern them."[29] This means that they present a method that can always be extended to other possible undertakings. The choices on which the subdivision of some very small portions of space are based are in fact analogous to those that could be used to reorganize the whole world. Space, "*als Substrat rationaler Organisation*,"[30] becomes the place in which a possible form of coexistence is put to the test, the place in which form appears as the image of a possible form of life. In space the abstraction of a pure hypothesis manifests itself with the maximum concreteness, in space ideas of community are made accessible and immediately subjected to the most direct test—that of using them. And so, as abstraction made concrete and therefore as a *hypothesis of community* that has acquired weight and material substance, architecture is always *political work*.

Architecture is the art of how to put together the concrete blocks that make up a garage, and architecture is art because the rule of the garage is the same as the rule of the world, if it were to be demolished and remade from scratch, for the garage is nothing but a test of the possible destruction and reconstruction of the world according to a design ultimately acceptable for human beings.[31] For this reason the ambition of architecture cannot help but be exaggerated and architects, at least the good ones, can only be megalomaniacs—and consequently frustrated (in this respect James Stirling came up with the useful acronym MFA: Megalomaniac Frustrated Architect[32]). Thus the problem of any building is always *the whole of architecture*. And this means that the problem of all buildings is always the same, that in every circumstance each building cannot fail to be responsible for (and to) the whole of architecture.[33] It also explains the unbelievable abundance of theory in the history of Western architecture (far greater than the amount of theory to be found in the parallel history of painting or sculpture—and theory that has almost always been produced by architects and written from the viewpoint of the designer, *of someone who produces the work*, while theory in the other arts has almost always been written from the viewpoint of *someone who experiences the work*). This invariably crude and badly written theory is in fact the inevitable by-product of buildings that are meant as a *representation of the rules that govern them*, that are meant to expose the universality and generosity that makes them at once so convincing and so surprising.[34]

This universal responsibility that crops up again and again in architecture is precisely the responsibility of the job, of the generic "means of earning a living," and could equally well apply to the cultivation of beans or the handling of divorce suits. Which is exactly why architecture acquires meaning, as reflection on work, the simplest and most generic work that is building. For this reason those who design buildings as solutions for specific problems, without distinguishing between the building and the image of the building, between the object and the rule expounded by the object, are ignoring the fundamental artistic and intellectual problem posed by architecture, which is the problem of work, of the transformation of the world, of reflection on the transformation of the world.

This way of looking at architecture also makes sense of a rather disheartening fact that you run up against in professional activity, the fact that the architect is *always unprepared*. The endless set of skills that Vitruvius declares necessary in the first lines of the first chapter of the first book of *De architectura*[35] is the blatant proof of this radical inadequacy. Architects give their opinion on questions to which they do not know the answer and their art is in fact that of tackling on each occasion problems for which their expertise is entirely inadequate, in order to derive from them rules (and images of rules) that are also valid above and beyond that specific problem. This is why the greatest architects are the ones that most clearly reveal the insecurity and vertigo that comes over them at the moment they embark on their ventures, the ones who have succeeded in preserving in the finished building all the doubts that had accompanied that building when it did not yet exist. Thus, in the absence of a professional technique already suited to a particular *environment*, this "intermediary at the lowest levels of specialization"[36] always ends up having to deal with the *world*.[37] The more that the choices that he or she makes lack immediately usable criteria, the more universal they become in outlining a possible mode of operation, one that is always potentially applicable to any other problem. Architecture is the art (and it is for this very reason that it is art) of taking decisions in the absence of a predetermined technique; *logical work*, and therefore *political work*.

40 Architecture as art

Architecture is *political work*, but there can be no doubt that it does not solve political problems. And above all it has nothing to *say* about political problems. Architecture does not take a stand, does not proclaim principles, does not become indignant, does not distinguish good from bad. Architecture is political work, but indirectly, *as art*. And it is *as works of art* that buildings are responsible for the events which take place inside and outside them. The Doric frieze is articulated according to the ideals of justice that should inform the constitution and the measurements of the Ionic door are based on the same need for equality that requires taxation to be progressive—and yet the partition of the frieze and the proportions of the door tell us nothing about the constitution and nothing about taxation. Above all they do not stop the executioner from entering through the Ionic door to slaughter all the poor orphans, right under the Doric frieze so perfectly designed according to the ideals of justice. Architectural forms do not correspond directly to the life that goes on in them. They are not entirely determined by life and neither do they determine it entirely. Forms are neither the cause nor the consequence of life; they simply define the stage on which it unfolds. Architecture does not coincide with the acts that occur inside it, and this disconnectedness allows it to present a whole world of other possible actions, other possible gestures. In a way architecture multiplies real life into a series of possible lives—which measure real life like an infinity mirror. And architecture is responsible solely for the chorus of mirror images of life that are associated with space, not for life itself. It follows that architecture, as *political work*, is indifferent to the immediate political conditions in which it is carried out. The political significance of architecture—the one directly imputable to the architect, the one by which his or her work is actually to be gauged—is only indirect, otherwise all the architecture of the past and the present, made for insane emperors, sadistic colonels, and merciless usurers, would be equally detestable. And Bramante's architecture would be particularly detestable, given that he worked chiefly for a duke who poisoned his relatives and a pope who liked to lead sieges in person.[38]

Architecture is not a way of changing history or society; architecture is a way of representing (and thus altering) a set of rules that correspond to that society. Architecture cannot oppose political power, but neither can it identify with it. It remains to some extent on the sidelines. In the account of the construction of the Tower of Babel in *De vulgari eloquentia*, Dante very clearly separates these two activities, closely related but in fact distinct: *pars imperabant, pars architectabantur.*[39] Architecture is not exactly power and neither is it execution of the designs of those in power: it is not commanding (*pars imperabant*) and it is not just being commanded (*pars muros moliebantur, pars amussibus regulabant, pars trullis linebant, pars scindere rupes ...*). Architecture shows a society what that society could be, if its rules were put into a coherent *form*. Architecture is fundamentally representation, in the dual sense of a social product based on a delegation on the part of a community and of an image that announces something it cannot make real.[40] So architecture, as an interweaving of levels of representation that is different each time, recoils continually on itself, as if to take away its reality at the very instant in which it is realized: architecture is representation of space that is produced in space and experience of space that can only be represented.

Whether architecture, as the spatial image of a just community, is an instrument of justice, or a substitute for it, is a question that remains outside the realm of architecture—and one that architecture can only address to the community that fosters it. And architecture can pose this question only if it remains what it is: art, the production of spaces and images of spaces that represent future communities—and we do not know whether, by representing them, they bring closer the just cities of which they claim to be the image or drive them further away.

In general, any opportunity to do architecture is good and nothing is more immoral than to turn those opportunities down because of the manner in which those who are willing to pay for architecture have obtained power or made their money.[41] Nothing is worse than to entrust the morality of architecture to the choice of the clients for whom the architect works. And, even more in general, it is not a good idea to expect an explicit moral or political commitment from architecture. In fact the demand for direct political engagement on the part of architecture always ends up eliminating its indirectly political character. If it were possible—to put it very simply—*to do good* through architecture, why bother to make beautiful buildings? Why waste time distinguishing an Attic base from a Samian base? Why go as far as Owatonna in Minnesota to see a bank built by an aging and despairing man? If it were really the job of architects to *solve problems*, they would only become indifferent to forms and follow criteria wholly indifferent to beauty in pursuit of their lofty aims (feeding poor children, comforting widows, saving panda bears from extinction). And if the goal of architecture were really to solve the problems of poor children, widows, and panda bears, it would have to refrain from expounding a more advanced political order than the one that now contents itself with very limited efforts on behalf of poor children, widows, and panda bears. There would be no progress in architecture if architects were to become nurses (just as there would be no progress in treating the sick if nurses were to set about designing hospitals). In architecture moral questions are always excuses: moralism is the "last refuge of the scoundrel," as Kirk Douglas would have put it,[42] if he had ever posed himself the problem. If we find the *maniera degli antichi* so convincing, it is because it is beautiful (*bella*), as Cellini says, not good and beautiful (*buona e bella*) as Palladio would have it.[43]

41 Demolishing St. Peter's

In his biography of *Bramante d'Urbino*, Francesco Milizia tells the story of the demolition and reconstruction of St. Peter's with succinct perfidy:

> Julius II had the grand idea of demolishing St. Peter's church and erect-
> ing a new one, whose equal had never been seen in Rome or in the world.
> ... Once this design was selected, he demolished half the church with his
> usual haste, and in 1513 bravely set to work on the new one...[44]

The date of foundation given by Milizia is wrong: the first stone was in fact laid on Saturday April 18, 1506.[45] For the occasion Julius II descend-ed *bravely* (*intrepidus accessit* says Buonanni) into the foundation sod-den with water, while thirty-one of the thirty-three cardinals present (two of them had been obliged to go down with the pope) looked on in puzzlement from the brink of the trench.[46] Despite the error of dating, Milizia recognized the *haste* with which Bramante demolished the old church and with his careful selection of adjectives was able to set the whole story in what feels just like the atmosphere of a Fascist newsreel. The eighteenth-century critic continued:

> But the magnificent structure of St. Peter's in the Vatican, which he
> planned to make immense and had begun with such ardor, remained,
> as it were, in its infancy.[47]

To anyone seeking to assign responsibility for this ill-considered ini-tiative, which at once proved a failure, the story of the new St. Peter's appears fairly obscure. In fact the intentions were never explicitly de-clared. Bold proclamations exist only in imaginary reconstructions, such as the historical scene clumsily dramatized by the Comte de Go-bineau, in which Julius addresses Bramante with these words:

> The old basilica ... is no longer worthy of us. Pull down, destroy, break,
> tear away, and show me, in place of what you will have effaced, all that
> you have the power to invent.[48]

Marteen van Heemskerck, view of St. Peter's,
ca. 1536, Kupferstichkabinett, Berlin.

It is unlikely that things went that way and today it is very hard to say either when the decision to demolish St. Peter's was taken[49] or whose idea it was. Everyone tells a different story and all seem to lie, and, as we know from *Rashomon*, the dead are the worst liars. According to Vasari, the decision was the pope's: Bramante, "having heard that he [Julius II] was thinking of knocking down St. Peter's in order to rebuild it,"[50] did no more than go along with the idea. Conversely, in the dialogue that, according to the *Simia*, takes place in heaven between St. Peter and Bramante, the architect is rebuked (and immediately accepts responsibility) for convincing Julius to demolish the church:

> *Tua fuit haec techna, tuo suasu, tuis artibus inductus iussit Iulius; te auctore, te duce evertere operarii.*[51]

Except for some anonymous texts, the officials of the Curia remained silent, keeping a safe distance, and adapted their version of the facts to the progress of the works: the farther away the conclusion of the enterprise seemed to be, the more they shifted blame for the demolition onto the shoulders of the architect.[52] It is no accident that functionaries of the Curia, such as Panvinio, Alfarano, and Buonanni, who were writing after fifty years of failures and had in front of their eyes the fragments of a project that appeared impossible to finish,[53] ended up assigning the responsibility entirely to Bramante, seeking to exonerate the pope and the Curia.[54]

When Giuliano della Rovere became pope in 1503, the old church of St. Peter's was in a parlous state. The possibility of demolishing it, at least in part, and then rebuilding, had already been raised several times in the fifteenth century. Not only has a record of this option survived in the architectural debate,[55] but at the time there were also evident material traces, like the foundations of the choir that Bernardo Rossellino had begun fifty years earlier. In addition, and this may have been the main motivation for the demolition, there was no room left in the church: the basilica was crammed with altars, tombs, and commemorative monuments and nothing else could be fitted in—certainly not the enormous memorial that Julius II wanted for himself.[56]

These were the conditions that made up the complicated *opportunity* offered to the architect. Faced with this intricate reality, Bramante's maneuver was a double one: first using the enormous tomb that Julius had commissioned from Michelangelo to get the old church demolished and immediately afterward setting it aside as incompatible with the new building:

> On the return of Giuliano [da Sangallo] to Rome, the question was being debated as to whether the divine Michelagnolo Buonarroti should make the tomb of Pope Julius; whereupon Giuliano exhorted the Pope to pursue that undertaking, adding that it seemed to him that it was necessary to build a special chapel for such a monument, and that it should not be placed in the old S. Pietro, in which there was no space for it, whereas a new chapel would bring out all the perfection of the work. After many architects, then, had made designs, the matter little by little became one of such importance, that, in place of erecting a chapel, a beginning was made with the great fabric of the new S. Pietro. There had arrived in Rome, about that time, the architect Bramante of Castel Durante, who had been in Lombardy; and he went to work in such a manner, with various extraordinary means and methods of his own, and with his fantastic ideas, having on his side Baldassarre Peruzzi, Raffaello da Urbino, and other architects, that he put the whole undertaking into confusion; whereby much time was consumed in discussions. Finally—so well did he know how to set about the matter—the work was entrusted to him, as the man who had shown the finest judgment, the best intelligence, and the greatest invention.[57]

Once authorized to start, Bramante proceeded with a determination that took everyone aback. He had control over the construction site and could count on the difficulty that a prompt interpretation of his moves posed for people without expertise in construction. Before the pope could change his mind, Bramante burned his bridges. Having convinced him was not in itself enough: the pope could backtrack or die, a successor might decide to spend the money in some other way. Bramante trusted nobody and, aware that he too was fairly old,[58] opted for the *fait accompli*. He laid waste to the tombs of popes and swept away the evidence of the history of the Church:

> ... he was so eager to see the work progress that he destroyed many fine things in St. Peter's, including tombs of popes, paintings, and mosaics,

and that as a result we have lost all trace of many of the portraits of prominent people that were scattered around the church, which is the most important in all Christendom. He spared only the altar of St. Peter ...[59]

Bramante seized the *opportunity* that chance offered him and exploited it without mercy. In 1506 work started on the first pier of the dome, the southwestern one, the so-called *pier of the Veronica*, outside the old basilica, but the ancient monastery of San Martino was destroyed to make way for it. Shortly afterwards commenced the construction of the northwestern pier and the choir (reusing the foundations of Rossellino's choir). Then, in 1510, work began on the piers facing onto the nave, which required the demolition of much of the transept and the western part of the old nave. It was at this moment (June 11, 1511) that the papal master of ceremonies Paris de Grassis jotted down in his diary Bramante's new nickname:

> ... interim contemplando ruinas et aedifitia, quae per eius architectum moliebantur nomine Bramantem, seu potius Ruinantem, ut communiter vocabatur a ruinis et demolitionibus, quae per ipsum tam Romae, quam ubique perpetrabantur.[60]

This program of demolitions cannot be explained by Bramante's inability to "think of anything new if he had not cleared the field through demolition," as Horst Bredekamp has argued:[61] Bramante spent his life adding pieces onto buildings already half constructed and certainly had no difficulty in working in settings crowded with preexisting elements. On the contrary—and precisely on the basis of his experience of often modest and fragmented building programs—Bramante recognized the exceptional *opportunity* presented by St. Peter's and set out to tackle it in adequate terms. Only through the destruction of the old church could the problem of St. Peter's be approached in a *quantitatively* correct manner; and only through an exact definition of its bulk could the new church exercise the desired effect on the city. It was the *size* of the old church that was incompatible with the aims of the new one.[62] In the face of this incompatibility, the motives for preserving at least some parts of the old basilica as a record of the history of the Church lost their validity for Bramante. Vestiges of the past were of secondary importance with respect to the correct definition of the scale of the new building.

At this point, even if we do not know precisely *who* nor *when* decided to have the old church demolished, it is worth asking *why* it was demolished. But the search for an ideological justification will not prove particularly fruitful either. Julius had at his disposal a fair number of intellectuals who could have been asked to explain and celebrate the undertaking, but who were never called on. There were no proclamations for the new St. Peter's; intentions were not declared. The celebration that was held on the *sabbato in Albis* of 1506, when the pope went down into the foundations to deposit there the medal engraved by Caradosso, was a decidedly sober one. There were none of those erudite speeches that the occasion might have seemed to warrant. Even the inscription carved on the first stone is fairly laconic: AEDEM PRINCIPIS APOSTORVM/IN VATICANO VETVSTATE, ET SITV/SQVALENTEM A FVNDAMENTIS/RESTITVIT IVLIVS LIGVR/PONT. MAX. AN. MDVI.[63] The bull of February 12, 1507 instituting the indulgence that was to fund the construction, and then the one of January 11, 1509 confirming it, confined themselves to asking for contributions *in pecunia numerata aut rebus aliis ad opus ipsum convertendis*[64] and did not go beyond extremely prosaic formulas.[65] Even the letters sent to inform the various rulers of Europe and to solicit offerings never contained any particularly clear ideological explanations. Indeed, they limited themselves to saying that the old church was about to collapse and it was necessary to return to a decorous situation.[66] For a discourse that spoke of the new church in somewhat loftier terms it was necessary to wait more than a year, until December 21, 1507, when Giles of Viterbo celebrated the victories of the Portuguese in India and made an effort to view these military successes and the construction of the new basilica as harbingers of a new golden age.[67]

The most programmatic document for the reconstruction of St. Peter's is probably the medal engraved by Caradosso with the inscription TEMPLI PETRI INSTAURACIO, but it reproduces a drawing and so refers to Bramante, without providing any discursive ideological defense of the operation. This absence of any adequate argumentation of the undertaking may be evidence that in the case of St. Peter's the decisions were actually taken by the architect, who, in a manner of speaking, *advanced in the open*, without theological backing, without ideological cover, alone in his enterprise, which no one else wanted a share in unless it proved a success.

To realize the full extent of the violence of the destruction of the old St. Peter's, it suffices to say that no similar case can be found in the history of religions. No civilization has ever razed to the ground its most important monument solely in order to be able to rebuild it *bigger and more beautiful*. Perhaps the only thing that can be compared to the demolition and reconstruction of St. Peter's is what is happening in these years in Mecca, where the spaces that surround the Kaaba are being devastated to build enormous hotels,[68] but in this case it would be hard to argue that there are significant aesthetic ambitions driving the project. Apart from the Saudis, no one has ever destroyed their holy places of their own free will. This is an activity reserved for enemies: the temple in Jerusalem was destroyed by Nebuchadnezzar and Titus, the Acropolis in Athens was devastated by the Persians, Reims Cathedral was shelled by the Germans, Dresden was razed to the ground by the British. In the case of St. Peter's, it was the pope who sanctioned the destruction of the church built over the tomb of the apostle.

There is something mad and glorious about the effort of an aging and megalomaniac architect to convince an aging and truculent pope to destroy the church that contained the tomb of St. Peter only because it was ugly. In their dream of beauty Julius and Bramante do not seem to have taken any consequences into account. The hopes which the form promised to fulfill led the political calculations astray, confounded the precepts of ritual, swept aside all religious circumspection. *Beauty at any cost*, Julius and Bramante seem to be saying, with the same caution with which Werner Herzog's Aguirre, surrounded by monkeys and dying soldiers, proclaims himself king on his raft drifting down the Amazon River.

The theatricality and wanton fury of the demolition of St. Peter's did not escape the notice of contemporaries. In the *Simia* it is said that Bramante would have stopped at nothing and would even have rebuilt heaven or, if St. Peter were unwilling, then hell instead: *"Ad Plutonem ibo, ibi mihi certum scio erit negotium."*[69]

In their observations on the destruction of the church (often exposed in a fairly discreet form, entrusted to diaries or anonymous pamphlets), writers of the time seem to have been fully aware of the ritual aspect of Julius and Bramante's performance. The demolition of St. Peter's had the appearance of a rite, although not a Christian one—perhaps just an abstractly universal one, a strangely catholic (in the most literal sense of the word) form of potlatch.[70] It is certainly hard to believe that Julius and Bramante hoped to boost their prestige by squandering the patrimony of the Church (after all they were not Kwakiutl chiefs, nor even the Sex Pistols), but they could not have been ignorant of the enormous symbolic impact that their initiative was going to have. Julius and Bramante assigned themselves the authority they needed to destroy the old church and pledged that they would have—almost by miracle—a new one rise in its place to buttress their unprecedented authority; an authority that would be confirmed, once the deed was done, more by the ardor of the demolition than by the ingenuity of the reconstruction. But they were not able to pull the giant rabbit out of the hat. Reconstruction was not as fast as hoped, and the image which sixteenth-century Europe was presented with—once the two elderly adventurers had died without leaving clear instructions—was that of the church in ruins.

For a long time, all that could be seen of Julius's and Bramante's *plan for the conquest of beauty* would be rubble. Maarten van Heemskerck's drawings portray the ruins of this war fought for the possession of beauty, the remains of a colossal and inexplicable *Sometimes Making Something Leads to Nothing*[71] performed in front of the appalled eyes of all the Christians of Europe. For over half a century, all that remained was a monstrous pile of wreckage:

> ... the remains of the old building and the unfinished parts of the new are bound together almost inextricably, and the ground is covered with rubble and debris, with architectural elements and spontaneous vegetation. Some tiny figures are wandering around this setting, as if lost: an image that calls to mind the contemporary accounts of the pope and his servers braving the weather to go and celebrate mass on the tomb of the apostle, protected by the *tegurio*.[72]

It is fairly difficult to speak of the demolition of St. Peter's, perhaps because it is hard to find a place for it in the "History of Art," which is always presumed to be a story of *creation*. And yet the demolition of St. Peter's is the most ambitious act in the art of the Italian Renaissance, its resplendent and terrifying masterpiece. Bramante devastated the old church without concealing the satisfaction he derived from it. The enthusiasm for beauty turned into a frenzy of destruction. Julius and Bramante seem to have tried to gain control of beauty through a sort of military operation. In the *Julius exclusus a coelo*,[73] the deceased Julius is waiting to assault Heaven with troops made up of the soldiers whose death he had caused in his wars. In the *Simia*, Alessandro (a prelate of the Roman Curia) sees Bramante and shows him to St. Peter, who immediately recognizes him as the destroyer of his church:

Petrus: Qui Bramantes?
Alexander: Architectus noster
Petrus: Templi eversor mei?
Alexander: Immo, et urbis atque orbis si potuisset.[74]

To destroy the church, all Bramante had needed to do was act ruth-lessly, taking advantage of the various *opportunities* and the (at least) lack of opposition from the pope. For its rebuilding, however, an archi-tectural project could not suffice. Ideology was needed too. And yet, incredibly, the question of the destruction and reconstruction of St. Peter's was treated by the pope and the Curia as a mere question of architecture. The motivation for the new church would lie entirely in the force of its tremendous mass and its indisputable beauty. That's all: Sigismondo de' Conti[75] says that the old basilica, as well as being dilapi-dated ("*ruinae proximam*"), had been built in an uncultured age, which had no idea of a more refined architecture ("*rudi saeculo et politiores architecturae ignaro conditam*") and that the enterprise had not been tackled earlier simply because of its prohibitive cost ("*maximi ac prope infiniti sumptus*"),[76] but now the munificent Julius ("*magnanimitas et pientissima liberalitas Julii II*") had found the courage to set about the work and the new building would surpass in beauty every monument of antiquity and its dome would be larger and higher than that of the Pantheon ("*omnem antiquitatem pulchritudine et magitudine superatu-ra videtur; in capite enim Basilicae testudo futura est latior et altior Tem-plo Pantheon*").[77] Vasari confirms this; the new church was supposed to be "immense and awesome" and "surpass in beauty, art, invention and design, as well as size, richness, and ornamentation, all the build-ings that had been erected in that city."[78] While this is little more than a brutally quantitative aesthetic lacking any kind of sophistication,[79] it is nevertheless an *aesthetic ideology*. No symbols, no traditions are called on to justify the operation; the building "suggests no ulterior motive."[80] Julius and Bramante do not appear to have set themselves any other objectives than immensity and beauty. There were no political or reli-gious motivations; the aims of this immense undertaking were solely aesthetic. Indeed the political and religious factors were all *opposed* to it, as it would not take long to find out. The faith placed in architecture has no parallel in other historical contexts. Von Pastor goes so far as to say that the demolition of the old St. Peter's was probably "due to the extravagant admiration"[81] for the new architecture. And in fact the official ideologues of the Curia all seem to have been fairly skeptical about the excessive credit given to an architect, not to mention annoyed by it.

By allowing Bramante to demolish the old St. Peter's, Julius chose to entrust the authority of the Church to the size and beauty of a building, rather than to the antiquity and authenticity of relics, to visual spectacle rather than to antiquarian erudition. Between the church as *symbol*, as testimony to the past, as memory of the lives of the saints, and the church as *form*, as glory in the visibility of a spectacle of space, Julius chose the latter. But was this construction of form at the cost of the destruction of the history of the Church theologically justifiable? And if so, how?

No one answered these questions.[82] When, after the Reformation and after the Sack of Rome, an effort was made to conclude the ill-omened initiative of the new St. Peter's, Catholic intellectuals would defend the use of images and the expense of constructing and decorating buildings with much more circumspect arguments, taking a line far behind the one at which Julius and Bramante had arrived and subordinating ecclesiastical architecture to a mission of propaganda infinitely more closely monitored and literal.[83] Conditions would be imposed on form and far more immediate and practical justifications required of it than the ones that defined Bramante's project. And the church of St. Peter's that would emerge from this realignment would be very different from the one to which Julius and Bramante had aspired. A church made to expound *glory* was replaced by a church made to proclaim *majesty*:

> St. Peter's nave is admirably calculated to impress the peasant from the Abruzzi, from the Tyrol, or from Brittany, as he is led about by his parish priest. It shows him how grandly the Holy Father once lived, and incites him to bitter hatred of those who now prevent him from living in such state as befits this, his private chapel.[84]

At St. Peter's the latest disciplinary methods were used to carry out an essentially medieval enterprise. Julius and Bramante thought they could construct the new building on the timescale of a Gothic cathedral

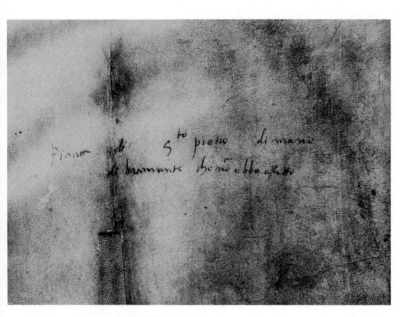

Antonio da Sangallo, note on the back of drawing
UA1 *(Pianta di S.to pietro di mano di bramante
che no ebbe effetto, Plan of St. Peter's by the hand
of Bramante that was not put into effect)*, unknown
date, Gabinetto Disegni e Stampe, Gallerie degli
Uffizi, Florence.

and adopting the same models of funding. The pope and the architect had that example in front of their eyes: Bramante had been an adviser for the cathedrals of both Milan and Pavia and had firsthand experience of the organization of their construction. But the sixteenth century was not the time for such ventures. The last major cathedral on which work started in Italy was the one in Milan (1386). If we exclude the Spanish cathedrals commenced after the *reconquista* (such as the ones in Granada, Salamanca, Segovia, and Valladolid), a few reconstructions (St. Paul's in London), and a few votive churches (the Sagrada Familia in Barcelona), there would be no new religious buildings of a comparable size and cost to the Gothic cathedrals in Europe after St. Peter's. In what was already such a *modern* century, the faith in the stability of society that the medieval ruling classes needed in order to embark on works that were going to take centuries to complete was lacking.[85] Julius and Bramante, from this point of view, were dreamers. These men, still so medieval, projected their innovations onto a society that they imagined wholly unchanged in every other aspect.[86] Viewed from a modern, individualist, and bourgeois perspective, the construction of St. Peter's, despite the dazzling modernity of the means employed, appears an incredibly archaic enterprise. St. Peter's is a cathedral that has passed its expiration date, just as *Orlando Furioso* is a chivalric romance after its time. But while Ariosto's literary project seems to be founded on an awareness of its impossibility, Bramante is still deluded. At times at least, Julius and Bramante seem to have believed in their impossible church.

Giulio and Bramante set out to produce a *visible beauty*, a *public spectacle* that would be staged in front of all, with the aim of imposing a cultural hegemony. The new church of St. Peter and the new city were to become the visible manifestation of the glory of the Church. The existing city had to be replaced by a new one, equally concrete but able to serve as an *image* to be presented to the rest of the Christian world. The real city was to become a weapon in the battle for the European imagination.

While Julius's actual politics was clearly unrealistic (but also, to tell the truth, fairly limited), his image politics was decidedly more sophisticated and credible—so much so that Thomas Hobbes seems still to have been afraid of it long after its defeat. In a wonderful passage in the last chapter of *Leviathan* (XLVII: "Of the Benefit that proceedeth from such Darknesse, and to whom it accreweth"), Hobbes evokes the spectre of a Catholic-Maoist resurgence (for which I hereby declare my full support, should it ever actually happen):

> But who knows that this Spirit of Rome, now gone out, and walking by Missions through the dry places of China, Japan and the Indies, that yield him little fruit, may not return, or rather an Assembly of Spirits worse than he, enter, and inhabite this clean swept house, and make the End thereof worse than the beginning?[87]

It looks like Julius was trying to anticipate the Reformation by setting up a triumphantly visual cultural hypothesis—one that was only *put on show*, and never really explained—but that could anyhow confuse and ridicule "this clean swept house." His plan was not very clear; the relations between the international religious and cultural capital (the capital of the *Church*) and the capital of the *State of the Church* and their respective administrative, ceremonial, and representative machineries remained wholly undefined.[88] And perhaps, setting aside all the moralism that has accumulated around these events, the project also failed *as representation*: St. Peter's was not able *to appear in time* to persuade the Germans to go on spending their money and the Italian Renaissance, as a *represented political project*, was in the end defeated by a political project that, more cautiously, refused to represent itself.

Jakob Burckhardt devoted the first part of *The Civilization of the Renaissance in Italy* to the "The State as a Work of Art." The only artist mentioned in this long discussion, which runs for nearly a hundred pages, is Bramante; the only work of art is St. Peter's. Burckhardt explains the undertaking of St. Peter's on the basis of Julius's desire to fulfill—at least in image—his imperial designs: "A ruler of this stamp needed some great outward symbol of his conceptions; Julius found it in the reconstruction of St. Peter's."[89] Julius's mere dream of an imperial policy (while his few soldiers muddled along as well they could around some small towns in Romagna) led to an architectural operation so colossal that it amounted to a genuine political initiative. The new church was not the *representation* of an imperial political design, but the expression of the desire for such.

St. Peter's is not the biggest building in European history; the royal palace of Versailles is decidedly larger, but Versailles reflects an already established political equilibrium. It does not try to construct it through architecture, as St. Peter's set out to do. At St. Peter's Bramante had an opportunity no one else in the history of architecture ever had. While his resources were not comparable to those at the disposal of the architects of ancient Rome,[90] the authority of his profession and the freedom he could allow himself as an intellectual were entirely different from those of antiquity. No architect has ever embarked on such a colossal task on the basis of such conscious aesthetic ambition: prior to the Renaissance it was not permitted to tackle this kind of problem with so much freedom; after it, the opportunity to take on problems of this kind would no longer be there. St. Peter's is not just an enormous building, but an attempt to realize *as a building*, and therefore as a work of art, something that as a political project was not at all clear. It is the incredible political instability and incredible ambition in which the design was developed that make St. Peter's so important to the history of architecture. No work on such a scale had ever been imagined in such a precarious political context.[91] Already in the subsequent stages of the construction of the church (for Michelangelo, for Maderno, for Bernini) the political aims and theological arguments on which the popes and the Curia drew were much clearer—and it is no coincidence that these initiatives would actually be brought to completion. In Rome, at the beginning of the sixteenth century, however, there was no well-defined political project; there was just a confused and contradictory ambition. Not coincidentally, Julius began his new church in April 1506, *before* any of his military ventures (the campaign against Perugia and Bologna commenced at the end of August 1506). St. Peter's was in fact, as Burckhardt put it, a "great outward symbol of his [Julius's] conceptions," a monument to monumentality itself. Architecture became the instrument of a process of institutionalization in which political ambitions were called on to be represented first, and known only later. The result of this inverted process was that the new church ended up representing "nothing more than the idea of representation."[92]

The universality and abstraction of Bramante's designs for St. Peter's are perfectly in keeping with this incredible absence of content which Julius II's Church seemed to exhibit in confirmation of its proclaimed universalism. Bramante went along with this *continuation of politics by other means*, which went from politics to art, in a reverse movement, in what seems to have been an attempt to appropriate the pragmatism of political action in order to transform artistic practice. In an essay entitled "The Perspective of Art," Charles Singleton argued that Machiavelli shifted the realm of politics from that of "doing" to that of "making," treating political action as artistic production.[93] Bramante seems to have arrived at the same point where artistic and political action turn into each other, even though proceeding in the opposite direction, starting from art and moving toward politics. He claimed for architecture the continual malleability of political action, securing for himself the maximum of reactivity and the maximum of opportunism. Most likely this was originally a tactical requirement: Bramante wanted to be able to adjust immediately to new balances of desires, in order to better exploit the opportunities that might come his way. This need ended up turning into a new strategy. In exchange for the possibilities that seemed to be offered him, Bramante was willing to get his hands dirty, to go along entirely with Julius's fanciful projects. Here, once again, the distance from Alberti is extreme: Bramante rejected any "ethical" notion of architectural practice. His gamble was a purely political one. Should it not come off, there would be no moral consolations. Bramante did not try to hang on to "desperate fragments of rationality, satisfied with their own *finitio*."[94] For him there were only furious assaults on the universe (whose predictable failure he acknowledged at once, and not without a good laugh).

There is nothing egocentric about Julius's and Bramante's megalomania.[95] The idea of demolishing and reconstructing St. Peter's was not a private venture but a collective gamble, a foolish attempt in which a whole civilization was involved—a civilization that would then be harshly punished for its reckless experiments and for not having been able to fulfill the expectations it had raised.[96] Julius and Bramante did not assume the responsibility of demolishing the old church in order to make a new but *bigger* and *more beautiful* one for themselves.[97] They took this responsibility *for everyone*. Their madness was contagious. St. Peter's was an autocratic and irresponsible enterprise, but it was nevertheless an enterprise for an entire community, for all the Christians of Western Europe. Even in more strictly artistic terms, Bramante was too humble to see the construction of St. Peter's as a personal matter (as Michelangelo did in the case of Julius II's tomb), but at the same time had no scruples about attributing boundless ambition to the architectural undertakings of the society in which he happened to live. Bramante's ambition was *for everyone*—and everyone, in one way or another, would be caught up in the vortex of destroying and rebuilding St. Peter's.

Bramante's series of drawings of St. Peter's seems to propose the same theme as the dialogue between Augustus and Virgil in Hermann Broch's *Death of Virgil*. Augustus and Virgil discuss the possibility of managing and dispensing beauty, accepting that power might coincide with truth, and that truth might speak with the frightening voice of power. Virgil wants to burn the *Aeneid* because it is aesthetically inadequate, to take it away from the empire for which it has been—from the start—produced; Augustus lays claim to it as an element in a political construction to which the emperor assigns the same aesthetic ambition as Virgil does to poetry. At St. Peter's, instead, it is Bramante who has to convince Julius to build a church that could provide an immediate experience of the glory of the Church, and who persuades him to undertake this construction in a most authoritarian and reckless manner. In the first case power needs beauty to be more perfectly power, in the second beauty needs power to be more perfectly beauty. Virgil does not want to finish the poem and Bramante wants at any cost to demolish the old church and start on the new one. Virgil tries to reject Augustus's extremely concrete empire; Bramante tries to pretend that Julius's improbable Eldorado can exist. And yet Bramante's problem is not so different from Virgil's: it is in any case a work that *has to be valid for all* and at the same time—and precisely for this reason—*cannot be valid for all*. Virgil tries to evade an almost complete design, Bramante binds himself hands and feet to a plan with no real possibility of success. Virgil resists the possibility of the empire using his poem to impose a law that cannot fully match the law to which the poem aspires and Bramante pursues a power that can give substance to a space that needs to be materialized in order to expound the law to which it aspires. Virgil has to take reality away from a poem that could be seen as perfect (and as a perfect translation of a perfect political power), Bramante wants to give reality to an image that can only be experienced if it is constructed—and so has to evoke a power capable of realizing it. Bramante knows that he will never live to see the church finished. He knows that only the tremendous beauty of the new church could justify the destruction that he perpetrates with such alacrity, without being able to provide any guarantee of that beauty, either for himself or for others.

The venture will not succeed. Beauty will not be achieved (*so viel verlorene Schönheit*, as the young Geymüller would say), and even if it had been, it could certainly not have justified all the disasters that arose in its wake. The particle of beauty was, perhaps, unforgivable—and perhaps it lay only in the war that was fought for beauty:

> The gods did not wish him to finish the verses, did not wish him to correct the incongruity, for every human work has to arise from twilight and blindness and therefore must remain incongruous; thus have the gods decided. And yet now he knew it; not only the curse but grace as well was mirrored in this incongruity, not only man's inadequacy but also his closeness to the divine, not only the soul's incompleteness but its magnitude, not only the blindness of the blindly-born human labor—otherwise it would never have been done at all—, but also its divining strength, for in the kernel of all human labor lay the seed of something that reached beyond itself and beyond him who had created it, and in this wise the worker was transformed into a creator; for the universal incongruity of circumstance began only when men became active in the universe—for there was no incongruity in the circumstances of the animal or of the gods—and only in this incongruity was revealed the fearful glory of the human lot which reached beyond itself; standing between the muteness of the animal and that of the gods was the human word, waiting to be silenced in ecstasy, beneath the radiant glance of that eye whose blindness has come in ecstasy to seeing: ecstatic blindness: the confirmation.[98]

43 Ninety-five theses

The demolition of St. Peter's was carried out by Bramante with the fury of a *coup d'état* and it was, in effect, a *coup d'état of form*, of the fragile reasons of form in the field of politics and religion. In demolishing St. Peter's, Bramante did not worry about invading territories that did not fall within his competence,[99] was not concerned about endangering equilibria that he could not hope to control. Thus architecture came so close to politics that it touched the point where the production of space urged the production of social relations. The bubble of spaces and images of space were entrusted with an immediate political task. And, even more urgently, this house of cards required concrete political actions to guarantee the huge financial resources needed to bring it to a conclusion. The possibilities that the forms were intended to bring to light came immediately into conflict with the conditions of their production. The building was so enormous and so costly that a specific political initiative was needed for it to be constructed. And this political initiative was not even all that sophisticated: it entailed selling indulgences around Europe.

Bramante promised to solve a political and ideological problem through form and he made this promise solely in order to obtain the means he needed to realize his incredible spatial concept. No doubt it was a vicious circle: the image of society presented by the new church was immediately destroyed by the configuration of society needed to find the resources required for its construction. The richness of coexistence shown to be possible in these spaces was based directly on robbery and on the practical negation of any civil coexistence. The *plan of conquest of beauty* required an action that at once contradicted the beauty that it proposed to bring to light. The new church ended up appearing to be the most obvious cause of the "centuries of calamities" that followed:[100] "No wonder that, in popular history, the building of St. Peter's is always made a principal cause of the Reformation!"[101]

Lucas Cranach the Elder, *Portrait of Martin Luther*, 1528, Kunstsammlungen der Veste Coburg, loan of Oberfrankenstiftung, Bayreuth.

On October 31, 1517, Martin Luther nailed a list of ninety-five theses to the door of the *Schlosskirche* in Wittenberg.[102] Four of these theses—50, 51, 82, and 86—refer to St. Peter's.[103] Their argument is more or less the same: the pope cannot desire the absurd depredations to which his faithful are subjected in order to collect the money intended for the construction of the new church of St. Peter. Thesis 50 says it all:

> *si Papa nosset exactiones venalium predicatorum, mallet Basilicam s. Petri in cineres ire quam edificari cute, carne et ossibus ovium suarum ...*

Luther's criticism was aimed not just at the waste of money and the means used to fund the Renaissance Church, but, more generally, at Julius's and Bramante's *plan of conquest of beauty*. Luther questioned not only the extremely dubious *means* but also the ineffable *ends* of the new St. Peter's. It was not just a matter of good administration; the theses raised the more general question of the value of beauty and its utility for the Christian community. Luther saw no reason to entrust beauty with all those hopes. He didn't see what difference beauty could make where salvation was concerned, didn't see why space should be so important, why architecture should not be subject to the laws of common sense. He didn't believe that the world would be saved by beauty. His critique was a radical one: if the contradictory political dimension of architecture cannot be resolved, if its offer of beauty provides no real answer, then it is better to renounce architecture, its cumbersome stupidity, its senseless costs, and its unjustifiable violence.[104] If salvation is a fundamentally private matter, if there is no need for a community to mediate between man and God, then buildings, spaces, and images of space are not needed either. If meaningful experiences are all inner experiences, then a public art like architecture is not required.

It is extremely difficult to ignore Luther's arguments, and hard not to see Bramante as at least marginally responsible for a political and religious catastrophe that divided European Christendom and plunged it into centuries of conflict. And yet, however problematic it may appear, a theory of architecture that sets out to present the void as space of the possible, and to consider the configuration of public space as an indirect, but explicit hypothesis of coexistence, cannot help but defend the need to imagine and represent spaces, cannot help but take the side of Bramante against Luther—and thus defend the autonomy of architecture against the brisk common sense of modernity, and still insist on squandering money for the sole purpose of producing *spectacles of space*.

NOTES

INTRODUCTION

1 G. C. Argan, "Il problema del Bramante," *Rassegna Marchigiana*, XII (1934), 212–233. Trans. into English as "Bramante's Problem" by H. Evans for the forthcoming *Bramante, an Introduction*, ed. K. Geers, V. Pizzigoni, and P. P. Tamburelli.

2 The expression used by Argan is "*spettacolo di spazialità*" or spectacle of spatiality (Argan, "Il problema del Bramante," 214). I will use the somewhat simplified and slightly more immediate expression "spectacle of space."

3 G. Vasari, "Bramante da Urbino," in *Le vite de' più eccellenti pittori scultori ed architettori scritte da Giorgio Vasari pittore aretino con nuove annotazioni e commenti di Gaetano Milanesi* (Florence: Sansoni, 1906), vol. IV, 145–146. English trans. by H. Evans in the forthcoming *Bramante, an Introduction*.

4 Vasari, "Bramante da Urbino," 146.

5 Scamozzi does not define "universale," which he sometimes uses in a strictly Aristotelan sense, see for example V. Scamozzi, *L'idea dell'architettura universale* (Milan: Forni, 1982), book I, ch. XXIV, 71, and sometimes simply as a synonym for "general."

6 Alberti used the expression "spatio" in a letter to Ludovico Gonzaga in which he proposed himself as the designer for Sant'Andrea (1470). Alberti hints at the need to "have a great space capable of accommodating a lot of people" (havere gram spatio dove molto populo capesse). *Space* in this case seems to have a purely quantitative meaning, yet it is interesting to note the link that, already in this first occurrence, is established between *spatio* and *populo*.

7 A. Schmarsow, "The Essence of Architectural Creation," in *Empathy,* *Form and Space: Problems in German Aesthetics, 1873–93*, trans. H. F. Mallgrave and E. Ikonomou (Los Angeles: Getty Research Institute, 1994), 281–297. Schmarsow's argument seems to have been anticipated by some considerations put forward by Geymüller about twenty years earlier, which significantly were developed in connection with Bramante's architecture. For Geymüller, Bramante sought "*die Harmonie der inneren Luft*" or, as is explained in more detail in the French version: "*l'harmonie des cubes d'air contenus et entourés par les différentes parties intérieures d'un édifice*" (the harmony of the volumes of air contained and surrounded by the different parts of the interior of a building). H. von Geymüller, *Les projets primitifs pour la basilique de Saint-Pierre de Rome* (Paris: Baudry/Vienna: Lehmann and Wentzel, 1875), 5, note 3. It is probable that Geymüller's reflections on Bramante's work contributed to the new interest in space in architectural theory at the end of the nineteenth century.

8 It may be possibile to concede something to anachronism, even without going so far as to propose, like Georges Didi-Huberman, an out-and-out *heuristics of anachronism* (G. Didi-Huberman, "L'histoire de l'art comme discipline anachronique," in idem, *Devant le temps: histoire de l'art et anachronisme des images* (Paris, Éditions de Minuit, 2000), 9–55; see too R. Koselleck, *Futures Past: On the Semantics of Historical Time*, trans. K Tribe (New York: Columbia University Press, 2004).

9 Fundamental on these aspects remain R. Sennett, *The Fall of Public Man* (New York: Norton, 1977), and C. Taylor, *A Secular Age* (Cambridge, MA: Harvard University Press, 2007).

10 For T. S. Eliot this was the fundamental characteristic of all art: "the emotion of art is impersonal." T. S. Eliot, "Tradition and the Individual Talent," in idem, *The Sacred Wood* (Mansfield, CT: Martino, 2015), 42–53. Rather than envying Eliot's certainties, we should be abandoning them. We cannot ignore the fact that all of contemporary art has refused to sign up to this commitment—and very often has made fun of it. Having said this, if it is possible for a public art to exist, it is certainly architecture.

11 The book is written in accordance with Vasari's rule—fairly unpopular in more recent studies of the history of architecture—that the eye is "a much better judge and guide than the ear" (G. Vasari, "Proemio alla parte seconda," in *Le vite de' più eccellenti pittori scultori ed architettori*, vol. II, 97. English ed., "Preface to the Second Part," in *Lives of the Painters, Sculptors and Architects*, trans. G. de Vere (London: David Campbell, 1996), vol. I, 248. Vasari's opinion was echoed in a beautiful passage from Jean-Baptiste Séroux d'Agincourt: "The history of the arts which have the eye for their judge, I would be tempted to say for their owner, should only be written by submitting their productions to it. I will add that the source of so many of the conjectures, sloppy ideas and errors that we encounter in the works of scholars, antiquarians and many others who have ventured to tackle the arts and their principles lies in the fact that they have written and spoken about them without having the monuments before their eyes, often substituting for them their particular opinions or fruitless discussions." J. B. Séroux d'Agincourt, "Discours préliminaire," in *Histoire de l'art par les monuments depuis sa décadence au IVe siècle jusqu'à son renouvellement au XVIe* (Paris: Treuttel et Wurtz, 1811–1820), VI; cited in G. Previtali, *La fortuna dei primitivi. Da Vasari ai neoclassici* (Turin: Einaudi, 1964), 166.

12 A. Bruschi, *Bramante* (London: Thames & Hudson, 1977). The so-called "big Bruschi" is A. Bruschi, *Bramante architetto* (Rome-Bari: Laterza, 1969).

13 The celebrations of Bramante (promoted by the National Committee set up by law no. 476 of April 2, 1968) were held in the fall of 1969. In fact the anniversaries— "of 1914 for the master's death and of 1944 for his birth—had both fallen in wartime," as noted in the "Relazione generale" that introduces the publication *Studi bramanteschi. Atti del Congresso internazionale. Milano-Urbino-Roma-1970* (Rome: De Luca, 1974), xiii. Significantly, despite the fact that it did not occur in wartime, the anniversary of 2014 was not marked by celebrations, nor still less by studies, apart from the enthusiastic but necessarily modest ones staged independently by the Accademia di San Luca, the Museo Palladio, and the magazine *San Rocco*.

14 R. Venturi, *Complexity and Contradiction in Architecture* (New York: Museum of Modern Art, 1966), 18.

15 The use of experiences in the past to inform the theory of contemporary architecture is in direct conflict with the more recent praxis in architectural historiography. Without bringing in Nietzsche, the situation with regard to architecture has been described in a very balanced way by Alan Colquhoun: "the use of the past to supply models for the present depends upon the ideological distortion of the past; and the whole effort of modern historiography is to eliminate these distortions."

A. Colquhoun, "Three Kinds of Historicism," in A. Colquhoun, *Collected Essays in Architectural Criticism* (London: Black Dog, 2009), 160.

16 A. Gramsci, *Prison Notebooks*, vol. II, trans. J. A. Buttigieg (New York: Columbia University Press, 1996), 186.

17 And things had not gone much better in Milan, at least judging by the disconcerting amount of disgraces listed by Leonardo in his note with the catalogue of buildings by Bramante (*Il castellano fatto prigione./ Il bissconte stracinato e poi morto el figliolo./ Gian della Rosa toltoli e denari./ Borgonzio principiò e nol uolle e però fuggì le fortune./ Il Duca perso lo stato e la roba e liberta,/ e nessuna sua opera si finj per lui*). The list is contained in Codex L; see L. da Vinci, Codex L, f. Iv. On the list, see R. Martinis, *Anticamente moderni. Palazzi rinascimentali di Lombardia in età sforzesca* (Macerata: Quodlibet, 2021), esp. 171–202.

18 baukuh is the architectural office that I have been running since 2004 together with Paolo Carpi, Silvia Lupi, Vittorio Pizzigoni, Giacomo Summa, and Andrea Zanderigo (www.baukuh.it). *San Rocco* is a magazine that I founded and edited from 2010 to 2019 (www.sanrocco.info).

19 G. Scott, *The Architecture of Humanism* (New York: Norton, 1974), 32.

INDIFFERENCE

1 Rome, *wie ich sie vorfand*

1 G. Vasari, "Bramante da Urbino," in *Le vite de' più eccellenti pittori scultori e architettori scritte da Giorgio Vasari pittore aretino con nuove annotazioni e commenti di Gaetano Milanesi*, vol. IV (Florence: Sansoni, 1906), 154.

I will draw throughout on the version of the "Life of Bramante" in the Giunti edition (1568), which is more complete than the Torrentino one (1550). As a consequence, all references to the "Life of Bramante" in this book are to the one edited by Milanesi, republished by Sansoni in 1973, and translated by H. Evans for the forthcoming *Bramante, an Introduction*, ed. K. Geers, V. Pizzigoni, and P. P. Tamburelli.

2 Bramante was certainly still in Milan on December 20, 1498, when he was paid for a model for the cloisters of Sant'Ambrogio. Ludovico Sforza left the city on September 2, 1499, and the French army occupied Milan on October 6 (one of the advisers accompanying Louis XII was Giuliano della Rovere, the future Julius II).

3 Although the opinion is exposed with great elegance, it does not seem to me that Bramante went to Rome to enjoy his retirement, as Creighton Gilbert writes (C. Gilbert, "Bramante on the road to Rome (with some Leonardo sketches in his pocket)," in *Arte Lombarda*, no. 66 (1983): 5–14. As soon as he arrived in Rome, Bramante painted a coat of arms for Alexander VI in San Giovanni in Laterano. He also made immediate contact with several cardinals and members of the papal court. On Bramante's reception in Rome see F. Andreani, "Bramante e gli amici lombardi a Roma," *Palladio* 53 (2014): 5–22. We do not know whether Bramante had visited Rome before moving there in 1499. If he did so, it could only have been for brief periods. A reconstruction of Bramante's movements can be found in A. Bruschi, "Identità di Bramante '… al mondo huom singolare,'" in *Donato Bramante: Ricerche, Proposte, Riletture*, ed. F. P. Di Teodoro (Urbino: Accademia

Raffaello, 2001), 7–18, and A. Bruschi, "Donato Bramante e i suoi amici pittori umbri," *Annali di Architettura*, no. 21 (2009): 11–26.

4 Bramante was the last architect of the Renaissance to encounter the Roman ruins without thorough prior preparation. His successors (partly as a result of his work) would come to Rome with a much clearer idea of what they might find there. Palladio, for example, "right from the first time, came to Rome with an already fairly well-developed idea of its architecture; he already knew a lot about Vitruvius, he was already, to a certain extent, familiar with the ancient and modern monuments of Rome through drawings, probably supplied to him by Trissino, and through Serlio's treatise." A. Bruschi, "Bramante, Raffaello e Palladio," in *Bollettino del Centro Internazionale di Studi di Architettura Andrea Palladio*, no. 15 (1973): 71.

5 On the somber climate of the reign of Alexander VI, see for example J. Burckhardt, *The Civilization of the Renaissance in Italy*, trans. S. G. C. Middlemore (London: George Allen & Unwin/New York: Macmillan, 1878), 46.

6 Giovanni Agosti and Dante Isella have shown that the author of the *Antiquarie* could not have been Bramante, as had already been suggested by Richard Schofield in 1979: see *Antiquarie prospetiche romane*, ed. G. Agosti and D. Isella (Milan: Guanda, 2006), with a long essay by Agosti on the critical reception and history of the attribution of the *Antiquarie*. See too D. Isella, "Le capre di Tivoli," in idem, *Lombardia stravagante* (Turin: Einaudi, 2005), 41–53. The opposite opinion is expressed in M. Giontella and R. Fubini, "Ancora sulle 'Antiquarie prospettiche romane'. Nuovi elementi per l'attribuzione a

Bramante," *Archivio Storico Italiano* 164, no. 609 (July–September 2006): 513–518.

7 "... painted sacred temples and sculpture / some of which are standing and some in total ruin, / making even the walls weep in sorrow," *Antiquarie prospetiche romane*, 7–8.

8 "Thus the 'as found' was a new seeing of the ordinary, an openness as to how prosaic 'things' could re-energise our inventive activity. A confronting recognition of what the postwar world actually was like. In a society that had nothing. You reached for what there was ..." (A. and P. Smithson, "The 'As Found' and the 'Found,'" in D. Robbins, *The Independent Group: Postwar Britain and the Aesthetics of Plenty* (Cambridge, MA: MIT Press, 1990), 201–202. See too "Rearrangements: A Smithsons Celebration," OASE, no. 51 (1999) and A. and P. Smithson, *The Charged Void: Architecture* (New York: Monacelli, 2005).

9 "As I found it." L. Wittgenstein, *Tractatus logico-philosophicus*, 5.631 (Frankfurt am Main: Suhrkamp, 1963), 90.

10 The population of Rome in 1500 was somewhere around 50,000 (J. Delumeau, *Vita economica e sociale a Roma nel Cinquecento*, Florence: Sansoni, 1979, 53), whereas in the second century CE the metropolis probably had a million and a half inhabitants. Between the end of the fifteenth century and the beginning of the sixteenth, the only cities in Europe to have more than one hundred thousand inhabitants were Istanbul, Milan, Naples, Paris, and Venice and, among these, only Istanbul—which in any case Bramante never saw—came close to half a million.

11 On the substantially negative evaluation of these enormous ancient buildings by the humanists see H. Günther, *Insana aedificia Thermarum nomine extructa,*

Die Diokletiansthermen in der Sicht der Renaissance, in A. Beyer, V. Lampugnani, and G. Schweikhart, *Hülle und Fülle. Festschrift für Tilmann Buddensieg* (Alfter: VDG, 1993), 252–283.

12 "… *io staria meglio a casa mia*." G. Agosti, *Su Mantegna* (Milan: Feltrinelli, 2005), 50. Mantegna in Rome looks as disappointed as Heidegger did in Greece, when he went there for the first time at the age of seventy, on a cruise trip with his wife.

2 As a snake sheds its skin

13 Bramante completed the design of the cloisters just before he left Milan, probably in September 1499. He built the refectory and not much more and left a preliminary model and perhaps some designs for the orders of the two cloisters. Construction on the cloisters would start after the middle of the sixteenth century and not be finished until the early decades of the seventeenth; see A. E. Werdehausen, "Bramante e il convento di Sant'Ambrogio," *Arte Lombarda*, no. 79 (1986): 19–48.

14 A contract dated August 17, 1500, governed the execution of eight pillars of the lower order (the complete documentation is in A. Bruschi, *Bramante architetto* [Rome-Bari: Laterza, 1969], 822–836 and C. Ricci, "Il chiostro della Pace. Documenti bramanteschi," *Nuova Antologia* I [1915], 361–667). So Bramante must have begun work on the project some time earlier. The cloister was completed in 1504, as the inscription on the Ionic frieze declares: … EREXIT ANNO SALVTIS CRISTIANE MDIIII.

15 There ought to be no debate over the date of the Tempietto, given that the year is clearly engraved on a stone slab in the crypt, which declares that the building was begun "by King Ferdinand and Queen Isabella of Spain in 1502." In reality, the slab has probably been moved and has a different inscription on the back; see C. L. Frommel, "Bramante, il Tempietto e il convento di San Pietro in Montorio," *Römisches Jahrbuch der Bibliotheca Hertziana* 41 (2013–2014): 130–132. No source speaks of the consecration of the building and it is hard to say when the Tempietto was completed. In this objectively complicated documentary context, scholars have taken the most varied positions. Murray (1972), Lotz (1974), and Nesselrath (1990) accept the date of the plaque. Italian scholars, on the other hand, have been more inclined to believe that a greater amount of time passed between the construction of the Tempietto and the cloister, leaving a long enough interval to imagine an evolution of his style. Thus for de Angelis d'Ossat (1966) the Tempietto dates from 1510, and for Bruschi (1969) and Portoghesi (1970) from 1508–1512. In 1977 Bruschi took up the question again and proposed an earlier date (1502-1506/07), while Spagnesi (1984) continued to propose 1508–1512. For Frommel (2014) the Tempietto was built between 1502 and 1508, Cantatore (2017) confirms this hypothesis.

16 R. Bonelli, *Da Bramante a Michelangelo. Profilo dell'architettura del Cinquecento* (Venice: Neri Pozza, 1960), 19.

17 Guglielmo della Porta, letter to Bartolomeo Ammannati. The letter is part of the notebook conserved in Düsseldorf; for a transcript of the letter, see W. Gramberg, *Die Düsseldorfer Skizzenbücher des Guglielmo della Porta* (Berlin: Mann, 1964), vol. I, 122–128.

18 C. Baroni, *Bramante* (Bergamo: Istituto Arti Grafiche, 1944), 21. For an

introduction to the context of fifteenth-century Milan see F. Malaguzzi Valeri, *La corte di Ludovico il Moro. Bramante e Leonardo da Vinci* (Milan: Hoepli, 1915) and L. Patetta, *L'architettura del Quattrocento a Milano* (Milan: CLUP, 1987); for Rome see instead P. Tomei, *L'architettura a Roma nel Quattrocento* (Rome: Multigrafica, 1942) and C. L. Frommel, *Der römische Palastbau der Hochrenaissance* (Tübingen: Ernst Wasmuth, 1973).

19 G. Grassi, "Analisi e Progetto," in *L'analisi urbana e la progettazione architettonica*, ed. A. Rossi (Milan: CLUP, 1969); now in G. Grassi, *L'architettura come mestiere e altri scritti* (Padua: Marsilio, 1979), 57.

20 By "recursive," here I mean a procedure "that is applied iteratively to the result of its previous application." P. Virno, *E così via, all'infinito. Logica e antropologia* (Turin: Bollati Boringhieri, 2010), 18.

21 Vasari, "Bramante da Urbino," 146.

22 See too S. Settis, "Did the Ancients Have an Antiquity? The Idea of Renaissance in the History of Classical Art," in A. Brown, *Language and Images of Renaissance Italy* (Oxford: Clarendon Press, 1995), 27–50.

3 *La bella maniera degli antichi*

23 E. Panofsky, "Renaissance and Renascences," in *The Kenyon Review* VI (1944): 201–236, and E. Panofsky, *Renaissance and Renascences in Western Art* (Stockholm: Almqvist & Wiksel, 1960).

24 This is a sentiment typical of Italian culture, of which perhaps the most succinct expression is Vito's lament in a famous line from the movie *Ecce bombo*: "I should have been born a hundred years ago, in 1848. The barricades in Leipzig.

By the age of twenty-two I'd have already been through the Paris Commune ..." (N. Moretti, *Ecce bombo*, 1978).

25 G. Beltramini, *Palladio privato* (Padua: Marsilio, 2008), 38.

26 "The beautiful manner of the ancients." The expression is Cellini's. See B. Cellini, "Della architettura," in *Opere di Baldassare Castiglione Giovanni della Casa Benvenuto Cellini*, ed. C. Cordié (Milan-Naples: Ricciardi, 1960), 1109. This expression appears in the title of a fundamental essay by Christof Thoenes: see C. Thoenes, "Bramante e la 'bella maniera degli antichi,'" in idem, *Sostegno e adornamento. Saggi sull'architettura del Rinascimento: disegni, ordini, magnificenza* (Milan: Electa, 1998), 59–65.

27 The ruins had to be studied, as Roberto Weiss so aptly put it: "not because they were ancient, but merely because they were conspicuous." R. Weiss, *The Renaissance Discovery of Classical Antiquity* (Oxford: Blackwell, 1969), 5.

28 A. Rossi, *A Scientific Autobiography*, trans. L. Venuti (Cambridge, MA: MIT Press, 1981), 16.

29 "[They] are saying, with a joyous face, that history / has a thousand faces, that the last / is often first": P. P. Pasolini, "The Religion of My Time," in idem, *Selected Poems*, trans. N. MacAfee and L. Martinengo (London: John Calder, 1984), 79.

30 The hose (by which I mean the kind of leggings that men wore during the Renaissance) are the ones which he mentioned so frequently in the poems he wrote during the Milanese period that they are now known as the *sonetti delle calze*, or "Sonnets of the Hose." The most recent edition of the sonnets is C. Vecce, *Donato Bramante. Sonetti e altri scritti* (Rome: Salerno Editrice, 1995).

31 Giuliano da Sangallo was born a year before Bramante and died a year after. He pursued a line of research that ran parallel to—and often intersected with—Bramante's. Hence Giuliano's production can be used to gauge Bramante's choices with respect to the cultural context in which they are set. What Giuliano *sought* offers an excellent starting point to evaluate what Bramante *found*. On Giuliano see S. Frommel, *Giuliano da Sangallo* (Florence: Edifir, 2014).

32 Giuliano's notes preserved in the *Taccuino Senese*, the *Libro dei Disegni* in the Biblioteca Apostolica, and the folios in the collection of the Uffizi are the proof of an anguished search: Giuliano *venerated* the architecture of the Romans, and sought its secret almost with dread, as if he were trying to find a way to transmute lead into gold. See C. Hülsen, *Il libro di Giuliano da Sangallo, Codice Vaticano Barberiniano Latino 4424*, 2 vol. (Leipzig: Harrasowitz, 1910).

33 Burckhardt recognized in the painting of Piero della Francesca a similar "want of a higher conception of the facts." J. Burckhardt, *The Cicerone* (London: John Murray, 1893), 71. All of Piero's art came after a rough leveling that reduced the things he painted to their most prosaic visual configuration. Piero's art is painting and painting shows things that can be seen. From this point of view the "leveling action of the European Renaissance" (*die nivellierende europäische Renaissance*) that Worringer lamented (W. Worringer, *Formprobleme der Gotik*, Munich: Piper, 1912, 126) was wholly conscious, just as Dante's invitation to "fly low" was conscious (D. Alighieri, *Convivio*, libro IV, VI, 20), 598; English trans. by Richard Lansing: https://digitaldante.columbia.edu/text/

library/the-convivio/book-04/; see too G. Agamben, *Categorie Italiane. Studi di poetica* (Padua: Marsilio, 1996), 27. On this even Ruskin got it right: Bramante actually proposed "an architecture which thus appealed not less to the lowest instincts of dullness, than to the subtlest pride of learning ..." J. Ruskin, *The Stones of Venice*, vol. III (Boston: Aldine, 1890), 67-68.

34 G. Contini, "Un'interpretazione di Dante," in G. Contini, *Un'idea di Dante* (Turin: Einaudi, 2001), 75.

35 D. Walcott, *Omeros*, LVI, III, 12-13 (London: Faber and Faber, 1990), 283.

36 Walcott, *Omeros*, LVI, III, 19-20, 283.

37 Walcott, *Omeros*, LVI, III, 24-32, 283.

4 No style

38 G. Grassi, *La costruzione logica dell'architettura* (Padua: Marsilio, 1967), 68.

39 Vitruvius, *De architectura*, IV, 3, 1. English ed., *Ten Books on Architecture*, trans. I. D. Rowland, commentary and illustrations by T. N. Howe (Cambridge: Cambridge University Press, 2015).

40 Even if those "correct solutions" do not, as Portoghesi would have it, correspond "to 'genres' of architectural language quite similar to literary genres." See P. Portoghesi, "La lingua universale: Cultura e architettura tra il 1503 e il 1527," in *Studi bramanteschi. Atti del Congresso internazionale. Milano-Urbino-Roma-1970* (Rome: De Luca, 1974), 356. Its translation will be published in the forthcoming *Bramante, an Introduction*.

41 See M. Baxandall, *Giotto and the Orators* (Oxford: Oxford University Press, 1971).

42 E. Auerbach, *Mimesis: The Representation of Reality in Western Literature*, trans.

W. R. Trask (Princeton: Princeton University Press, 1953), 185.

43 D. Bramante, "Bramanti opinio supra domicilium seu templum magnum," in *Annali della Fabbrica del Duomo*, Session June 27, 1490, published by G. Mongeri, "Bramante e il Duomo," in *Archivio Storico Lombardo*, yr. 5, no. 3 (1877); now in *Studi bramanteschi*, 22–24. Its translation will be published in the forthcoming *Bramante, an Introduction*. The only other text of Bramante's to have survived, apart from the sonnets, is a short report on the fortifications of Crevola in Val d'Ossola. The report was so badly done that Ludovico Sforza immediately ordered it to be done again.

44 Bramante, "Bramanti opinio supra domicilium seu templum magnum," 24.

45 The *Opinio* is even clearer if we consider that the Gothic cathedral provided a perfect opportunity to indulge in a facile classicist polemic of the type that Palladio was unable to refrain from in the case of the completion of the façade of San Petronio in Bologna.

46 Bramante, "Bramanti opinio supra domicilium seu templum magnum," 23.

47 The copied capital is the one on the pilaster of the portico, as shown in drawing UA6670, probably made by Antonio da Sangallo the Younger. According to a contract of March 1, 1508, the capitals then had to be "approved by Barbante [*sic*]." The complete text of the contract is in K. Frey, "Zur Baugeschichte des St. Peter: Mitteilungen aus der Reverendissima Fabbrica di S. Pietro," *Jahrbuch der Königlich Preussischen Kunstsammlungen*, no. 31 (1911): 44; see too C. Denker Nesselrath, *Die Säulenordnungen bei Bramante* (Worms: Römische Studien der Bibliotheca Hertziana, 1990), 79–84.

48 The most striking example of the promotion of a new style through the discarding of all previous ones is provided by Le Corbusier: "Architecture has nothing to do with 'styles' ... The styles of Louis XV, Louis XVI, Louis XIV or the Gothic are to architecture what a feather is to a woman's head ..." Le Corbusier, "Trois rappels à MM. LES ARCHITECTES," *L'Esprit Nouveau* (Paris, 1920), 90–95.

49 The classic formulation of the problem is Heinrich Hübsch's "in what style should we build?": H. Hübsch, *In welchem Style sollen wir bauen?* (Karlsruhe: C. F. Müller Hofbuchhandlung und Hofbuchdruckerei, 1828). A contemporary edition is W. Herrmann, *In What Style Should We Build? The German Debate on Architectural Style* (Santa Monica, CA: Getty Center for the History of Art and Humanities, 1992).

50 "Universal" and "universalism" are used here in a fairly generic sense, without addressing the criticism of the "universal" as an alternative to the "common" and of the consequent contrast between a "realism of the Common" and a "nominalism of the Universal" made by Paolo Virno in his essay "Angels and the General Intellect: Individuation in Duns Scotus and Gilbert Simondon," *Parrhesia*, no. 7 (2009): 58–67.

5 Architecture implies the city

51 This would be the position adopted, with great clarity, by Piranesi: "Piranesi's argument for the superiority of the Romans lay not in the fact that they invented 'from their own resources' but that they invented from the resources of others." (I. Small, "Polarités. Piranesi's Shape of Time," *Image [&] Narrative*

[e-journal], 18 (2007). http://www. imageandnarrative.be/inarchive/ thinking_pictures/small.htm.

52 "... *congiugnitore delli miei generanti, che con esso parlavano.*" Dante, *Convivio*, book 1, chap. 13. English trans. by Richard Lansing: https://digitaldante. columbia.edu/text/library/the-convivio/book-01/#13.

53 A. Rossi, *L'architettura della città* (Padua: Marsilio, 1966), 25. English ed., *The Architecture of the City*, trans. D. Ghirardo and J. Ockman (Cambridge, MA: MIT Press, 1984), 113. This fundamental statement by Aldo Rossi defines the most clear-cut alternative in the theory of architecture: whether architecture is founded on the city and thus operates on the basis of a complex and already given system of mutual references or it is architecture that is the foundation of the city, which would then consist of a sum of elements produced independently of one another and that can all be ascribed to an outside cause. The alternative between a city founded on architecture and an architecture founded on the city is the basis of the contrast between an "atomistic" school (Alberti and Palladio and Perrault and Laugier and Ledoux and Durand and Gropius and Price) and a "dialectical" school (Bramante and Vignola and Bernini and Fischer von Erlach and Piranesi and Loos and Rossi and Koolhaas).

54 The perspective describes what a viewer sees when inserted into a space already transformed by human hand. The perspective, *as symbolic form*, was born as reflection on a city that already existed, as a tool of knowledge that, even when it represents the city of the future, does it on the basis of the existing one. See H. Damisch, *The Origin of Perspective*, trans. J. Goodman (Cambridge, MA: MIT Press, 1994), 168-197.

55 "[C]ertain buildings were appropriate for the public as a whole, others for the higher members of society, and others for the lower ones." L. B. Alberti, *On the Art of Building in Ten Books*, trans. J. Rykwert, N. Leach, and R. Tavernor (Cambridge, MA: MIT Press, 1988), 117.

56 S. Serlio, *Libro VI*, unpublished (see V. Hart and P. Hicks, ed. and trans., *Sebastiano Serlio on Architecture. Volume Two: Books VI and VII of "Tutte L'Opere D'Architettura et Prospetiva" with "Castrametation of the Romans" and "The Extraordinary Book of Doors"* (New Haven-London: Yale University Press, 2001). For Serlio Lomazzo's judgment still holds: "*Veramente Sebastiano Serlio ha fatto più ammazzacani architetti che non aveva egli peli in barba*" (Truly Sebastiano Serlio made more dog-catchers into architects than he had hairs in his beard). G. P. Lomazzo, *Trattato dell'arte della pittura, diviso in VII libri* (Milan: P. G. Pontio, 1584), 407.

57 S. von Moos, "The Palace as a Fortress: Rome and Bologna under Julius II," in *Art and Architecture in the Service of Politics*, ed. H. A. Millon and L. Nochlin (Cambridge, MA: MIT Press, 1978), 74.

58 Founding architecture on the city does not mean ignoring the fact that the city is a response to a natural environment, to a *climate* (to use Tetsuro Watsuji's fascinating terminology), but rather stressing that this response is neither automatic nor necessary, that the possible interpretations of a climate are diverse and that all coincide with a hypothesis of civilization.

59 G. De Finetti, *Milano. Costruzione di una città* (Milan: Hoepli, 2002), 198.

6 Pantheon + Basilica of Maxentius

60 See F. Graf Wolff Metternich and C. Thoenes, *Die frühen St.-Peter-Entwürfe 1505-1514* (Tübingen: Wasmuth, 1987), 82, note 135, with a discussion of the sources.

61 St. Peter's, as Creighton Gilbert succinctly put it, was "a very large building of immense symbolic importance." C. Gilbert, *Michelangelo: On and Off the Sistine Ceiling* (New York: Braziller, 1994), 31.

62 *The Golden Legend of Jacobus de Voragine*, trans. and adapted by Ryan Granger and Helmut Ripperger (New York: Longmans, 1941), 46-51. This legend was very widespread in the Middle Ages and Renaissance and is quoted for example in Giovanni Rucellai's *Zibaldone Quaresimale*, where it is written of the Temple of Peace (the name given at the time to the Basilica of Maxentius), that "it is said to have been a temple of idols, and that the Romans said that it lasted until a virgin gave birth, and that it fell into ruin the night that Our Lord Jesus Christ was born." See R. Weiss, *The Renaissance Discovery of Classical Antiquity* (Oxford: Blackwell, 1969), 74.

63 The letters of Pietro Bembo and Giovan Francesco Pico date from 1512. They are published in G. Santangelo, *Le epistole de imitatione di Giovanfrancesco Pico della Mirandola e di Pietro Bembo* (Florence: Olschki, 1954). The passage quoted here is on p. 45. On this subject see too J. S. Ackerman, "Imitation," in *Antiquity and Its Interpreters*, ed. A. Payne, A. Kuttner, and R. Smick (Cambridge: Cambridge University Press, 2000), 9-16, and E. Battisti, "Il concetto di imitazione nel Cinquecento italiano," in idem, *Rinascimento e Barocco* (Turin: Einaudi,

1960), 175-215. The letters are discussed in P. Portoghesi, "La lingua universale: cultura e architettura tra il 1503 e il 1527," in *Studi bramanteschi*, 354.

64 A. Guarna, *Scimmia. Edizione emendata e corretta*, ed. G. Battisti (Rome: Istituto Grafico Tiberino, 1970), 118. The *Simia* is a satirical dialogue whose protagonists are members of the Roman Curia; the dialogue was published by Andrea Guarna in 1517 and probably borrows motifs from Erasmus's *The Julius Exclusus*, which was already circulating anonymously in 1514. See Desiderius Erasmus, *The Julius Exclusus*, trans. P. Pascal (Bloomington, IN: Indiana University Press, 1968).

UNIVERSALISM

7 Universal language

1 J. Summerson, *The Classical Language of Architecture* (London: Methuen, 1963), 20. Summerson defines classicism as "the Latin of Architecture" (*The Classical Language of Architecture*, 7). Even the titles of the various chapters insist on a linguistic metaphor ("The Grammar of Antiquity," "Sixteenth-century Linguistics," "The Rhetoric of the Baroque"), but the metaphor is never made clear, just as the title chosen for the book is never explained. Summerson certainly had no grand theoretic ambitions and the popularizing tone of the radio broadcasts on which the book is based did not help him make headway in such discourses. Ten years later the ideas in Summerson's book were opposed by Bruno Zevi with his *Il linguaggio moderno dell'architettura*. Nor did Zevi show much concern about the problem and, right at the beginning of

his book, declared that he felt no need to justify the use of "language" in relation to architecture, moving on at once to the argument that was the guiding thread of his whole project: "For better or worse, architects communicate. And the fact remains that they speak architecture, whether it is a language or not. Thus we must set down precisely what it implies to speak architecture in an anticlassical key. If we can do this, the theoretical apparatus will come by itself ..." (B. Zevi, *Il linguaggio moderno dell'architettura. Guida al codice anticlassico*, Turin: Einaudi, 1973, 9). English ed., *The Modern Language of Architecture* (Seattle, WA: University of Washington Press, 1978), 4.

2   R. Bonelli, "Avvicinamento a Bramante," in *Palladio*, nos. III–IV (July–December 1952): 144.

3   A. Bruschi, *Bramante architetto* (Rome-Bari: Laterza, 1969), 670.

4   P. Portoghesi, "La lingua universale: Cultura e architettura between il 1503 e il 1527," in *Studi bramanteschi. Atti del Congresso internazionale. Milano-Urbino-Roma-1970* (Rome: De Luca, 1974), 351–371.

5   W. Lotz, *Architecture in Italy 1500-1600*, ed. D. Howard, 2nd revised ed. (New Haven, CT: Yale University Press, 1995), 12.

6   From the mid-1960s, history of architecture began to come under the influence of contemporary studies of semiotics, proposing to treat "all cultural phenomena as if they were systems of signs." U. Eco, *La struttura assente* (Milan: Bompiani, 1968), 15. This strange marriage of architecture and semiotics occurred as a result of the natural attraction of opposites, as in this way architecture could satisfy its narrative ambitions and semiotics could

take on "one of the sectors in which semiotics finds itself most challenged" (Eco, *La struttura assente*, 191). This period of studies had at least the merit of obliging historians to revise their use of certain expressions. Confining ourselves to a small selection, see: G. K. Koenig, *Analisi del linguaggio architettonico* (Florence: LEF, 1964); G. Baird and C. Jencks, *Meaning in Architecture* (New York: George Braziller, 1970); C. Jencks, *The Language of Postmodern Architecture* (New York: Rizzoli, 1977).

7   "In fact, the nature of the architectural discipline and its social role did not permit a purely restorative intent, as in the case of Latin. Alongside the problem of correctness architects had to tackle those of meeting completely new requirements and of the accessibility of aesthetic experiences and techniques which had become such a deep-rooted part of the social heritage that they could neither be fully erased nor easily translated into the terms of classicistic orthodoxy. In essence architects had to grapple with and resolve in their choices of language the difficulties of both the Latinists and the supporters of the vernacular. In fact, the architectural language of the Renaissance, unable to completely set aside the influences of medieval culture, which emerged continually at the level of the economic structure and [building] typology, was born out of constant attempts to make the 'Latin' of the classical tradition fit in with the 'vernacular' of the tradition of late-antique, Romanesque and Gothic construction." P. Portoghesi, "La lingua universale," 356-357.

8   E. Forssman, *Dorico, ionico, corinzio nell'architettura del Rinascimento* (Rome-Bari: Laterza, 1973 [Original Swedish edition, 1961]), 111.

9   On the more general possibility of treating architecture as a language see N. Goodman, "How Buildings Mean," in *The Philosophy of the Visual Arts*, ed. Philip Alperson (New York: Oxford University Press, 1992), 368-376, G. Baird, "Semiotics and Architecture," in idem, *Writings on Architecture and the City* (London: Artifice, 2015), 70-75, and M. Donougho, "The Language of Architecture," *Journal of Aesthetic Education* 21, no. 3 (Autumn 1987): 53-67. An attempt to view the orders as "bearers of meaning" has been made by John Onians in a book with that title: J. Onians, *Bearers of Meaning: The Classical Orders in Antiquity, the Middle Ages and the Renaissance* (Princeton: Princeton University Press, 1988). In the course of his long argument Onians himself admits that these *meanings* are neither easy to ascertain nor constant in time. Some very balanced considerations can also be found in M. L. Scalvini, *L'architettura come semiotica connotativa* (Milan: Bompiani, 1975), where however the author seems to limit and complicate the sense in which architecture can be called language to such an extent as to render the project of a semiotics of architecture completely useless. A reconstruction of the origin and use of the expression "architectural language" in relation to modern architecture is hinted at in A. Forty, *Words and Buildings. A Vocabulary of Modern Architecture* (London: Thames and Hudson, 2004), in particular 63-85. It would be interesting to extend this study to classical architecture and its historiography.

10 The premises for an operation of this kind can already be found in an old and wonderful book by Geoffrey Scott, curiously entitled *The Architecture of Humanism*, while in reality it is more of an introduction to the study of it, a sort of *prolegomena to any future study of the architecture of humanism*. Setting out to clear up the misconceptions that impede an understanding of the architecture of the Italian Renaissance, the book provides a merciless criticism of Romantic and positivist historiography and art theory, repeatedly derided in chapters that bear titles like "The Romantic Fallacy," "The Romantic Fallacy (continued)," "The Mechanical Fallacy," and "The Ethical Fallacy." For Scott, the biggest obstacle to understanding the architecture of the Renaissance is symbolism: "the first fallacy of Romanticism, then, and the gravest, is to regard architecture as *symbolic*." G. Scott, *The Architecture of Humanism* [1914] (New York: Norton, 1974), 50.

11 "The long and arduous route from Vitruvius's early studies to the definitive elaboration of the system of the five orders is reflected in the history of the words. As far as I can tell, the word 'order' in the sense in which it is understood here was used for the first time in the so-called letter from Raphael to Leo X, and then gradually taken up by Serlio, Bartoli, Bertani and others, until in Vignola's Regola it supplanted all the older synonyms, such as *specie (spetie), genere (genus), generatione, qualità, maniera (mos), opera, lavoro, ragione (ratio), modo, misura, forma, sorta*. It should be noted that originally it was a logical classification (first, second, third order of columns) and not, as is often thought today, a specific way of 'ordering' the members of the building, in the sense of Vitruvius's *ordinatio*." (C. Thoenes, "'Spezie' e 'ordine' di colonne nell'architettura di

Brunelleschi," in *Filippo Brunelleschi: la sua opera e il suo tempo*, vol. II (Florence: Centro Di, 1980), 317, note 14. See too C. Thoenes, "La 'Regola delli cinque ordini' del Vignola," in idem, *Sostegno e adornamento* (Milan: Electa, 1998), 76–107.

12 A good definition of "order" is the one provided by Scamozzi toward the end of the development of Renaissance classicism: "a well-regulated precedence, and succession of the parts; so that they have their own place." V. Scamozzi, *L'idea dell'architettura universale* (Milan: Forni, 1982), book I, ch. II, 8; see too book VI, ch. I, 2.

13 "[A]ny semiotic system works out a code to transmit a message, and architecture does not convey this message: the information that can be derived or somehow obtained from it is not the message that would assure its semiotic nature." C. Brandi, *Struttura e architettura* (Turin: Einaudi, 1967), 35. See too C. Brandi, *Le due vie* (Bari: Laterza, 1966).

14 "No geometry without the word." P. Valéry, "Eupalinos," in P. Valéry, *Eupalinos. L'Ame et la danse. Dialogue de l'arbre* (Paris: Gallimard, 1945), 54. English ed., "*Eupalinos, or The Architect*," in P. Valéry, Dialogues, trans. W. M. Stewart (New York: Pantheon, 1956), 105.

15 Something similar happens in music: "Images of the objective world appear in music only in scattered, eccentric flashes, vanishing at once; but they are, in their transience, *of music's essence*." (T. W. Adorno, *Beethoven. The Philosophy of Music* [Cambridge: Polity Press, 1998], 8). Just before, Adorno had given a beautiful example: "In the first movement of Schubert's Symphony in C major, at the beginning of the

development, we feel for a few moments as if we were at a rustic wedding; an action seems to begin unfolding, but then is gone at once, swept away in the rushing music which, once imbued with that image, moves onwards to a quite different measure."

8 Architecture non parlante

16 Vitruvius, *De Architectura*, IV, 1, 6–8. English edition, Vitruvius, *Ten Books on Architecture*, trans. I. D. Rowland, commentary and illustrations by T. N. Howe (Cambridge: Cambridge University Press, 2015).

17 Vitruvius, *Ten Books on Architecture*, IV, 1, 8–12.

18 Bruschi recognized that the pedestals project decidedly more at the front than they do at the sides. See Bruschi, *Bramante architetto*, 267–285.

19 Vitruvius, *Ten Books on Architecture*, IV, 1, 6–7.

20 "Imagine a really ripe fig,/and you'll understand everything of their shape,/ and consider the eyelets of the laces/ the gnawed battlements of a city wall./ If we were to speak of the heels,/the groin, the shins and the knees,/a whole estate of writing would be needed./And the seams are filled with lice,/and look like a garment from Germany,/or rather the windows or oculi of the Cathedral." "Sonetto XVIII," in C. Vecce, *Donato Bramante. Sonetti e altri scritti* (Rome: Salerno Editrice, 1995), 50. Translated into English by H. Evans for the forthcoming *Bramante, an Introduction*.

21 Piranesi rebukes Montesquieu for not knowing "how limited are the gains that can be made from Architecture." G. B. Piranesi, *Parere sull'Architettura* (Naples: CLEAN, 1993), 27.

22 G. Vasari, "Bramante da Urbino," in *Le vite de' più eccellenti pittori scultori ed architettori scritte da Giorgio Vasari pittore aretino con nuove annotazioni e commenti di Gaetano Milanesi* (Florence: Sansoni, 1906), vol. IV, 158–159. Translated into English by H. Evans for the forthcoming *Bramante, an Introduction*. See too E. Bentivoglio, "Bramante e il geroglifico di Viterbo," in *Mitteilungen des Kunsthistorischen Institutes in Florenz 6*, no. 2 (1972): 167–174.

23 The duck is the one that Robert Venturi, Denise Scott Brown and Steven Izenour talk about in *Learning from Las Vegas* (Cambridge, MA: MIT Press, 1972), 88–91. See too H. Stadler, M. Stierli, and P. Fischli, *Las Vegas Studio. Bilder aus dem Archiv von Robert Venturi und Denise Scott Brown* (Zurich: Scheidegger & Spiess, 2008).

24 The expression, used to characterize Ledoux's approach to architecture, appeared for the first time in 1852 in an anonymous essay published in *Magasin Pittoresque*; see E. Kaufmann, *Three Revolutionary Architects: Boullée, Ledoux, and Lequeu* (Philadelphia: American Philosophical Society, 1952), 447, 514, 517, 520, 535. By *architecture parlante* I mean (to borrow the words of Boffrand, who does not, however, use the expression *architecture parlante*) buildings that "have to announce their purpose to the viewer": G. Boffrand, *Livre d'Architecture* (Paris: Guillaume Cavalier, 1745), 16.

9 Text envy

25 Vitruvius, *Ten Books on Architecture*, I, 1, 5. Here the translation on p. 22 of the English edition simplifies the meaning of the original, where the word *historias* implies "stories" as well as "history." "*Historias autem plures novisse oportet, quod multa ornamenta saepe in operibus architecti designant, de quibus argumentis rationem, cur fecerint, quaerentibus reddere debent.*"

26 L. B. Alberti, "Prologue," in *Leon Battista Alberti, On the Art of Building in Ten Books*, trans. J. Rykwert, N. Leach, and R. Tavernor (Cambridge, MA: MIT Press, 1988), 31. See too G. Wolf, *Body and Antiquity in Alberti's Writings*, in A. Payne, A. Kuttner, and R. Smick, *Antiquity and its Interpreters* (Cambridge: Cambridge University Press, 2000), 174–190, and P. Falguières, "Alberti, l'ornement, la nature et le droit (L. B. Alberti, *De re aedificatoria*, VI, 2, 93)," in *Albertiana XX*, no. 1 (2017): 97–145.

10 Architecture as painting

27 Bruschi suggests the possibility of a meeting between Alberti and Bramante in Urbino or Mantua (A. Bruschi, *Bramante architetto*, 8 and 151). Bruschi returned to the subject on more than one occasion; see for example A. Bruschi, "Alberti e Bramante: un rapporto decisivo," in *Leon Battista Alberti e il Quattrocento. Studi in onore di Cecil Grayson e Ernest Gombrich*, ed. L. Chiavoni, G. Ferlisi, and M. V. Grassi (Florence: Olschki, 2001), 354–358, and A. Bruschi, "Identità di Bramante '... al mondo huom singolare'," in *Donato Bramante Ricerche, Proposte, Riletture*, ed. F. P. Di Teodoro (Urbino: Accademia Raffaello, 2001), 7–18. English translation by H. Evans in the forthcoming *Bramante, an Introduction*.

28 F. Graf Wolff Metternich, "Der Kupferstich Bernardos de Prevedari

aus Mailand von 1481. Gedanken zu den Anfängen der Kunst Bramantes," *Römisches Jahrbuch für Kunstgeschichte* XI (1967–1968): 18, 42, 69, and 99, note 186, and F. Graf Wolff Metternich, "Bramante, Skizze eines Lebenbildes," in idem, *Bramante und St. Peter* (Munich: Wilhelm Fink, 1975), 194.

29 On the relationship between rhetoric and the figurative arts in the Italy of the fourteenth and fifteenth centuries the contributions of Michael Baxandall remain decisive. See his *Giotto and the Orators* (Oxford: Oxford University Press, 1971) and *Painting and Experience in Fifteenth-century Italy* (Oxford: Oxford University Press, 1972).

30 See the considerations of Cecil Grayson and Lucia Bertolini in the introductions to their respective editions of Alberti's text: C. Grayson, "Introduction," in L. B. Alberti, *On Painting and On Sculpture: The Latin texts of De Pictura and De Statua* (London: Phaidon, 1972) and L. Bertolini, "Introduzione," in L. B. Alberti, *De Pictura* (Florence: Polistampa, 2012). See too L. Bertolini, "Sulla precedenza della redazione volgare del *De pictura* di Leon Battista Alberti," in *Studi per Umberto Carpi*, ed. M. Santagata and A. Stussi (Pisa: Edizioni ETS, 2000), 7–36, and L. Bertolini, "Come 'pubblicava' l'Alberti: ipotesi preliminari," in *Storia della lingua e filologia. Per Alfredo Stussi nel suo sessantacinquesimo compleanno*, ed. M. Zaccarello and L. Tomasin (Florence: Edizioni del Galluzzo, 2004), 219–240.

31 Grayson, "Introduction," xvi–xvii. See too C. Thoenes, "Postille sull'architetto nel *De re aedificatoria*," in *Leon Battista Alberti. Architettura e cultura* (Florence: Olschki, 1999), 27–32, and M. Trachtenberg, "Ayn Rand, Alberti and the Authorial Figure of the Architect,"

California Italian Studies 6, no. 2 (2016).

32 His sixteenth-century biographers cite only painters as Bramante's teachers. For Vasari, Fra Carnevale (Vasari, "Bramante da Urbino," 147); for Sabba da Castiglione, Piero della Francesca and Mantegna: S. Castiglione, "Ricordo CXI," in S. Castiglione, *Ricordi ovvero Ammaestramenti di Monsignor Saba da Castiglione Cavalier Gerosolimitano ne quali con prudenti, e christiani discorsi si ragiona di tutte le materie honorate, che si ricercano a un vero gentil'huomo* (Venice: Paolo Gherardo, 1554), 139.

33 "[E]loquent in the rhyming verses of the vernacular poets, although he was unlettered." Vitruvius, *De Architectura. Translato, commentato et affigurato da Cesare Cesariano*, ed. A. Bruschi, A. Carugo, and F. P. Fiore (Milan: Il Polifilo, 1981), fol. 70v. There have been various interpretations of the meaning of *illiterato* in this context, ranging from the strict interpretation of Metternich, for whom Bramante was simply unable to read or write, to the more nuanced opinion of Bruschi, who understood this observation by Cesariano to be a reference to Bramante's lack of formal education.

34 It has always been difficult for art historians to reconcile Bramante's incomplete education with his unequivocal intellectualism. The problem, which is framed with great critical intelligence in Cesariano's synthetic formula (*facundo/illiterato*, "eloquent/unlettered"), is one that all the most attentive scholars, from Vasari to Bonelli, from Metternich to Bruschi, have run up against. The tragicomic situation in which the unlettered artists of the Renaissance found themselves is described perfectly in a passage that Carlo Dionisotti devoted to Cesariano's

Commentary: "... the mere fact that an artist not from Tuscany, and not a man of letters, could undertake and perform such a task [the translation of *De architectura* into Italian] goes to show what enormous reserves Italian culture had accumulated. The fact remains that Cesariano, while wishing to write in the vernacular, could not. At times, in desperation, he resorted to Latin, but overall his efforts as a translator and commentator were in vain. For the language that he professed to write in could not but be the one that he, a Lombard, spoke, and it was not moreover a tongue that someone inexpert could adapt, so vague and unconstrained by any rule as it still was, to the requirements of a difficult Latin text. Inevitably the original impressed itself with an effect of involuntary parody on the soft texture of the vernacularization and commentary." C. Dionisotti, "Tradizione classica e volgarizzamenti," in idem, *Geografia e storia della letteratura italiana* (Turin: Einaudi, 1967), 134. See too G. C. Spivak, "Can the Subaltern Speak?," in *Marxism and the Interpretation of Culture*, ed. C. Nelson and L. Grossberg, (Chicago, IL: University of Illinois Press, 1988), 271–313.

35   G. C. Argan and C. Grayson, "Leon Battista Alberti," in *Dizionario biografico degli italiani*, vol. I (Rome: Istituto dell'Enciclopedia Italiana, 1960), 709–713, http://www.treccani. it/enciclopedia/leon-battista-alberti_ (Dizionario-Biografico)/.

36   A. Bruschi, "Una tendenza linguistica 'medicea' nell'architettura del Rinascimento," in A. Bruschi, *L'antico, la tradizione, il moderno. Da Arnolfo a Peruzzi, saggi sull'architettura del Rinascimento* (Milan: Electa, 2004), 299.

37   In the Letter to Leo X, Raphael distances himself from Bramante on just this point: "Thus, even if it so happens that architecture has been awakened from its slumbers in our day and comes very close to the style of the ancients, as one sees in many beautiful works of Bramante, nonetheless the ornaments are in less precious material than those of the ancients, who, it seems, with endless expense ..." Several versions of the text of the Letter to Leo X can be found in F. P. Di Teodoro, *Raffaello, Baldassar Castiglione e la Lettera a Leone X, con l'aggiunta di due saggi raffaelleschi* (Bologna: Minerva, 2003).

38   A sign of the ever more exclusive privacy and diminished ambitions of contemporary architecture is the increasing importance assigned to the tactile aspect of buildings. In more recent architecture this tendency has given rise to a genuine cult of the roughness of brick, the softness of leather, the smoothness of marble. This cult coincides with a brazen refusal to look at reality and recognize the conditions under which architecture is produced, and a willingness to settle (and get others to settle) for a handful of garbage—as if a dusting of moss on a chipped brick would be enough to make life less wretched. The intellectual poverty and the complicity with the most odious forms of exploitation of this pure display of samples of precious pieces (or, worse still, pieces that are not even precious) do not need to be emphasized further. On the contrary, it is worth recalling how the groundwork for this resistible triumph of touch was laid down by a dogged campaign of denigration of vision, to which the learned masters of French Theory have not failed to make their own contribution: see M. Jay, *Downcast Eyes: The Denigration of Vision in Twentieth-Century French Thought*

(Berkeley: University of California Press, 1993). The paradoxical unrealism of touch and the corresponding desire not to see the world had already been pointed out by Arendt: "It is characteristic of all theories that argue against the world-giving capacity of the senses that they remove vision from its position as the highest and most noble of the senses and substitute touch or taste, which are indeed the most private senses, that is, those in which the body primarily senses itself while perceiving an object." H. Arendt, *The Human Condition* (Chicago-London: University of Chicago Press, 1998), 114, note 63.

39 C. Thoenes, "Renaissance St. Peter's," in *St. Peter's in the Vatican*, ed. W. Tronzo, (Cambridge: Cambridge University Press, 2005), 81.

40 These interventions were carried out during the papacy of Leo X (after March 1513) and thus under a new cultural climate. Bramante had not been able to draw for a long time due to palsy and would die in April 1514. In Loreto he was also obliged to work with the sculptor Andrea Sansovino, whom Leo X had already entrusted with the supervision of the works on June 22, 1513. F. Grimaldi, *L'ornamento marmoreo della Santa Cappella di Loreto* (Loreto: Carilo, 1999), 42.

41 R. Longhi, "Piero de' Franceschi e lo sviluppo della pittura veneziana," now in *Scritti giovanili I (1912-1922)* (Florence: Sansoni, 1980), 100.

42 "*In tota re aedificatoria primarium certe ornamentum in columnis est*" (In the whole art of building the column is the principal ornament without any doubt): Alberti, *De re aedificatoria*, VI, 13. English ed., *On the Art of Building in Ten Books*, 188.

43 J. Fischer, "Mark Rothko: Portrait of the Artist as an Angry Man," *Harper's Magazine* (July 1970): 16-23.

11 Order of all the orders

44 F. Milizia, "Bramante d'Urbino," in idem, *Vite de' più celebri Architetti d'ogni nazione e d'ogni tempo* (Rome: Paolo Giunchi Komarek, 1768), 180. Milizia repeats a similar judgment by Vasari.

45 G. Grassi, *La costruzione logica dell'architettura* (Padua: Marsilio, 1967), 70.

46 Something similar happened in the staircase of the Belvedere, where once again Bramante made the effort to insert *all* the architectural orders. The singular combination of precision and imprecision with which Renaissance architects tackled the theme of the orders is evident from the discrepancies between different descriptions of the stairs. According to Vasari there are three orders: Doric, Ionic, Corinthian (G. Vasari, "Bramante da Urbino," 158); for Palladio there are four: Doric, Ionic, Corinthian, and Composite (A. Palladio, *I Quattro Libri dell'Architettura*, I, 64); while for Serlio there seem to be five: Tuscan, Doric, Ionic, Corinthian, and Composite (S. Serlio, *Il terzo libro di Sabastiano Serlio Bolognese, nel qual si figurano, e descrivono le antiquità di Roma, e le altre che sono in Italia, e fuori de Italia*, CXLVII, fol. 120r, now in *Sebastiano Serlio on Architecture Volume One: Books I-V of "Tutte L'Opere D'Architettura et Prospetiva*," ed. V. Hart and P. Hicks (New Haven-London: Yale University Press, 1996), 237). While none of these authors recall the recipe for the cocktail of columns precisely, all are clear that the staircase contains *all the orders*, and all bring it down to *a*

single rule (Christof Thoenes has shown how the staircase of the Belvedere was the premise of Vignola's *Regula*: see C. Thoenes, "La 'Regola delli cinque ordini' del Vignola," in idem, *Sostegno e adornamento* [Milan: Electa, 1998], 76–107), see too C. Denker Nesselrath, *Die Säulenordnungen bei Bramante* (Worms: Römische Studien der Bibliotheca Hertziana, 1990), 28, notes 131, 132, 133.

47 The search for the origins of the orders had already been the target of Bramante's sarcasm in the Canonica of Sant'Ambrogio, where he put tree-trunk-shaped columns not so much to tell something about the presumed evolution of columns from tree trunks, but to expose the visual inconsistency between the two objects when placed side by side—and this with the express intention of mocking the literary connection between them.

48 C. Lévi-Strauss, *The Raw and the Cooked*, vol. I, trans. J. and D. Weightman (New York: Harper & Row), 1975, 14.

49 T. S. Eliot, "What Dante Means to Me," in *To Criticize the Critic and Other Writings* (New York: Farrar, Straus and Giroux, 1965), 133.

50 P. P. Pasolini, "La volontà di Dante a essere poeta," in *Saggi sulla letteratura e sull'arte*, vol. I (Milan: Mondadori, 1999), 1390.

51 "[C]ommon to all yet owned by none." Dante, *De vulgari eloquentia*, I, XVIII. English ed., *Dante: De vulgari eloquentia*, ed. and trans. S. Botterill (Cambridge: Cambridge University Press, 1996), 43.

13 Eclecticism and classicism

52 R. Wittkower, *Architectural Principles in the Age of Humanism* (New York: Norton, 1949), 1.

53 Ibid.

54 D. Watkin, *Morality and Architecture: The Development of a Theme in Architectural History and Theory from the Gothic Revival to the Modern Movement* (Oxford: Clarendon Press, 1977).

55 Observing "the state of the arts from the beginning of the nineteenth century on," Mario Praz has noted the frenzy in which they seem to plunge: "we shall then see Painting asking support from Literature, and vice versa, and Architecture calling on both for aid, but in vain." M. Praz, *Mnemosyne: The Parallel between Literature and the Visual Arts* (Princeton: Princeton University Press, 1967), 157.

56 The eclecticism of the nineteenth century functioned in exactly the same way as contemporary identitarian artistic practices in which only the members of a certain group are authorized to produce art on particular themes and this art is addressed solely to a certain section of the public. For an example of all this see the incredible controversy over Dana Schutz's painting *Open Casket* at the Whitney Biennial in 2017: https://www.theguardian .com/artanddesign/2017/mar/21/whitney-biennial-emmett-till-painting-dana-schutz.

57 W. Benjamin, "Die Aufgabe des Übersetzers" (1923), now in *Gesammelte Schriften* IV/1, (Frankfurt: Suhrkamp, 1972). English ed., "The Task of the Translator," trans. H. Zohn, in W. Benjamin, *Selected Writings*, vol. 1: 1913–1926, ed. M. Bullock and M. W. Jennings (Cambridge, MA: Belknap Press of Harvard University Press, 1996).

14 Classicism, colonialism

58 This is why Bramante, as Geymüller did not fail to point out, ended up having

"une importance bien supérieure à celle de tous les autres architectes." H. von Geymüller, *Les projets primitifs pour la basilique de Saint-Pierre de Rome* (Paris: Baudry/Vienna: Lehmann & Wentzel, 1875), 82.

59 Vasari, "Bramante da Urbino," 146.

60 J. W. O'Malley, "Fulfilment of the Christian Golden Age under Pope Julius II: text of a discourse of Giles of Viterbo, 1507," in *Traditio* 25 (1969): 338. Taprobane was the name given to Sri Lanka in antiquity.

61 O'Malley, "Fulfilment of the Christian Golden Age," 265–338. The speech ("nimis longa" and given "primo Latinum, deinde contra bonas caerimonias vulgarem" according to the always well-disposed de Grassis; see Vat. MS Vat. Lat. 12268 fols. 143v–144r) was made on December 21, 1507, on the occasion of the celebration of three victories of the Portuguese: the landing on Ceylon and submission of the local rulers, the victory of Lourenço de Almeida over the Zamorin of Calicut, and the "discovery" of Madagascar. The same pattern was followed in the oration given on May 3, 1512, as an introduction to the fifth Lateran Council. But Giles was much less triumphalist in his private letters: "*Aurum ergo habet antiques etatis, non nostre.*" Egidio da Viterbo, "Lettera a Serafino Ferri," in *Lettere familiari*, I (1494–1506) (Rome: Fontes Historiae Ordinis Sancti Augustini, Series altera: epistolaria aliique fonts, 1990), 304–305. See too J. W. O'Malley, *Giles of Viterbo on Church and Reform* (Leiden: Brill, 1968), 108 and C. Thoenes, "'Il Primo tempio del Mondo'. Raffaello, S. Pietro e il denaro," in *Casabella*, no. 654 (1998): 59, note 39. The connection between the rebuilding of St. Peter's and the colonial ventures of the day was probably even closer than is proposed here in fairly general terms. In fact the resources needed for the rebuilding of the church were found through the issue of various Bulls of the Crusade. The bulls were documents that attested to the purchase of indulgences, pardons, or exemptions in exchange for the payment of a sum of money. They were granted by the state authority on behalf of the Church and allowed the kingdoms to which they were referred to raise funds for the "Crusade" (a concept whose breadth was defined case by case). Part of the money collected in this way was then transferred to the Church. At times the European kingdoms came to an agreement to make fixed annual contributions to be used for the rebuilding of the church of St. Peter's in exchange for the right to collect the offerings made possible by the Bull of the Crusade. In the case of Spain and Portugal (the main contributors, at least from the second half of the sixteenth century onward), much of the resources obtained in this way came from their colonial possessions. So it would be possible to demonstrate a direct link between colonial enterprises and the funding of the new St. Peter's. For an analysis of the mechanisms of this funding see R. Sabene, *La Fabbrica di San Pietro in Vaticano. Dinamiche internazionali e dimensione locale* (Rome: Gangemi, 2012); see too the considerations in J. Delumeau, *Vita economica e sociale a Roma nel Cinquecento* (Florence: Sansoni, 1979), in particular 248.

62 The Renaissance cult of antiquity should also be viewed from the perspective of the parallel refusal to recognize the contemporaneity of the non-European peoples with which the conquerors came into contact in those same years. At the

moment in which European intellectuals were trying to establish a relationship of equality with the ancients, to extract them from the past and bring them into the contemporary world, the very same people rejected any relationship with the representatives—who really were contemporary—of the civilizations they encountered, relegating them, against all evidence, to a wholly ideological past; on this "denial of coevalness," see J. Fabian, *Time and the Other: How Anthropology Makes Its Object* (New York: Columbia University Press, 1983), and W. D. Mignolo, *The Darker Side of the Renaissance: Literacy, Territoriality and Colonization* (Ann Arbor: University of Michigan Press, 2003). But perhaps it is not even necessary to look as far as America: in his famous letter to Francesco Vettori of December 10, 1513, Machiavelli seems to reject in the same way the contemporaneity of the people with whom he plays cards at the inn during the day: "With them I become a rascal for the whole day, playing at cricca and at tric-trac," only to seek the friendship of the ancients at night: "At the door I take off my clothes of the day, covered with mud and mire, and I put on my regal and courtly garments; and decently reclothed, I enter the ancient courts of ancient men." N. Machiavelli, "Letter to Francesco Vettori," in *The Prince*, trans. H. Mansfield Jr. (Chicago-London: Chicago University Press, 2nd ed., 1998), 109.

ABSTRACTION

15 Distance

1   A. Choisy, *L'art de bâtir chez les Romains* (Paris: Ducher, 1873), 2. See too H. Schlimme, "Auguste Choisy and the Architecture of Italian Renaissance," in *Auguste Choisy (1841–1909). L'architecture et l'art de bâtir*, ed. J. Girón and S. Huerta (Madrid: Instituto Juan de Herrera, 2009), 387-404.

2   Bramante and the other architects of the Renaissance did not copy the Roman structures, but instead exactly their decorations, for which, following Choisy, the Romans reserved their *indifférence dédaigneuse*. On this, too, see C. Thoenes, "Bramante e la 'bella maniera degli antichi,'" in idem, *Sostegno e adornamento. Saggi sull'architettura del Rinascimento: disegni, ordini, magnificenza* (Milan: Electa, 1998), 59-65. Translated into English by H. Evans for the forthcoming *Bramante, an Introduction*.

3   F. R. Ankersmit reached a similar conclusion, recognizing the possibility of political action as lying precisely in the lack of correspondence between represented and representative. See F. R. Ankersmit, *Aesthetic Politics: Political Philosophy Beyond Fact and Value* (Stanford, CA: Stanford University Press, 1996).

4   J. Burckhardt, *Il Cicerone* (Florence: Sansoni, 1963), 329.

5   The value of the past as a measure of the present was very clear to the supporters of the ancients in the *Querelle des Anciens et des Modernes* ("Dispute of the Ancients and the Moderns"). The beginning of the dispute is conventionally dated to 1687, with the presentation of Charles Perrault's *Le siècle de Louis le Grand* to the Académie Française, but its origins lie in the Renaissance. On the *Querelle*, see M. Fumaroli, "Les abeilles et les araignées," in *La Querelle des Anciens et des Modernes. XVIIe–XVIIIe siècles*, ed. A. M. Lecoq (Paris: Gallimard, 2001).

16 Difficultà grandissima

6   G. Vasari, "Bramante da Urbino," in
    *Le vite de' più eccellenti pittori scultori
    ed architettori scritte da Giorgio Vasari
    pittore aretino con nuove annotazioni
    e commenti di Gaetano Milanesi*, vol.
    IV (Florence: Sansoni, 1906), 146.
    Translated into English by H. Evans
    for the forthcoming *Bramante, an
    Introduction*. It is worth noting the
    honesty with which Vasari, despite
    belonging to an artistic clan that was not
    at all well-disposed toward Bramante,
    acknowledged the fact that he had
    learned from him ("taught us").

7   Bruschi understood perfectly
    Bramante's passion for the risk
    associated with the game of forms in
    the case of the Belvedere staircase, "in
    which the machine, the perfect device,
    seems, as its elements are gradually
    identified, to start to blow up in the
    hands of its inventor. But Bramante
    does not throw it away as a broken or
    dangerous toy. On the contrary, he
    appears to relish the game; he wants to
    see, by taking it all the way, what are
    the consequences of going along—in a
    process that is logical and consistent,
    even rigid in its coherence—with the
    "natural" law of development implicit
    in the mechanism. He does not want
    to conceal the problems that cannot be
    solved, the paradoxical consequences;
    he does not wish to put himself in
    simpler situations in order to arrive at
    more obvious results through easily
    predictable consequences." A. Bruschi,
    Bramante architetto (Rome-Bari:
    Laterza, 1969), 425.

8   H. James, "The Figure in the Carpet," in
    Complete Stories. 1892–1898 (New York:
    The Library of America, 1996), 591.

9   It was, of course, a *golden age* that
    remained entirely within the confines of
    the discipline, and moreover coincided
    with a time of extreme political crisis for
    Italy.

10 P. Portoghesi, "La lingua universale:
    cultura e architettura tra il 1503 e il
    1527," in *Studi bramanteschi*, 363. A
    partial translation can be found in the
    forthcoming *Bramante, an Introduction*.

11 P. Letarouilly, *Les édifices de Rome
    moderne* (Paris: Didot, 1840–55; reprint,
    Princeton: Princeton Architectural
    Press, 1997).

12 In the *Letter to Leo X* Raphael speaks of
    "bones ... without flesh." Several versions
    of the text of the Letter to Leo X can
    be found in F. P. Di Teodoro, *Raffaello,
    Baldassar Castiglione e la Lettera a Leone
    X, con l'aggiunta di due saggi raffaelleschi*
    (Bologna: Minerva, 2003). There is
    an English translation of one of these
    versions in the appendix of *Palladio's
    Rome: A Translation of Andrea Palladio's
    Two Guidebooks to Rome*, trans. V. Hart
    and P. Hicks (New Haven-London: Yale
    University Press, 2006), 177–192.

17 Remote future

13 Don Quixote's argument is this: if
    other knights go mad for a reason, then
    I who have no reason to go mad am
    all the more noble: "Therein lies the
    virtue," responded Don Quixote, "and
    the excellence of my enterprise, for a
    knight errant deserves neither glory nor
    thanks if he goes mad for a reason. The
    great achievement is to lose one's reason
    for no reason, and to let my lady know
    that if I can do this without cause, what
    should I not do if there were cause? ..."
    M. de Cervantes, *Don Quixote* (1615),
    trans. E. Grossman (New York: Ecco/
    HarperCollins, 2003), 211–212.

14   C. Cattaneo, *Alcuni scritti*, 267–268,
     quoted in L. Einaudi's introduction to
     C. Cattaneo, *Saggi di economia rurale*
     (Turin: Einaudi, 1975), xxxvii.

15   W. Benjamin, *The Arcades Project*
     (Cambridge, MA: Belknap Press,
     2002), 392.

16   "[L]a forza rivoluzionaria del passato,"
     in P. P. Pasolini, *Poesia in forma di una
     rosa* (Milan: Garzanti, 1964).

17   The "anachronic" aspect of
     Renaissance art has been underscored
     in an interesting, but sometimes rather
     sensationalist, book by Alexander
     Nagel and Christopher S. Wood:
     Anachronic Renaissance (New York:
     Zone Books, 2010).

18   Here it would appear that the
     contemporary situation is completely
     different from that of the Renaissance
     and, more generally, the whole of the
     premodern era. And it is undeniable
     that the expected life of buildings today
     is much reduced (just long enough for
     them to reach the conclusion of the
     business cycle that brought them into
     the world without falling apart). But
     it is equally true that these shoddy
     buildings are not suddenly swept away,
     but continually rehabilitated, renovated,
     and repaired. In other words, while
     the vast majority of contemporary
     constructions are not *made to endure*, we
     need to recognize the incredible inertia
     that somehow or other keeps them in
     the world, however ugly and poorly
     designed they may be. And this inertia
     can only grow with the foreseeable rise
     in the cost of waste disposal. Thus, even
     without supposing a greater ambition
     for our cities, even without imagining
     a true policy of sustainability, it is hard
     to believe that Sant'Elia's prophecy
     ("Our houses will last less time than we
     do. Every generation will have to make

its own city anew") is ever going to
come true. Contemporary architecture
continues to face long-term problems,
even if it doesn't want to admit it. For
Sant'Elia's arguments, see A. Sant'Elia,
Manifesto dell'architettura futurista,
no. 8, July 11, 1914. English translation,
"Futurist Architecture," in *Futurism: An
Anthology*, ed. L. Rainey, C. Poggi, and
L. Wittman (New Haven-London: Yale
University Press, 2009), 201.

19   This became apparent, at the end of
     their careers, even to the most strenuous
     propagandists of modernism, like
     Giedion and Le Corbusier.

20   A demonstration of the clarity of some
     of the theoretical presuppositions that
     would remain constant over the long
     experience of classical architecture
     can be found in the contemptuous
     responses that an exasperated Bernini
     gave to Colbert's extremely precise
     questions. Examining the plans for
     the Louvre, the French minister asked
     the elderly Italian architect where the
     stock of butter would go and where the
     firefighting equipment would be stored.
     Extremely irritated, Bernini replied that
     he didn't know and that in the Vatican
     Palaces everything was reorganized
     each time a pope died, and that the
     minister should be asking the master
     of ceremonies about these things and
     not the architect. Colbert wanted to
     know exactly what architecture could
     do. He wanted to be able to gauge the
     quality of its services before they were
     provided, to be *insured* against the
     unpredictability of life inside buildings.
     For Bernini, on the other hand, it
     was the long lifespan of architecture
     that made buildings indeterminate,
     unpredictable, and therefore also
     capable of reacting to a variety of
     scenarios. The incredible generosity of

Renaissance architecture was possible solely because the questions that Colbert put to Bernini were not asked of these buildings. Precisely what architecture did, what services it offered, what kind of justification it needed, the architects and clients of the Renaissance did not ask themselves. A good objective for a contemporary theory of architecture would be to find a way of demonstrating the stupidity of Colbert's questions without taking refuge in Bernini's wounded silence, of making—in a context that is fully modern, or rather already non-modern once again—the argument that Bernini refused to make. See P. Fréart de Chantelou, *Journal du voyage du Cav. Bernin en France*, ed. M. Stanic (Paris: Macula, 2001), and P. P. Tamburelli, "Italian Cowboys Go France: Some Remarks on the Diary of the Cavaliere Bernini's Visit to France," *Hunch*, no. 14 (2010): 78–91.

18 The object is simple

21 "The possibility of its occurring in states of affairs is the form of an object." L. Wittgenstein, *Tractatus logico-philosophicus* (Frankfurt: Suhrkamp, 1963), 13. English translation by D. F. Pears and B. F. McGuinness (London: Routledge and Kegan Paul, 1961, rev. ed., Routledge Classics, 2001), 7.

22 "Objects are simple." Ibid. (In contrast to the D. F. Pears and B. F. McGuinness translation, the sentence in the original German text is in the singular: "the object is simple.")

23 Phalaris, tyrant of Akragas in the mid-sixth century BCE, is famous for his so-called "brazen bull," a hollow sculpture made of brass or bronze in which those who had annoyed him were placed and then a fire lit underneath, making the bull bellow with their screams as they were roasted. Phalaris arrived in Akragas after being entrusted with the job of building a new temple to Zeus on the acropolis. He used the money for the construction of the temple to arm the builders and seize power. According to Cicero, he was *crudelissimus omnium tyrannorum* (the most cruel of all tyrants).

24 See for example the endless literature eulogizing Mies van der Rohe, such as M. Cacciari, "Res aedificatoria. Il 'classico' di Mies van der Rohe," *Casabella*, no. 629 (1995): 3-7.

19 Form follows function

25 A very persuasive criticism of the political economy of functionalism (conducted from the viewpoint of an evolutionary biologist) can be found in R. Prum, *The Evolution of Beauty: How Darwin's forgotten theory of mate choice shapes the animal world—and us* (New York: Doubleday, 2017).

26 Bruschi, *Bramante architetto*, 525.

20 Abstract architecture is public

27 "When all the pitchers are smashed, / What's left of the tears in the pitchers?" I. Bachmann, "Scherbenhügel," in idem, *Anrufung des großen Bären* (Munich: Piper, 1956). English translation by P. Filkins, "Shard Mound," in I. Bachmann, *Darkness Spoken: The Collected Poems* (Brookline, MA: Zephyr Press, 2006), 165.

28 J. S. Ackerman, "Architectural Practice in the Italian Renaissance," *Journal of the Society of Architectural Historians* XXIII, no. 3 (1954): 9.

INTERMEZZO:
Dante, Giotto, Piero, Bramante

I

1   F. Guicciardini, *Storia d'Italia* (Turin:
    Einaudi, 1971), book II, ch. XII–XIII,
    888–901.
2   On the story of Julius II's beard see M. J.
    Zucker, "Raphael and the Beard of Pope
    Julius II," *Art Bulletin* 59, no. 4 (1977):
    524–533.
3   The statement was made in a dispatch
    from Stazio Gadio, tutor of the young
    Federico Gonzaga, at the time held
    hostage by Julius II (letter to Tolomeo
    Gonzaga, Bologna, December 13, 1510).
    See A. Luzio, "Isabella d'Este di fronte a
    Giulio II," *Archivio Storico Lombardo* 17
    (1912): 278–279.
4   G. Visconti, *Rithmi* (Milan, 1493), 19,
    cited in L. Beltrami, *Bramante poeta.
    Colla raccolta dei sonetti in parte inediti*
    (Milan: Colombo e Cordani, 1884), 8.
    On Gaspare Visconti see R. Renier,
    "Gaspare Visconti," *Archivio Storico
    Lombardo* 13 (1886): 509–562 and
    777–824, and R. Schofield, "Gaspare
    Visconti, mecenate di Bramante," in
    *Arte, committenza ed economia a Roma e
    nelle corti del Rinascimento, 1420–1530*,
    ed. A. Esch and C. L. Frommel (Turin:
    Einaudi, 1995), 295–324. The relationship
    between Bramante and Dante was
    crudely celebrated, from a Fascist
    perspective, by Gustavo Giovannoni.
    In an entry for the 1930 edition of the
    Enciclopedia Italiana, Giovannoni
    wrote: "Certainly for the Italians the
    figure with which Bramante can in some
    ways be most closely compared is that of
    Dante. In the name of Latin civilization
    and under the banner of the Empire the
    latter renewed the language and molded
    Italian thought: Bramante, starting

from the modest formula of 'reviving
the good architecture of antiquity'
and looking to the future, gave our
tradition such a powerful impetus
that it restored it to its domination of
the world (as had been the case in the
Roman period) in the most enduring
expressions of civilization, such as those
of architecture."See too G. Giovannoni,
"Bramante e l'architettura italiana," in
G. Giovannoni, *Saggi sulla architettura
del Rinascimento* (Milan: Treves, 1931),
61–98, and C. Thoenes, "Bramante—
Giovannoni. Il Rinascimento
interpretato dall'architettura fascista,"
Casabella, no. 633 (1996): 64–73.

II

5   Vasari mentions Bramante's
    apprenticeship with Fra Carnevale,
    and Sabba da Castiglione says: "He
    was a disciple of Mantegna & a great
    prospective painter, as created by Pietro
    del Borgo" (S. Castiglione, *Ricordi overo
    Ammaestramenti di Monsignor Saba da
    Castiglione Cavalier ...* [Venice: Paolo
    Gherardo, 1554], 139).
6   Cellini describes Bramante as "un
    pittoraccio di poco credito," or "a bad
    painter of little credit" (B. Cellini,
    "Trattato dell'oreficeria," in *Opere di
    Baldassarre Castiglione Giovanni della
    Casa Benvenuto Cellini*, ed. C. Cordié
    (Milan-Naples: Ricciardi, 1960), 1022.
    English trans. C. R. Ashbee, *The Treatises
    of Benvenuto Cellini on Goldsmithing and
    Sculpture* (Mineola, NY: Dover, 1967),
    52. See too C. Pedretti, "Bramante,
    'un pittoraccio di poco credito,'" in
    *Donato Bramante: ricerche, proposte,
    riletture*, ed. F. P. Di Teodoro (Urbino:
    Accademia Raffaello, 2011), 207–214. For
    Longhi, too, the giant figures of "Casa

Panigarola" are mediocre. Longhi also notes Bramante's Mantegnesque "*desire for cracks and thorniness*," and wonders about the absence of the "*peace and chromatic largeness laid over the volumes*" that would be expected of a decent pupil of Piero della Francesca (R. Longhi, Review of Malaguzzi Valeri, "La corte di Ludovico il Moro," in *L'Arte*, 1916, now in *Scritti giovanili I (1912-1922)*, 293). But it is a bit unfair to look for traces of Piero in Bramante's painting, where he could not do much; instead, the traces are there—and evident—as soon as Bramante moved to an environment more suited to the luxuriant aridity of his muse, in architecture. Bramante seems to have been well aware of his limits as a painter. In the *Prevedari Engraving* he hides the feet of the monk in the foreground in his habit. This choice not only distinguishes the figure from its explicit model (the apostle kneeling on the left in Mantegna's *Ascension*, now part of the *Triptych* in the Uffizi), but flies in the face of any naturalism (the monk would certainly not have been able to walk in such a long habit). If we consider the extraordinary importance Mantegna assigned to the feet of the apostle as a pictorial theme—an importance that could not have eluded Bramante—and then look at Bramante's very ungainly version, both the clumsiness of his painting and his awareness of it are evident. On the relationship between Mantegna's apostle and Bramante's friar see F. Graf Wolff Metternich, "Der Kupferstich Bernardos de Prevedari aus Mailand von 1481. Gedanken zu den Anfängen der Kunst Bramantes," *Römisches Jahrbuch für Kunstgeschichte* XI (1967-1968): 57-58 and 59, ill. 42.

7 For example the ones for Resor House at Jackson Hole (1941) or for the Bacardi

headquarters in Cuba (1957).

8 "Painting is nothing but a demonstration of surfaces." Piero della Francesca, *De prospectiva pingendi*, ed. C. Gizzi (Venice: Edizioni Ca' Foscari-Digital Publishing, 2016), 190.

9 G. Vasari, "Piero della Francesca," in *Le vite de' più eccellenti pittori scultori ed architettori scritte da Giorgio Vasari pittore aretino con nuove annotazioni e commenti di Gaetano Milanesi* (Florence: Sansoni, 1906), vol. II, 496. English trans. by G. Bull, *Vasari: Lives of the Artists* (Harmondsworth: Penguin, 1965), 195.

10 D. Arasse, "Piero della Francesca: peintre d'histoire?," in *Piero. Teorico dell'arte*, ed. O. Calabrese (Rome: Gangemi, 1985), 108.

11 The first person to have no interest in discovering the identity of the mysterious figures in the *Flagellation* is Piero.

12 B. Berenson, *The Italian Painters of the Renaissance* (London: Phaidon, 1952), 109-110.

13 Without going further into the subject here, it will suffice to say that the technique of fresco requires a preliminary planning of the painting and thus discourages any form of improvisation or immediacy in its execution. Frescoes are in fact painted by fairly large groups of craftsmen who work quite quickly and on the basis of a rigorously coordinated plan of action. So the fresco is an unemotional, calculated, and impersonal medium, congenitally architectural and by and large inclined to depict collective scenes, rather than personal experiences.

III

14 F. Villani, *Liber de civitatis Florentiae famosis civibus*, ed. G. C. Galletti

(Florence: Mazzoni, 1847), 35. English trans. in Michael Baxandall, *Giotto and the Orators: Humanist observers of painting in Italy and the discovery of pictorial composition, 1350–1450* (Oxford: Clarendon Press, 1971), 70. Hubert Damisch has underlined the concept in these terms: "*les figures que l'art de Giotto met en jeu ne sauraient être dissociées de l'action où elles sont engagées.*" H. Damisch, "Figuration et représentation. Le problème de l'apparition," *Annales: Économies, sociétés, civilisations* 26, no. 3 (1971): 674.

15 See too P. P. Tamburelli, "Giotto, or Beauty in Space," *San Rocco*, no. 13 (Spring 2017): 111–127.

16 The number of scenes has been calculated here excluding the *Judgment* on the counter-façade and *God Sends Gabriel to the Virgin* above the arch of the choir, which remain difficult to classify in terms of an alternative between nature and city.

17 S. Sandström, *Levels of Unreality. Studies in Structure and Construction in Italian Mural Paintings during the Renaissance* (Uppsala: Almqvist & Wiksells, 1963), 59.

18 R. Evans, *The Projective Cast: Architecture and Its Three Geometries* (Cambridge, MA: MIT Press, 2000), 133.

19 An exception in Giotto's case is the extraordinary delicacy of the *Scenes from the Story of Isaac*, but this is perhaps also the main argument against their attribution to Giotto. A sophisticated analysis of the *Isaac Stories* can be found in S. Romano, *Giotto's O* (Rome: Viella, 2015).

20 "In painting Cimabue thought he held/the field, and now it's Giotto they acclaim/the former only keeps a shadowed fame." *The Divine Comedy of Dante Alighieri, Purgatorio*, XI, 94–96, trans. A. Mandelbaum (Berkeley, CA:

University of California Press, 1982).

21 As far as the problem of the presumed "portrait of Dante" is concerned, the situation in the debate is still the one perfectly encapsulated by Gombrich in 1979 as "a question of Giotto's portrait of Dante in a fresco hardly by Giotto where Dante could hardly have figured." E. H. Gombrich, "Giotto's Portrait of Dante," *The Burlington Magazine* 121, no. 94 (1979): 471–483.

22 For example by Giovanni Previtali; see G. Previtali, *Giotto e la sua bottega* (Milan: Fabbri, 1967), 13. See too L. Bellosi, *La pecora di Giotto* (Milan: Abscondita, 2015).

23 "Then I like there to be someone in the 'historia' who tells the spectators what is going on, and either beckons them with his hand to look, or with ferocious expression and forbidding glance challenges them not to come near, as if he wished their business to be secret, or points to some danger or some remarkable secret, or by his gestures invites you to laugh or to weep with them." L. B. Alberti, *De Pictura*, II, 42 (Rome-Bari: Laterza, 1975), 72. English trans. by C. Grayson, *On Painting*, ed. M Kemp (London: Penguin Classics, 1991), 78. On these aspects see too M. Baxandall's *Giotto and the Orators*.

24 "Un esempio di poesia dantesca (Il canto XXVIII del Paradiso)," in G. Contini, *Un'idea di Dante* (Turin: Einaudi, 2001), 198.

25 "*La chose humaine par excellence.*" C. Lévi-Strauss, *Tristes Tropiques* (Paris: Plon 1955), 127. English trans. by J. Russell, *Tristes Tropiques* (New York: Criterion Books, 1961), 127. See too the fundamental interpretation of this passage in A. Rossi, *L'architettura della città* (Padua: Marsilio, 1966), 27, note 2.

26 *Inferno*, III, 39.

IV

27 Or as it was originally written, *comedìa* (*Inferno*, XVI, 128, and *Inferno*, XXI, 2). The addition of the adjective "divine" to the original title was made in the edition by Ludovico Dolce (Venice, 1555). Dolce was following a very bad idea of Boccaccio's. On the title of the *Commedia* see too M. Tavoni, "Il titolo della 'Commedia' di Dante," *Nuova rivista di letteratura italiana* I, no. 1 (1998): 9–34, and G. Agamben, *Categorie Italiane* (Rome-Bari: Laterza, 2011), 3–28.

28 S. Bettinelli, "Dieci Lettere di Publio Virgilio Marone scritte dagli Elisi all'Arcadia di Roma sopra gli abusi introdotti nella poesia italiana," in S. Bettinelli, *Lettere virgiliane e lettere inglesi, Lettera seconda* (1758) (Milan: Rizzoli, 1962), 41.

29 The authenticity of the letter has been extensively debated, without philologists ever coming to a shared conclusion. In general, it seems that that those who do not like the title of Dante's poem tend not to accept the authenticity of the *Epistle to Cangrande*, and vice versa. Recently Carlo Ginzburg has argued that part of the letter (the one that contains among other things the words quoted here) is the result of an interpolation by Giovanni Boccaccio: see C. Ginzburg, "Dante's Epistle to Cangrande and its Two Authors," in *Proceedings of the British Academy*, no. 139 (2006): 212. An opposing opinion is expressed in S. Bellomo, "L'Epistola a Cangrande, dantesca per intero: 'a rischio di procurarci un dispiacere,'" *Rassegna Dantesca*, special issue, no. 45, year LVI (January–July 2015): 5–20.

30 "Easy and humble, because it is in the vulgar tongue, in which also women communicate." D. Alighieri, "Epistula

XIII," in D. Alighieri, *Opere*, vol. II (Milan: Mondadori, 2014), 1494–1521, with commentary by C. Villa, 1563–1592. English trans. by J. Marchand, *From Dante's letter to Can Grande della Scala*, http://www.english.udel.edu/dean/cangrand.html.

31 G. Contini, "Un'interpretazione di Dante," in idem, *Un'idea di Dante* (Turin: Einaudi, 2001), 104.

32 T. S. Eliot, "What Dante Means to Me" (1950), in *T. S. Eliot: Essays from The Southern Review* (Oxford: Clarendon Press, 1988), 232. See too P. P. Pasolini, "La volontà di Dante a essere poeta," in *Saggi sulla letteratura e sull'arte*, vol. I (Milan: Mondadori, 1999), 1376.

33 S. Bettinelli, "Dieci Lettere di Publio Virgilio Marone …" 43–44.

34 "The phenomenon of greatest extension … in the whole body of our literary language. E. Sanguineti, "Il realismo di Dante," in idem, *Dante reazionario* (Rome: Editori Riuniti, 1992), 275.

35 G. Contini, "Sul XXX dell'Inferno," in idem, *Un'idea di Dante*, 159–170.

36 The *Comedy*, with its absurd pretension of judging who must be damned and who must be saved, is possible only because Dante, as *protagonist of the Comedy*, is no one special. Dante is not Faust; if he visits the hereafter it is precisely because there is no reason he should be the one to make the journey. Contini leaves no doubts: the fellow who wanders in the afterlife is "not a select, not a socially high-status 'narrator,' as then the style would be tragic; [he is] an ordinary 'narrator,' in order to fairly represent the whole of humanity." G. Contini, "Dante come personaggio-poeta della Commedia," in idem, *Un'idea di Dante*, 39.

37 G. Contini, "Preliminari sulla lingua del Petrarca," in F. Petrarca, *Canzoniere* (Turin: Einaudi, 1964), vii–xxxviii.

38 See C. Vasoli, "Introno al Petrarca e ai logici 'moderni,'" in *Miscellanea Mediaevalia IX, Antiqui et Moderni* (Berlin: De Gruyter, 1974), 142–154; C. Vasoli, *La dialettica e la retorica dell'Umanesimo* (Milan: Feltrinelli, 1968), in particular 9–77; and E. Garin, *Rinascite e rivoluzioni* (Rome-Bari: Laterza, 2007), in particular 51–88. On Dante's lack of interest in philology, see G. Padoan, "Dante di fronte all'umanesimo letterario," *Lettere italiane* XVII, no. 3 (July–September 1965): 237–257, and R. Weiss, "Dante e l'umanesimo del suo tempo," *Lettere italiane* XIX, no. 3 (1967): 279–290.

39 "It was Petrarch's introversion that permitted his reductive innovation through a calm renunciation of extremes. Let us use rough-and-ready terms and say: his romanticism is the condition of his classicism." Contini, "Preliminari sulla lingua del Petrarca," XIV. See too A. Berardinelli, Il fantasma di Petrarca, *Nuovi argomenti* 16 (October–December 2001): 276–283.

40 This project was grasped perfectly by Benedetto Croce. The objective of Croce's interpretation of the *Comedy* was in fact to undermine the Catholic, plebeian and inordinately anti-tragic machinery of the poem by eliminating its most earthbound and doctrinaire parts. Croce takes Dante's illiberal masterpiece apart in order to find in the *Comedy* what Dante had so plainly been loath to put into it: a bit of bourgeois psychology. "Croce's grand machination, which distinguishes structure and poetry, can be explained as the brilliant invention of a secular, late-Romantic, and bourgeois reader who, faced with a text so tenaciously imbued with what is for him an unacceptable ideology, devises a cursory

but effective, sophisticated but practical way of neutralizing that ideology while preserving intact, but in a suitably neutralized, and thus vigorously distorted form, its poetry." Sanguineti, "Il realismo di Dante," 282–283.

V

41 The attribution to Bramante of the frescoes in "Casa Panigarola," now in the Accademia di Brera and probably executed in 1480–1482, was made by Lomazzo: G. P. Lomazzo, *Trattato dell'arte della pittura, scultura e architettura*, book VI, XL (Milan, 1584), 273; see L. Beltrami, "La sala dei Maestri d'Arme nella casa dei Panigarola in San Bernardino (ora via Lanzone) dipinta da Bramante," *Rassegna d'Arte* II (July 1902) and D. Kiang, "Bramante's Heraclitus and Democritus: the Frieze," *Zeitschrift für Kunstgeschichte* 51, no. 2 (1988): 262–268. The traditional identification of the house's owner as Gottardo Panigarola has been questioned by Grazioso Sironi; see G. Sironi, "Gli affreschi di Donato d'Angelo detto Bramante alla Pinacoteca di Brera di Milano: chi ne fu il committente?," *Archivio Storico Lombardo*, series 10, vol. 4 (1978), 199–207. For Metternich the globe that separates the two philosophers has been repainted, bringing it up to date with new notions of cartography; see F. Graf Wolff Metternich, "Der Kupferstich Bernardos de Prevedari aus Mailand von 1481. Gedanken zu den Anfängen der Kunst Bramantes," *Römisches Jahrbuch für Kunstgeschichte* XI (1967–1968): 42 and 75. Gabriella Ferri Piccaluga is opposed to the attribution of the frescoes to Bramante and has also raised doubts about the reconstruction of the

room made by Beltrami prior to their detachment; see G. Ferri Piccaluga, "Gli affreschi di casa Panigarola e la cultura Milanese tra Quattro e Cinquecento," *Arte Lombarda* 86–87, no. 3–4, Bramante a Milano (1988): 14–25. See too G. Mulazzani and M. Dalai Emiliani, "D. Bramante: gli uomini d'arme," *Quaderni di Brera*, no. 3 (1977), R. V. Schofield, "Bramante dopo Malaguzzi Valeri," *Arte Lombarda* 167, no. 1 (2013): 5–51, and R. Martinis, *Anticamente moderni. Palazzi rinascimentali di Lombardia in età sforzesca* (Macerata: Quodlibet, 2021), 57–73.

42 The contrasting of Democritus with Heraclitus derives from a passage in a dialogue by Lucian of Samosata, known as the *Sale of Creeds*; see Lucian of Samosata, *The Works of Lucian of Samosata*, trans. H. W. Fowler (Oxford: Clarendon Press, 1905). On the same theme, in 1505 Antonio Fregoso, a friend of Gaspare Visconti, published in Milan the moralizing poem *Il riso di Democrito e pianto di Eraclito* (see R. Renier, "Gaspare Visconti," *Archivio Storico Lombardo* 13 (1886): 793–802. See too S. Ferrari, A. Cottino, *Forestieri a Milano. Riflessioni su Bramante e Leonardo alla corte di Ludovico il Moro* (Busto Arsizio: Nomos, 2013).

43 G. Allegranza, "Lettera a V. De Pagave Sopra una cifra creduta di Bramante," in idem, *Opuscoli eruditi latini e italiani* (Cremona, 1781), 293. At the time Casa Visconti was owned by the Borri family.

44 C. Pedretti, "The Sforza Sepulchre," part I, *La Gazette des Beaux-Arts* 125 (1977): 121–131.

45 The identification of Euclid as Bramante is related by Vasari: G. Vasari, "Raffaello da Urbino," in *Le vite de' più eccellenti pittori scultori ed architettori scritte da Giorgio Vasari pittore aretino con nuove annotazioni e commenti di Gaetano Milanesi*, vol. IV (Florence: Sansoni, 1906), 331 English trans. by G. C. de Vere, "Raffaello da Urbino," in *Lives of the Painters, Sculptors and Architects*, vol. 1 (London: Everyman Library, 1996), 718. For Joel, see C. Robertson, "Bramante, Michelangelo and the Sistine Ceiling," *Journal of the Warburg and Courtland Institutes* XLIX (1986): 105. Another portrait of Bramante, as proposed by Suida in 1936, might be the man seated at the table on the left in the tapestry by Bramantino dedicated to the month of August. The man and the woman opposite him are the only sober people at a table strewn with pieces of melon skin and overturned glasses, where all the other diners are asleep or drunk. The tapestry is reproduced in G. Agosti and J. Stoppa, *I mesi del Bramantino* (Milan: Officina Libraria, 2012), 51–57.

46 That Bramante was explicitly recognized as an intellectual in the circles of the Sforza court can be deduced, for example, from a sonnet by Gaspare Visconti in which the author, defending himself against accusations of a lack of originality, says among other things: *Chi dice: egli è Bramante che gli insegna*. "[There are people] who say: it is Bramante who teaches him." In another sonnet Visconti says: *e non sol me stupisse, ma Bramante/quel sai che non è pur poeta umil*: "and it is not just me he amazes, but Bramante/who you know is no modest poet." See Renier, "Gaspare Visconti," 534 and 807, and R. Martinis, *Anticamente moderni. Palazzi rinascimentali di Lombardia in età sforzesca* (Macerata: Quodlibet, 2021).

47 G. Contini, "Dante oggi," in Contini, *Un'idea di Dante*, 63. The two "Guidos" Contini refers to are Guido Guinizelli (1237–1276) and Guido Cavalcanti (1258–1300).

VI

48 "[L]ove is the seed in you of every virtue/
and of all acts deserving punishment."
Purgatorio, XVII, 104–105.

49 "... what love is: you have reduced/to
love both each good and its opposite."
Purgatorio, XVIII, 14–15.

REALISM

21 After seeing the cathedral

1 In Geymüller's view, Vasari's account
has not even the slightest claim to
credibility ("*nicht den geringsten
Anspruch auf Glaubwürdigkeit*"). See
E. von Geymüller, *Les projets primitifs
pour la basilique de Saint-Pierre de Rome*
(Paris-Vienna: Baudry, Lehmann and
Wentzel, 1875), 19–20.

2 G. Vasari, "Bramante da Urbino," in
*Le vite de' più eccellenti pittori scultori
ed architettori scritte da Giorgio Vasari
pittore aretino con nuove annotazioni
e commenti di Gaetano Milanesi* vol.
IV (Florence: Sansoni, 1906), 146.
Trans. into English by H. Evans for the
forthcoming *Bramante, an Introduction.*

3 Vasari, "Bramante da Urbino," 148.

4 Vasari, "Bramante da Urbino," 148–149.

5 In this insert Vasari includes a very short
and sad (as well as marvelously written)
life of Cesare Cesariano, "reputed a
good geometer and architect, who wrote
a commentary on Vitruvius, and, driven
to despair at not having received the
recompense he had imagined, became
so strange that he refused to work
anymore, turning so unsociable that
he died more like a beast than a man."
Vasari, "Bramante da Urbino," 149–150.

6 Vasari, "Bramante da Urbino," 152–153.

7 A dialect expression in Lombardy and

northwestern Italy for a vagabond,
idler, petty criminal, or misfit. Bruschi
writes: "Bramante on close examination
was in reality an outsider; a vagabond
uprooted from the place of his birth;
where he must have felt, since he fled it,
a stranger. He did not have a true, single
teacher; he was an outsider in Milan;
as in the end he would also be in Rome;
even if sought after by the powerful and
followed by disciples and admirers." A.
Bruschi, *Bramante architetto* (Rome-
Bari: Laterza, 1969), 165.

8 Vasari, "Bramante da Urbino," 146.

9 D. Bramante, "Bramanti opinio supra
domicilium seu templum magnum,"
in "Annali della Fabbrica del Duomo,"
Seduta 27 giugno 1490, now in *Studi
bramanteschi. Atti del Congresso
internazionale. Milano-Urbino-Roma-
1970* (Rome: De Luca, 1974), 23–24.
Translated into English by H. Evans
for the forthcoming *Bramante, an
Introduction.*

10 The brusque directness with which
everyday language intrudes into a half-
Latin technical terminology is the same
as that of the marvelous first sentence of
the *De prospectiva pingendi*: "*La pictura
contiene in sé tre parti principali, quali
diciamo essere disegno, commensuratio
et colorare*" Piero della Francesca,
De prospectiva pingendi, ed. C. Gizzi
(Venice: Edizioni Ca' Foscari/Digital
Publishing, 2016), 81.

11 The *Opinio* is a short text of just 1121
words. Of these 412 are devoted to
"congruence" and only 45 to "lightness."

12 The *Opinio* seems to highlight the
same class of phenomena as James
Stirling identifies in his axonometrics.
Bramante's prose has the same tone as
these drawings. Stirling uses axonometry
in a wholly counterintuitive manner
to map out and reveal the mechanism

that controls his spatial configurations. A means of representation originally devised for describing volumes (mechanical parts and structural elements) is used to analyze voids. Stirling chooses axonometry rather than perspective, which in the tradition of the discipline is the most obvious technique for the representation of space, to give his descriptions an objective character, almost as if he wished to treat space *a parte obiecti*. Thus he produces extremely simple, even stark drawings in which he records nothing but *architectural phenomena*: only the volumes, the hollows, and the local alterations such as steps, ramps, windows that—almost like Lilliputian notes—redefine the paths and the perception of the rooms and the solids, functioning as instructions for the interpretation (and destabilization) of space. See R. Banham, "Introduction," in *James Stirling*, "RIBA Drawings Collection," catalogue of the exhibition at the Heinz Gallery, London, April 24–June 21, 1974 (London: RIBA Publications, 1974), 5–14; L. Stalder and M. Gleich, "Stirling's Arrows," *AA Files*, no. 72 (2016): 57–67; and J. Declerck, K. Geers, C. Grafe, R. Molendijk, P. P. Tamburelli, and T. Vandeputte, *OASE 79/The Architecture of James Stirling 1964–1992: A Non-Dogmatic Accumulation of Formal Knowledge* (Rotterdam: NAi Publishers, November 2009).

13 Bramante, "Bramanti opinio supra domicilium seu templum magnum," 23–24.

14 Ibid., 24.

15 In this case the starting data were the models submitted to the "competition" for the completion of the cathedral.

22 *Angeborener kritischer Verstand*

16 Wolff-Metternich speaks of "angeborener kritischer Verstand" (innate critical intellect). See F. Graf Wolff-Metternich, "Bramante, Skizze eines Lebensbildes," in idem, *Bramante und St. Peter* (Munich: Wilhelm Fink, 1975), 203.

17 "On the other hand my learned Bramante / Bites me when my verse is clumsy and mean." R. Renier, "Gaspare Visconti," *Archivio Storico Lombardo*, 13 (1886), 806.

18 The *Flagellation* is located in the sacristy of the oratory of the Disciplinati di San Francesco in Perugia. See L. Bellosi, "Una 'Flagellazione' del Bramante a Perugia," in *Prospettiva* 9 (1977): 61–68, and, for an opinion contrary to the attribution, *Melozzo da Forlì. L'umana bellezza tra Piero della Francesca e Raffaello*, ed. D. Benati, M. Natale, and A. Paolucci (Cinisello Balsamo: Silvana Editoriale, 2011), 159–161.

19 This may have been the basis of the friendship between Bramante and Julius II. In fact Matteo Bandello writes that Pope Julius "was descended of very mean folk and was not ashamed to say oftentimes that whenas he was a boy, he had sundrywhiles carried onions in a little boat from Arbiziola, a village of the Savonese, to sell at Genoa ..." M. Bandello, "Novella XXXI," in idem, *Novelle* (Turin: Einaudi, 1990) http://www.letteraturaitaliana.net/pdf/Volume_4/t77.pdf. English ed., "Various Sallies and Repartees Promptly Made of Divers Persons," in *The Novels of Matteo Bandello: Bishop of Agen*, vol. 2, trans. John Payne (London: Villon Society, 1890), 127.

20 The passion for grammar (and thus a certain tendency to pedantry as well) is typical of intellectuals from the subaltern classes, the ones who,

not having been endowed with grace by birth, have to impose rules on themselves so as not to be left at the mercy of their barbarism. In his analysis of *distinction*, Pierre Bourdieu quotes a culinary treatise from 1931 which could not be clearer: "There is such a thing as bad taste … and persons of *refinement* know this *instinctively*. For those who do not, rules are needed." See P. Bourdieu, *Distinction: A Social Critique of the Judgement of Taste* (Cambridge, MA: Harvard University Press, 1984), 68.

21 F. Graf Wolff-Metternich, "Kuppelentwurf Bramantes für die Peterskirche," in idem, *Bramante und St. Peter*, 84. See too L. H. Heydenreich, "Bramante's 'Ultima maniera'. Die St. Peter-Studien Uff. arch. 8 v und 20," in *Essays in the History of Architecture presented to Rudolf Wittkower*, ed. D. Fraser, H. Hibbard, and M. J. Lewine (London: Phaidon, 1967), 60–63, and C. Thoenes, "S. Lorenzo a Milano, S. Pietro a Roma: ipotesi sul 'piano di pergamena,'" *Arte Lombarda* 86–87, nos. 3-4 (1988): 94.

22 Perhaps a trace of this story can be found in this passage from the "Life" of Giuliano: "Giuliano resenting this, for it appeared to him that he had received an affront from the Pope, in view of the faithful service that he had rendered to him when his rank was not so high, and of the promise made to him by the Pope that he should have that building [St. Peter's], sought leave to go (G. Vasari, "Giuliano e Antonio da Sangallo," in *Le vite de' più eccellenti pittori scultori ed architettori*, 282–283). Trans. into English by G. de Vere as "Giuliano and Antonio da San Gallo," in *Lives of the Painters, Sculptors and Architects*, vol. 1 (1912; London: Everyman Library, 1996), 705.

23 The drawings for St. Peter's have been studied with extraordinary refinement by Christof Thoenes; for a summary, see first of all C. Thoenes, "Nuovi rilievi sui disegni bramanteschi per San Pietro," in idem, *Sostegno e adornamento. Saggi sull'architettura del Rinascimento: disegni, ordini, magnificenza* (Milan: Electa, 1998), 201–225, and C. Thoenes, "Elf Thesen zu Bramante und St. Peter," in *Römisches Jahrbuch der Bibliotheca Hertziana* 41 (2013–2014): 209–226.

24 S. Serlio, *Il terzo libro di Sabastiano Serlio Bolognese, nel qual si figurano, e descrivono le antiquità di Roma, e le altre che sono in Italia, e fuori de Italia*, ill. XXXVII (folio 65r), (Venice: 1544), now in *Sebastiano Serlio on Architecture. Volume One: Books I–V of "Tutte l'opere d'architettura et prospetiva,"* ed. and trans. V. Hart and P. Hicks (New Haven-London: Yale University Press, 1996), 127.

23 *Prevedari Engraving*

25 The contract between the painter Matteo Fedeli and the engraver Bernardo Prevedari is dated October 24, 1481 and provided for the execution of the engraving after a drawing by Bramante by Christmas of the same year. At this date, Bramante was probably already at work on Santa Maria presso San Satiro, although he does not appear in the documents until 1482, as witness to a deed of sale.

26 Reconstructions of the building depicted in the *Prevedari Engraving*, with plans and sections, can be found in F. Graf Wolff-Metternich, "Der Kupferstich Bernardos de Prevedari in Mailand von 1481. Gedanken zu den Anfängen der Kunst Bramantes," *Römisches Jahrbuch für Kunstgeschichte* XI (1967–1968): 26–27, and in A. Bruschi, *Bramante*

architetto (Rome-Bari: Laterza, 1969), 154-155. Whether it is a building on a central (Bruschi) or a basilica plan (Wolff-Metternich) can only be decided on the basis of a more general idea of Bramante and of Renaissance architecture; the drawing, in itself, could easily refer to either layout (moreover, if we are to judge solely by the drawing, the building could even consist of just a nave and one aisle).

27   The figure may also be a representation of St. Barnabas. See C. Alberici, "Bernardo Prevedari incisore di un disegno del Bramante," *Arte Lombarda* 86-87 (1988): 5-13.

28   The head would, according to Geymüller's somewhat fanciful hypothesis, subsequently taken up by Wolff-Metternich, be that of Leon Battista Alberti (Wolff-Metternich, "Der Kupferstich Bernardos de Prevedari aus Mailand von 1481," 105). In fact, this head, which faces away from the viewer, has short and curly hair and since everybody knows that Alberti was the only man of his time to have short and curly hair (!), it can only be his (!!) As if all this were not already absurd enough, we also need to consider the fact that it is explicitly stated in *De re aedificatoria* that the ancients only used quadrangular windows. L. B. Alberti, *De re aedificatoria*, VII, XII, ed. G. Orlandi and P. Portoghesi (Milan: Il Polifilo, 1966), 619. Also from this point of view, then, the insertion of Alberti's bust in a round window seems a very strange form of tribute.

29   B. Berenson, *The Italian Painters of the Renaissance* (London: Phaidon, 1952), 110.

30   A. Chastel, *Le Grand Atelier d'Italie, 1460-1500*, 2 vols. (Paris: Gallimard, 1965). The passage has been translated from the Italian edition, *La grande officina. Arte italiana 1460-1500* (Milan: Rizzoli, 1966), 192.

31   Squarcione's workshop was active roughly from the 1430s to the 1460s. A period spent in Padua and the frequentation of circles linked to Squarcione toward the end of the 1450s or in the first half of the 1460s is compatible with the chronology of Bramante's life (he was born in 1444). Sabba da Castiglione says, moreover, that Bramante was a "pupil of Mantegna" (S. Castiglione, "Ricordo CXI," in S. Castiglione, *Ricordi ovvero Ammaestramenti di Monsignor Saba da Castiglione Cavalier Gerosolimitano ne quali con prudenti, e christiani discorsi si ragiona di tutte le materie honorate, che si ricercano a un vero gentil'huomo* [Venice: Paolo Gherardo, 1554], 139) and Mantegna, even after leaving Squarcione, worked in Padua, at least up until he moved to Mantua in 1460. On the possible links among Bramante and Venice, see V. Pizzigoni, "Donato Bramante e Venezia," in *Annali di architettura*, no. 21 (2009): 27-30.

32   R. Longhi, "Lettera pittorica a Giuseppe Fiocco," in R. Longhi, *Opere complete*, vol. 2: *Saggi e Ricerche, 1925-1928* (Florence: Sansoni, 1967), 92.

33   An iconographic interpretation of the engraving can be found in G. Mulazzani, "'Ad civitatem Mediolani veni': Il senso dell'incisione Prevedari," in *Studi sulla cultura lombarda in onore di M. Apollonio*, vol. I (Milan: Vita e Pensiero, 1972). There is also an analysis of the engraving in A. Nagel and C. S. Wood, *Anachronic Renaissance* (New York: Zone, 2010), 309-312.

34   According to Wolff-Metternich's and Bruschi's reconstructions the space occupied by the building is around 20 × 20 m. See Bruschi, *Bramante architetto*,

154-155 and Wolff-Metternich, "Der Kupferstich Bernardos de Prevedari aus Mailand von 1481," 83, note 47.

35 Wolff-Metternich, "Der Kupferstich Bernardos de Prevedari aus Mailand von 1481," 63-64.

24 Opportunities and propaganda

36 N. Machiavelli, *Il Principe* (Turin: Einaudi). English ed., *The Prince*, trans. W. K. Marriott (Woodstock, ON: Devoted Publishing, 2016), ch. VI, 19. Machiavelli returns to the example of Moses, Cyrus and Theseus in the final chapter of his treatise (XXVI). See too "Capitolo dell'Occasione," in N. Machiavelli, *Capitoli: Introduzione, testo critico e commentario di G. Inglese* (Rome: Bulzoni, 1981), 157-158.

37 Vasari, "Bramante da Urbino," 145-146.

38 C. Baroni, *Bramante* (Bergamo: Istituto Arti Grafiche, 1944), 21. Baroni also speaks of "second-hand motifs" (*Bramante*, 10).

39 R. Longhi, "Recensione a Malaguzzi Valeri, La corte di Ludovico il Moro," *L'Arte* (1916); now in R. Longhi, *Scritti giovanili I (1912-1922)* (Florence: Sansoni, 1980), 297.

40 Moving St. Peter's tomb was too much even for Julius II: "*immota oportere esse sacra dictitare, movere non movenda prohibere ... se sacra prophanis, religionem splendori, pietatem ornamentis esse praepositurum.*" See Egidio da Viterbo, *Historia viginti saeculorum*, Bibl. Ang., Ms. lat. 502 fol. 194r and L. von Pastor, *The History of the Popes*, vol. VI, ed. and trans. F. I. Antrobus (London: Kegan Paul, Trench, Trübner & Co., 1901), 479-480 and app. no. 89, 655-656. The obelisk, formerly part of the Circus of Nero, used to be located

about 250 m from its present position in St. Peter's Square. It was moved by Domenico Fontana in 1586, during the papacy of Sixtus V (D. Fontana, *Della trasportatione dell'obelisco vaticano (1590)*, ed. A. Carugo and P. Portoghesi (Verona: Il Polifilo, 1979). Since, unlike Fontana, he did not possess the technical skills that would have allowed him to move the obelisk and line it up with the church, Bramante tried to solve the problem at the level of ideology: if the obelisk couldn't be moved, then the church could always be turned round.

41 This characteristic places architecture in a completely different position to the other contemporary arts, which, since the nineteenth century at least, have dumped their patrons and gone to sell their products directly on the market.

42 B. Zevi, *Architectura in nuce* (Macerata: Quodlibet, 2018), 143.

43 The Abbé Sieyès pointed out this resemblance in the months preceding the Revolution, see E. J. Sieyès, *Vues sur les moyens d'exécution dont les représentants de la France pourront disposer en 1789*, https://gallica.bnf.fr/ark:/12148/bpt6k41688x/f76.item#, 31.

44 Bramante was called Donato (Donato di Pascuccio d'Antonio). Some biographies (for instance Milizia's) also give the surname Lazzari, although it does not appear in the documents. "Bramante" ("longing," "yearning") seems to have been his father's nickname (sometimes in the versions "Abramante" and "Barbante"), which was then inherited by Donato and his brothers. On the question see Bruschi, *Bramante architetto*, xxiii, and F. Sangiorgi, *Bramante "hastrubaldino." Documenti per una biografia bramantesca* (Fermignano, Urbino: STEU, 1970).

45 For an overall picture of Bramante's

ill repute see J. S. Ackerman, "Notes on Bramante's Bad Reputation," in *Studi bramanteschi. Atti del Congresso internazionale. Milano-Urbino-Roma-1970* (Rome: De Luca, 1974), 339–349.

46 The choir was finished by the Easter of 1514, one year after the death of Julius and exactly at the time of Bramante's death; see F. Graf Wolff-Metternich, "Bramante, Skizze eines Lebenbildes," 52, and K. Frey, "Zur Baugeschichte des St. Peter," *Jahrbuch der königlich preussischen Kunstsammlungen* 31 (1911): 57.

47 C. Thoenes, "I tre progetti di Bramante per S. Pietro," in idem, *Sostegno e adornamento. Saggi sull'architettura del Rinascimento: disegni, ordini, magnificenza* (Milan: Electa, 1998), 156.

48 Folio 24v [Ashby 31] of the Codex Coner (now in the Soane Museum and attributed to Bernardo della Volpaia) illustrates the grotesque state of the construction site on Bramante's death.

49 Bramante's plans would fail and the choir, with the adoption of the giant order on the outside, would end up giving Michelangelo the idea for a radical distortion of Bramante's spatial concept for St. Peter's. In fact, Michelangelo would reduce the whole church to the essential monumentality of the exterior of the choir, in the end saving what Bramante would have chosen to sacrifice.

50 Paolo Portoghesi, "La lingua universale: cultura e architettura tra il 1503 e il 1527," in *Studi bramanteschi*, 362. Translated into English by H. Evans for the forthcoming *Bramante, an Introduction*.

51 M. Tafuri, "Via Giulia: storia di una struttura urbana," in L. Salerno, L. Spezzaferro, and M. Tafuri, *Via Giulia* (Rome: Staderini, 1975), 75.

25 Tempietto

52 "Public" here means a very small circle of people; the "society of the spectacle" addressed by Bramante was certainly not a mass society.

53 J. M. Lotman, *Culture and Explosion*, trans. Wilma Clark, ed. Marina Grishakova (Berlin: De Gruyter Mouton, 2009).

54 On March 23, 1989, Professors Fleischmann and Pons of the University of Utah announced that they had achieved what came to be known as *cold nuclear fusion*. Only three years had passed since the disaster at Chernobyl and it would have been great to have found a safe and inexpensive source of energy. However, it appears that Professors Fleischmann and Pons had not discovered anything.

55 H. Günther, "La ricezione dell'antico nel Tempietto," in *Donato Bramante. Ricerche, Proposte, Riletture*, ed. F. P. Di Teodoro (Urbino: Accademia Raffaello, 2001), 294–295.

56 The affinities between Renaissance Rome and Hollywood were recognized by M. McLuhan: "Renaissance Italy became a kind of Hollywood collection of sets of antiquity." *The Gutenberg Galaxy: The Making of Typographic Man* (New York: Signet, 1969), 146.

57 In a completely different context of interpretation from this one, Renato De Fusco and Maria Luisa Scalvini have noted the skill with which Bramante assembled the (in their opinion symbolic) elements with which he started: "To the realm of symbols belong for example, in the case of San Pietro in Montorio, the centrality of the plan, the presence of the dome and the crypt, the use of the Doric order, the recurrence of particular numerical ratios, the

figurations of the metopes ... And all these factors ... constituted ... a set of givens 'a priori' to the configuration of the specific work we are examining." R. De Fusco, M. L. Scalvini, "Segni e simboli del tempietto di Bramante," in *op. cit.*, no. 19 (1970): 5–18.

26 *Kolossal*

58 *Kolossal* is a term used in Italian cinematic language for spectacular, high-budget movies, launched with costly advertising campaigns. The name *kolossal* does not apply to a genre in its own right, but to a range of different genres and formulas: from religious, historical, or mythological epics to war films, melodramas, and westerns. The characteristics of the *kolossal* are an exaggerated length, scenes with casts of thousands and lavish sets and costumes. Examples of the *kolossal* include *The Ten Commandments* (C. B. De Mille, 1956), *Ben-Hur* (W. Wyler, 1959), *Lawrence of Arabia* (D. Lean, 1962), *Tora! Tora! Tora!* (R. Fleischner, 1970) and *Dune* (D. Lynch, 1984) *(translator's note)*.

59 This possibility of establishing urban relations on a large scale also depended on the topography of Rome. In the absolute geographical uniformity of Milan such work on urban space could certainly not have been imagined.

60 C. Thoenes, "Nuovi rilievi sui disegni bramanteschi per San Pietro," in C. Thoenes, *Sostegno e adornamento. Saggi sull'architettura del Rinascimento: disegni, ordini, magnificenza* (Milan: Electa, 1998), 219. In the end, the dome of St. Peter, as built, would be slightly smaller than that of the Pantheon (ca. 42 m in diameter as opposed to ca. 43.40 m).

61 The name of its engraver is unknown, but according to Roberto Weiss the medal dates from the period 1504–1508: R. Weiss, "The Medals of Pope Julius II (1503–1513)," *Journal of the Warburg and Courtauld Institutes* VVVIII (1965): 180–181. For the contrasting opinion of Ackerman, who dates it instead to the latter part of Julius's pontificate, see J. S. Ackerman, *The Cortile del Belvedere* (Vatican City: Biblioteca Apostolica Vaticana, 1954), 192. See too C. L. Frommel "I tre progetti bramanteschi per il cortile del Belvedere," in idem, *Architettura alla corte papale nel Rinascimento* (Milan: Electa, 2003), 98, and F. Testa, "'ut ad veterum illa admiranda aedificia accedere videatur'. Il Cortile del Belvedere e la retorica politica del potere pontificio sotto Giulio II," in *Donato Bramante: ricerche, proposte, riletture*, 238.

62 These solutions would be used extensively in the following centuries: the Belvedere is the toolbox of baroque urbanism.

63 F. Milizia, "Bramante d'Urbino," in F. Milizia, *Vite de' più celebri Architetti d'ogni nazione e d'ogni tempo* (Rome: Paolo Giunchi Komarek, 1768), 181.

64 The importance of the Sanctuary of Fortuna in Palestrina for Bramante and the originality of his interest in this monument, which up to then had not attracted much attention, cannot be exaggerated. It was from the ancient sanctuary at Praeneste that Bramante derived an idea of architecture as a sequence of devices for the control of movement and vision, an art capable of constructing a choreography of actions associated with corresponding views of the landscape. On the influence of the sanctuary in Palestrina on Bramante, see J. S. Ackerman, "The Belvedere as a Classical Villa," *Journal of the Warburg*

and *Courtland Institutes* XIV (1951): 70–
91. On the sanctuary itself see G. Gullini
and V. Fasolo, *Il santuario della Fortuna
Primigenia a Palestrina* (Rome: Istituto
di Archeologia, University of Rome,
1952); H. Kähler, "Das Fortunaheiligtum
von Palestrina Praeneste," *Annales
Universitatis Saraviensis* 7, nos. 3–4
(Saarbrücken, 1958): 189–240; and
F. Coarelli, *I santuari del Lazio in età
repubblicana* (Rome: Carocci, 1987).

27 The conquest of Beauty

65 The whole of the Roman art world of the
early sixteenth century was not immune
to this interest in the colossal, which
appears to have been shared, although
with different accents, by Leonardo,
Bramante, Michelangelo, Raphael and
even Titian. See C. Gilbert, "A New
Sight in 1500: The Colossal," in idem,
Michelangelo: On and Off the Sistine Ceiling
(New York: Braziller, 1994), 227–251. See
too H. Wölfflin, *Renaissance and Baroque*,
trans. K. Simon (Ithaca, NY: Cornell
University Press, 1967), 44–57.

66 Besides a beautiful but minuscule
sketch on the verso of UA20, where
the dome emerges from an immense
cubic block without any articulation,
the medal struck by Caradosso is
the only image of the exterior of
Bramante's design for St. Peter's.
The medal has a diameter of 5.65 cm.
There are specimens of the medal in
the Museo Civico Archeologico of
Bologna, the Cabinet des Medailles of
the Bibliothèque National in Paris, the
National Gallery in Washington and
the British Museum. On Caradosso,
see C. M. Brown and S. Hickson,
"Caradosso Foppa," *Arte Lombarda*,
new series, 119 (1997): 9–39, and G. F.

Hill, *A Corpus of Italian Medals of the
Renaissance before Cellini* (London:
British Museum, 1930), 168–171.

67 R. Koolhaas, *The Surface*, unpublished
manuscript (1969), cited in G. Mastrigli,
"Modernity and Myth: Rem Koolhaas in
New York," *San Rocco*, no. 8 (2013): 84–98.

68 "It is the greatest building that has ever
been seen, and it will cost more than a
million in gold; and I know that the Pope
has decided to spend annually sixty
thousand ducats on the fabric, and that he
thinks of nothing else." Raffaello, "Lettera
a Simone Ciarla" (July 1, 1514), in S. Ray,
Raffaello architetto (Rome-Bari: Laterza,
1974), 357–358. The letter is quoted in C.
Thoenes, "'Il Primo tempio del Mondo.'
Raffaello, S. Pietro e il denaro," *Casabella*,
no. 654 (1998): 56, note 8, and has been
translated into English in E. McCurdy,
Raphael Santi (London: Hodder and
Stoughton, 1917), 52.

69 According to Rem Koolhaas it is a
"discredited intellectual problem."
R. Koolhaas, "Bigness or the Problem
of Large," in R. Koolhaas and B. Mau,
S,M,L,XL (New York: Monacelli,
1997), 496.

70 U. Foscolo, "Ragion poetica e sistema
generale del Carme alle Grazie esposti
dall'autore," in idem, *Opere edite e
postume*, vol. 9 (Florence: Successori Le
Monnier, 1836), 210.

71 "*[C]he porgesse a que' che vi entrano
dentro stupefatti, spavento.*" Alberti, *De re
aedificatoria*, libro VII, cap. 3. English ed.,
On the Art of Building in Ten Books, 194.

72 This is also the reason why architecture
has nothing in common with the applied
arts. The design of things so large that
you can enter them has to be different
from the design of things so small that
you can pick them up in your fingers:
the experience of someone who meets
a butterfly in a forest is different from

the experience of someone who meets a bear in a forest. From this point of view any confusion between architecture and product design leads to a renunciation of the ambition inevitably associated with the spatial and temporal dimension of architecture. Architecture is one of the "major arts," i.e., an art that at once arrogates to itself an immense ambition and has to reckon with this ambition (with the responsibility of this ambition). And it is precisely as an art in the highest—and obviously most ridiculous—sense that architecture also contributes to the system of production in which it operates. André Chastel has described with great understanding the sense of experimentation and civilization that the artistic research of the Renaissance was able to introduce into the industries of Italian cities at the end of the fifteenth century: "now the mason had to learn to carve the deep grooves that had fallen out of use: the stonecutter had to execute new moldings, and the painter, new drapery." (A. Chastel, *La grande officina. Arte italiana 1460-1500*; Milan: Feltrinelli, 1966, 324.) It is the minor arts that derive their standards of precision and coherence from the major arts. Doing things the other way round can only lead us to escape our responsibilities.

73 The terror that is an undeniable part of architecture has often been mistakenly seen as something unequivocal and monolithic, giving all too much credit to architecture's claim to domination, without recognizing how ridiculous this pretense is. Architecture's capacity for control and anticipation as an instrument of policing has for instance been greatly exaggerated by Michel Foucault and Henri Lefebvre. But all it takes is a bit of experience to know that without the

assiduous contribution of the guards, prisons would be unable to exercise surveillance over anything, and indeed can easily be turned into museums, conference centers and luxury hotels as soon as convicts are relocated. So it is not true that "stones can make people docile" (M. Foucault, *Discipline and Punish*, trans. A. Sheridan; New York: Vintage Books, 1995, part III, ch. 2, 172), nor can architecture function as a "machine for creating and sustaining a power relation independent of the person who exercises it" (Foucault, *Discipline and Punish*, Part III, ch. 3, 201) or impose "blind, spontaneous and *lived* obedience" (H. Lefebvre, *The Production of Space*; Malden, MA: Blackwell, 1974, 143). Architecture has never had this unlimited power; its uses in repression are decidedly overestimated.

SPACE

28 Walls

1 With the exception of the *Prevedari Engraving* and a few scribbles, the architectural drawings by Bramante that have come down to us are all plans.

2 Rem Koolhaas quotes Raymond Hood's definition, emphasizing its "tautological bravura." See "Typical Plan," in OMA, R. Koolhaas, and B. Mau, *S,M,L,XL* (New York: Monacelli, 1995), 334. See too, R. Koolhaas, "Field Trip, A(A) Memoir (First and Last ...): The Berlin Wall as Architecture," in the same volume, 212-233.

3 Once again Bramante chose to take a different position from Alberti, who in fact saw the roof as the fundamental element in architecture: "Roofs are the most important elements": L. B. Alberti,

On the Art of Building in Ten Books, trans. J. Rykwert, N. Leach, and R. Tavernor (Cambridge, MA: MIT Press, 1988), 26; "For unless I am mistaken, the roof of its very nature was the first of all building elements to provide mankind with a place of shelter: so much so that it was for the sake of the roof that the need arose not only for the wall and all that goes with it, but also for anything constructed below ground, such as water conduits, rainwater channels, sewers, and the like." Alberti, On the Art of Building in Ten Books, 34–35. The alternative between an architecture conceived on the basis of the walls and one conceived on the basis of the roof is explained very clearly by Schmarsow: "The principal concern is always the spatial enclosure of this subject, that is, the enclosure or walling in along the sides—not the roofing from above ..." A. Schmarsow, "The Essence of Architectural Creation," in Empathy, Form and Space: Problems in German Aesthetics, 1873–93, trans. H. F. Mallgrave and E. Ikonomou (Los Angeles: Getty Research Institute, 1994), 289.

4   G. C. Argan, "Il problema del Bramante," Rassegna Marchigiana, XII (1934), 220. Translated into English as "Bramante's Problem" by H. Evans for the forthcoming Bramante, an Introduction.

5   Argan, "Il problema del Bramante," 218. English trans. "Bramante's Problem."

6   Piero della Francesca, De prospectiva pingendi, ed. C. Gizzi (Venice: Edizioni Ca' Foscari Digital Publishing, 2016), 190.

7   This undifferentiated material is well represented by the orange molass filling the boundaries of the wall portions represented in drawing UA1.

8   C. Baroni, Bramante (Bergamo: Istituto Arti Grafiche, 1944), 28.

9   The cloisters of Sant'Ambrogio are a painterly critique of the sculptural elementarism of the Ospedale degli Innocenti. Brunelleschi seems to have wanted to make the upper story disappear, keeping the wall smooth and articulating it solely with the frames of the windows in order to make it clearly subordinate to the columns of the lower story. In Bramante's building, on the contrary, it is the wall above, uniformly built out of brick and much more extensively articulated than in the Ospedale degli Innocenti, that dominates the portico below.

10   The relationship between the solution adopted for the corner between nave and transept of Santo Spirito and the one adopted in Pavia Cathedral has been pointed out by Bruschi: See A. Bruschi, Bramante architetto (Roma-Bari: Laterza, 1969), 182–185.

11   "[E]lements in themselves amorphous and lacking individuality." F. Graf Wolff Metternich, "Le premier projet pour St.-Pierre de Rome," in idem, Bramante und St. Peter (Munich: Wilhelm Fink, 1975), 24.

12   About 9 m (a Roman palm measured 22.34 cm).

13   In the drawing UA20 there is also a hint of a possible alternative with niches carved out of bigger pillars, a solution very similar to the one adopted later in "Raphael's plan."

14   The deliberate ambiguity of Bramante's design is most evident in some of Giuliano da Sangallo's drawings, such as Codex Vat. Barb. Lat. 4424 f. 56v and f. 64v and above all UA7r, where the two halves of the drawing illustrate a church with a nave and two aisles and a church with a nave and six aisles, taking the possible interpretations of Bramante's design to an extreme. The variations introduced by Giuliano serve to shed

light on the status of the small aisle that, in Bramante's version, results from the enfilade of opposing apses carved out of the pillars that bound the nave. Giuliano wanted to define the number of aisles in the church precisely, eliminating all the ambiguities of Bramante's layout, where the number of aisles seems to remain undefined, almost varying in relation to the position chosen by the observer.

15 Argan, "Il problema del Bramante," 223.

29 Spectacle of space

16 A. Bruschi, "Bramante, Raffaello e Palladio," *Bollettino del Centro Internazionale di Studi di Architettura Andrea Palladio*, no. 15 (1973): 69–87.

17 On depth as the specific dimension of architecture see A. Schmarsow, *Zur Frage nach dem Malerischen. Sein Grundbegriff und seine Entwicklung* (Leipzig: Hirzel, 1896).

18 This blurring, although not identical to Leonardo's *sfumato*, was certainly influenced by it.

19 Piero della Francesca's influence on the choir of Santa Maria del Popolo lies more in this almost imperceptible interval than in the presence of the conch.

20 The large altar was inserted in 1627.

21 Quite what the *function oblique* actually was no one has ever been able to understand, but it was certainly something generous and unexpected that was made manifest in space. On the *fonction oblique* see C. Parent, *Vivre à l'oblique* (Paris: L'Aventure Urbaine, 1970).

22 The context for the search for the right proportion in Renaissance Italy has been clarified by Michael Baxandall in an important passage of his work on the painting of the fifteenth century:

"Problems of proportion include: pasturage, brokerage, discount, tare allowance, the adulteration of commodities, barter, currency exchange. These were very much more prominent than they are now. For instance, exchange problems were of an extraordinary complexity because each substantial city had not only its own currency but its own weights and measures ... So fifteenth-century people became adept through daily practice in reducing the most diverse sort of information to a form of geometric proportion: A stands to B as C stands to D. For our purpose, the important thing is the identity of skill brought both to partnership or exchange problems and to the making and seeing of pictures. Piero della Francesca had the same equipment for a barter deal as for the subtle play of intervals in his pictures." (M. Baxandall, *Painting and Experience in Fifteenth-century Italy* [Oxford: Oxford University Press, 1972, 2nd ed. 1988], 96–97)

23 Metternich made it clear that "Bramante's design was not by any means an ideal project determined only by the rules of absolute proportion, conceived in the empty space on the drawing board, but rather a concrete plan that met technical, topographical, liturgical and artistic requirements in equal measure" F. Graf Wolff Metternich, "Kuppelentwurf Bramantes für die Peterskirche," in idem, *Bramante und St. Peter* (Munich: Wilhelm Fink, 1975), 81.

24 R. Wittkower, *Architectural Principles in the Age of Humanism* (New York, Norton 1971), 26. For a criticism of Wittkower's views, see C. Thoenes, "Nuovi rilievi sui disegni bramanteschi per San Pietro," in idem, *Sostegno e adornamento. Saggi sull'architettura del Rinascimento:*

disegni, ordini, magnificenza (Milan: Electa, 1998), 222, note 22.

25 C. Thoenes, "Pianta centrale e pianta longitudinale nel nuovo San Pietro," in idem, *Sostegno e adornamento,* 187–199; and C. Thoenes, "San Pietro. Storia e ricerca," in idem, *Sostegno e adornamento,* 237–251.

26 Beckett uses this formula to describe Baudelaire's unity, in contrast to Proust's: S. Beckett, *Proust* (New York: Grove Press, 1978), 60.

27 See the drawings of Maarten van Heemskerck, in particular 79 D2, fol. 8r and 79 D2, fol. 52r in the Kupferstichkabinett in Berlin and the drawing by Ammanati (?) in the Kunsthalle Hamburg, as well as Geymüller, Metternich, and Portoghesi's drawings of reconstruction in F. Graf Wolff Metternich and C. Thoenes, *Die frühen St.-Peter-Entwürfe 1505–1514* (Tübingen: Wasmuth, 1987), 37, 86–87, and P. Portoghesi, *Roma del Rinascimento* (Rome: Electa, 1970), 64–65.

28 R. Bonelli, "Avvicinamento a Bramante," *Palladio,* nos. 3–4 (July–December 1952), 146. English translation by H. Evans, "Approaching Bramante," in the forthcoming *Bramante, an Introduction.*

29 Bramante cites San Lorenzo and Milan Cathedral in drawing UA8v. He was familiar with Hagia Sophia too. In fact, among the drawings included in a letter sent to Ascanio Sforza by the members of the Board of Trustees of Pavia Cathedral on August 17, 1487, and probably inspired by Bramante, there were some of Hagia Sophia. See S. Foschi, "Santa Sofia di Costantinopoli: immagini dall'Occidente," *Annali di architettura,* 14 (2002), 7–34. Drawings of Hagia Sophia, derived from Cyriacus of Ancona, also appear in Giuliano da Sangallo's book (Biblioteca Apostolica Vaticana, cod. Vat. Barb. Lat. 4424, fol. 28r and fol. 44r). In Hagia Sophia the centrifugal effect is even stronger than in Bramante's plans for St. Peter's, since the directions of expansion of the central space toward the minor spaces coincide neither with the axes nor with the diagonals of the square on which the central dome is set, but are shifted toward the outside. In fact, the apses and the minor semidomes depend on the two major apses, separated from the central square by the ample intervals of the great arches. In addition, the axes on which the two "minor diagonal apses" are set do not coincide even with the diagonals of the two squares into which the major apses can be inscribed. These adjustments, which took any rigorous coherence of a geometrical and structural kind away from the plan, met with strong disapproval from Sinan, who in his large mosques systematically sought to correct Hagia Sophia from this point of view. From Hagia Sophia Bramante seems to have drawn completely opposite conclusions to those of Sinan. Bramante, in all likelihood, would even have been happy with the absurd pile of unmatched buttresses that defines the building's exterior, and which produces an effect not so different from the one suggested on Caradosso's medal.

30 C. Thoenes, "Bramante a San Pietro: i 'deambulatori,'" in F. P. Di Teodoro, *Donato Bramante Ricerche, Proposte, Riletture* (Urbino: Accademia Raffaello, 2001), 312. See too A. Bruschi, "I primi progetti di Antonio di Sangallo il Giovane per San Pietro," in *Architektur und Kunst im Abendland,* ed. M. Janesen and K. Winands (Rome: Herder, 1992), 63–81, and A. Bruschi, "Problemi del S. Pietro bramantesco ... 'admodum

surgebat non inopia pecuniae sed cunctatione Bramantis architecti ...'" in *Quaderni dell'Istituto di Storia dell'Architettura*, new series, 1–10 (1983–87 [1987]), 273–292.

31 In the fall of 1518, Antonio da Sangallo drew up a *memoriale* in eleven points on St. Peter's, "to show how the money spent in St. Peter's is being spent with little honor of God and of Your Holiness." It is not known whether Antonio actually transmitted the memorial to the Curia or to the pope. The memorial, now in the Uffizi drawing collection (UA33), was published by Milanesi in his commentary on Antonio da Sangallo's life, see G. Milanesi, "Commentario alla vita di Antonio da Sangallo," in *Le vite de' più eccellenti pittori scultori ed architettori scritte da Giorgio Vasari pittore aretino con nuove annotazioni e commenti di Gaetano Milanesi*, vol. V (Florence: Sansoni, 1906), 476–477. For a dating of the memorial see C. L. Frommel, "Sul metodo progettuale nei disegni di Bramante, Raffaello e Antonio da Sangallo il Giovane per San Pietro," in H. Burns et al., "Palladio e la Roma di Antonio da Sangallo il Giovane, Atti del Seminario" (Vicenza, 2016), *Annali di architettura* 30 (2018), 131. See too *The Architectural Drawings of Antonio da Sangallo the Younger and his Circle. II: Churches, Villas, the Pantheon, Tombs, and Ancient Inscription*, ed. C. L. Frommel and N. Adams (Cambridge, MA: MIT Press, 2010), 65–67 and 275, and S. Ray, *Raffaello architetto* (Rome-Bari: Laterza, 1974), 114–115.

32 Antonio complained that "if it is continued as it was begun the nave will be so narrow and tall that it will look like an alley." (Milanesi, "Commentario alla vita di Antonio da Sangallo," 477).

33 G. Miarelli Mariani, "Aspetti della ricerca bramantesca," in *Bramante tra umanesimo e manierismo, Mostra storico-critica, settembre 1970, Milano, Palazzo Reale*, ed. R. Bonelli and A. Bruschi (Comitato Nazionale per le Celebrazioni Bramantesche) (Rome: Istituto Grafico Tiberino, 1970), 46. See, in the same volume, S. Benedetti, "Lo spazio architettonico in Bramante," 90–91. By buildings with a "Italian deutero-Byzantine Greek-cross plan" are meant some of the buildings of eleventh- to twelfth-century Byzantine culture already likened to Bramante's by Metternich, such as San Vittore alle Chiuse at San Vittore, in the municipality of Genga (AN), Santa Croce at Sassoferrato (AN), Santa Maria delle Moie at Moie (AN) and San Claudio al Chienti at Corridonia (MC). As well as in these buildings, the solution later adopted by Bramante appears in *The Bringing of the Rods to the Temple, The Suitors Praying*, and *The Marriage of the Virgin* in the Scrovegni Chapel, and in Piero della Francesca's *Montefeltro Altarpiece*.

34 The sole exception is the exterior of the sacellum of San Satiro, where the niches are carved directly into the wall, although flanked at the sides by slightly distanced pilasters.

30 Space and images of space

35 C. Brandi, "Considerazioni sulla spazialità in Bramante pittore e in Bramante architetto," in *Studi bramanteschi*, 84.

36 The monumentalizing effect of the *sotto in sù* view had been explored by Piero della Francesca (*Flagellation*), Mantegna (*Scenes from the Lives of St. Christopher and St. James*) and Melozzo (*Sixtus IV*

Appointing Bartolomeo Platina as Prefect of the Vatican Library). The extreme architectural consequences of this operation can be seen in Bramantino's Trivulzio Chapel, where the sarcophagi are located in the second row of niches, suspended five meters above the ground.

37 Starting from the probable height of this soldier (eight Roman palms, or about 1.78 m) Metternich has reconstructed the dimensions of the entire building: see F. Graf Wolff Metternich, "Der Kupferstich Bernardos de Prevedari aus Mailand von 1481. Gedanken zu den Anfängen der Kunst Bramantes," *Römisches Jahrbuch für Kunstgeschichte*, XI (1967–1968): 15, illustration 5, and 25, note 26.

38 See V. Pizzigoni, "Flat Grid: The Nature of the Floor in the *Prevedari Engraving*," *San Rocco*, no. 11 (2015), *Happy Birthday Bramante!*: 51–54.

39 B. Zevi, *Saper vedere l'architettura* (Turin: Einaudi, 1948), 147. English ed., *Architecture as Space: How to Look at Architecture*, trans. M. Gendel (New York: Da Capo Press, 1993), 220.

40 All the "ideal" reconstructions of San Satiro gloss over this aspect. See the drawing entitled *demonstrative scheme of the organization of the ideal illusionistic structure of Santa Maria di S. Satiro* in Bruschi, *Bramante architetto*, 134, fig. 79, and the even more implausible *Bramante's hypothetical Greek-cross design with apsidioles* in L. Patetta, *L'architettura del Quattrocento a Milano* (Milan: CLUP, 1987), 185.

41 Bonelli, "Avvicinamento a Bramante," 145. English trans. "Approaching Bramante," in the forthcoming *Bramante, an Introduction*.

42 While Bramante was strongly influenced by Mantegna, it does not seem to me that there is any real connection between the choir of San Satiro and the *Camera*

degli Sposi in Mantua, where the frescoes make no attempt to modify the space of the room. An early and extraordinary reinterpretation of Bramante's work at San Satiro is the façade of the Scuola Grande di San Marco in Venice, which Pietro Lombardo and his collaborators began in 1485. See W. Stedman Sheard, *Bramante e i Lombardo: ipotesi su una connessione*, in C. Pirovano, *Venezia e Milano. Storia, civiltà e cultura nel rapporto tra due capitali* (Milan: Electa, 1984), 25–56.

43 Longhi pointed out the terminological embarrassment that the spaces represented in the two frescoes have created for art historians. Among the names used to describe the two spaces, perhaps the most telling is *ripostigli* ("closets," "cubicles") used by Giovanni Battista Cavalcaselle. Cited in R. Longhi, "Giotto spazioso," in R. Longhi, *Da Cimabue a Morandi* (Milan: Mondadori, 1973), 68.

44 Longhi, "Giotto spazioso," 68.

45 Ibid., 71.

46 Ibid., 71–72.

47 The altar was not placed in its current position until 1611 and then it was radically altered during the restoration work carried out by Felice Pizzagalli between 1819 and 1820. See G. Ferri Piccaluga, "Il Rinascimento in Lombardia: Bramante e la chiesa di Santa Maria presso San Satiro," in *Piero. Teorico dell'arte*, ed. O. Calabrese (Rome: Gangemi, 1985), 143. See too G. Lise, *Santa Maria presso San Satiro* (Milan: Silvana Editoriale, 1975).

31 Evidence of space

48 Wittkower, *Architectural Principles in the Age of Humanism*, 8. An interesting

critical interpretation of the *Architectural Principles* can be found in the first chapter, "Perturbed Circles," of R. Evans, *The Projective Cast* (Cambridge, MA: MIT Press, 2000), 3–53. See too M. Tafuri, *Ricerca del Rinascimento* (Turin: Einaudi, 1992), 3–32. English ed., *Interpreting the Renaissance: Princes, Cities, Architects*, trans. D. Sherer (New Haven, CT: Yale University Press/Cambridge, MA: Harvard GSD Publications, 2006), 1–22, and A. Payne, "Rudolf Wittkower and Architectural Principles in the Age of Modernism," *Journal of the Society of Architectural Historians* 53 (1994): 322–342.

49 According to Anton Francesco Doni, Bramante wrote a treatise called *Pratica* (a marvelous title for a book of theory) in which he described a way of making proportions obvious: "whoever reads this, as soon he sees a building, immediately knows whether it is in proportion or not." (A. F. Doni, *Libraria seconda* [Venice: De Ferrari, 1551], 187). There is no other record of this Bramante treatise and Doni might, not without a certain subtlety, have invented it.

50 A. Gehlen, *Man: His Nature and Place in the World*, trans. C. McMillan and Karl Pillemer (Columbia University Press, 1988), 146. In this passage Gehlen cites K. Lorenz, "Die angeborenen Formen möglicher Erfahrung," *Zeitschrift für Tierpsychologie* 5, no. 2 (1943): 235–409. At the end of the passage cited above, Gehlen says something that, in the way it makes frailty coincide with boldness, seems the emblem of all classicism: "One can ultimately explain the preference for symmetrical figures only by their improbability."

51 What for Rudolf Arnheim is "the immediate impact of perceptual form. And it is this impact that distinguishes art

from other kinds of communication." R. Arnheim, *The Power of the Center: A Study of Composition in the Visual Arts* (Berkeley, CA: University of California Press, 1982.

32 Experience of space

52 "*Der künstler aber, der architekt, fühlt zuerst die wirkung, die er hervorzubringen gedenkt, und sieht dann mit seinem geistigen auge die räume, die er schaffen will. Die wirkung, die er auf den beschauer ausüben will, sei es nun angst oder schrecken, wie beim kerker; gottesfurcht, wie bei der kirche; ehrfurcht vor der staatsgewalt, wie beim regierungspalast; pietät, wie bei grabmal; heimgefühl, wie bei wohnhause; fröhlichkeit, wie in der trinkstube.*" A. Loos, "The Principle of Cladding," in *Spoken into the Void: Collected Essays 1897–1900*, trans. J. O. Newman and J. H. Smith (Cambridge, MA: MIT Press, 1982), 66.

53 "*Nos édifices, surtout les édifices publics devraient être, en quelque façon, des poèmes. Les images qu'ils offrent à nos sens devraient exciter en nous des sentiments analogues à l'usage auquel ces édifices sont consacrés*": E. L. Boullée, *Architecture. Essai sur l'architecture* (Paris: Hermann, 1968), 73. English ed., E. L. Boullée, "Architecture, Essay on Art," trans. Sheila de Vallée, in *Boullée and Visionary Architecture*, ed. Helen Rosenau (London: Academy Editions/New York: Harmony Books, 1976), 82.

54 Any theory that sees architecture as an act of communication has to reduce the experience of space to the description and anticipation of it. This hypothesis has been advanced by Umberto Eco: "what permits the use of architecture (passing, entering, staying, going up, lying down, looking out, leaning against, gripping,

etcetera) is not just its possible functions, but first of all the meanings connected with it that prepare me for its functional use." It is because the experience of space can be fully defined in advance that it can then be communicated as well. See U. Eco, *La struttura assente* (Milan: Bompiani, 1968), 195.

55 G. C. Argan, *Pier Luigi Nervi* (Milan: Il Balcone, 1955), 13.

56 M. Merleau-Ponty, *Phenomenology of Perception*, trans. C. Smith (London: Routledge, 2002), 412.

57 Aristotle, *Nicomachean Ethics*, trans. W. D. Ross (Kitchener, ON: Batoche Books, 2001), Book 6, 2, 92.

33 A brief and not all that complicated theory of space

58 H. Lefebvre, *The Production of Space* (Malden, MA: Blackwell, 1974).

59 A. Schmarsow, *Das Wesen der architektonischen Schöpfung, Antrittsvorlesung, gehalten in der Aula der K. Universität Leipzig am 8. November 1893* (Leipzig: Hiersemann, 1894), 9. English trans. by H. F. Mallgrave and E. Ikonomou, "The Essence of Architectural Creation," in *Empathy, Form, and Space: Problems in German Aesthetics* (Santa Monica, CA: Getty, 1994), 291.

60 G. W. Leibniz, "Initia rerum mathematicarum metaphysica," in *Mathematische Schriften*, vol. VII, ed. C. I. Gerhardt (Hildesheim: Georg Olms, 1963), 18.

34 Form of the void

61 Here we cannot help but trace the difficulty back to the one peremptorily raised by Aristotle: *infinitum enim ad finitum in nulla proportione est*; see Aristotle, *De caelo* I 6, 274a 7-8, 275a 1-2, ed. D. J. Allen (Oxford: Clarendon Press, 2005), n.p., and St. Thomas Aquinas, *In Aristotelis librum de coelo et mundo*, I, 1, Lectio XII and XIV (Turin-Rome: Marietti, 1952), 54-70. The possibility of establishing a relationship between these terms through the *praecisio absoluta* and the corresponding *docta ignorantia* was at the center of the attempt made by Nicholas of Cusa; see Cassirer, *The Individual and the Cosmos in Renaissance Philosophy*. For a recent perspective, see too T. Tho, "The Void Just Ain't (What It Used to Be): Void, Infinity and the Indeterminate," *Filozofski vestnik* 34, no. 2 (2013): 27-48.

COMMUNITY

35 Public work

1 "*Neque enim minus operosum est artem aliquam omni ex parte consummari quam urbem. Itaque sicuti nulla urbs ab uno, immo nec a paucis condi potest, ita neque ars ulla, sed a multis atque a plurimis, neque his inter se ignotis—nam aliter quomodo aemulari possent et de laude contendere—sed notis et ante omnia eiusdem linguae commercio coniunctis. Quoniam ab urbe extruenda comparationem ac similitudinem sumpsi, nonne ita e sanctis libris accepimus, eos qui immanem illam turrim Babel extruebant, ideo ab extruendo cessasse, quod alius alium loquentem amplius non intelligebat?*" L. Valla, "Orazione per l'inaugurazione dell'anno accademico 1455-56 (18 Ottobre 1455) / Oratio clarissimi viri Laurentii Valle habita in principio [sui] studii die XVIII Octobris

MCCCCLV," *Roma nel Rinascimento* (1994), 192–201. Translated in M. Baxandall, *Giotto and the Orators: Humanist Observers of Painting in Italy and the Discovery of Pictorial Composition, 1350–1450* (Oxford: Clarendon Press, 1986), 119.

2   The collective character of Bramante's work was already recognized by Giovannoni in an essay written in 1914, although his conclusions about the *bottega* and its persistence after the death of the master may be somewhat fanciful. See G. Giovannoni, "Il palazzo dei Tribunali del Bramante in un disegno di Fra Giocondo," *Bollettino d'Arte* 7, no. 6 (1914): 193–194.

3   Richard Schofield has attempted to distinguish exactly what was done by Bramante and what by Giovanni Antonio Amadeo in Santa Maria delle Grazie, appraising all the decorative elements and trying to assign them to one of the two architects. R. Schofield, "Bramante and Amadeo at Santa Maria delle Grazie in Milano," *Arte Lombarda* 78, no. 3 (1986): 41–58. It seems to me a rather pointless exercise, in that it claims to recognize the hybrid nature of the production of monuments in the Milan of the Sforzas but ends up reducing the whole affair to just the two "artists" involved, without giving any role to the artisans who worked on these buildings. Moreover, Schofield fixes his gaze only on the decorative elements, without ever looking at the spatial organization of the complex, and draws questionable conclusions, for instance that the vault of the choir had been raised (by Amadeo) with respect to a presumed original design (by Bramante?) in which the oculus at the center of the archivolt that faces the nave opened onto the sky like the other three. In reality, the relation of this oculus to the vault of the choir can be explained very well by the desire to modulate the view of the choir from the nave, revealing and at the same time concealing the last element in the sequence—a solution that reflects a way of articulating depth that is typical of Bramante.

4   In December 1649 the men working on San Giovanni in Laterano, on the orders of Francesco Borromini, beat to death a certain Marco Antonio Bussoni, who had damaged a slab of marble. Borromini was put on trial and then pardoned by the pope. See J. Connors, "Francesco Borromini. La vita 1599–1667," in *Borromini e l'universo barocco*, ed. R. Bösel and C. L. Frommel (Milan: Electa, 1999), 15.

36   Impresario

5   C. Reed, *The Agony and the Ecstasy*, 1965. On *The Agony and the Ecstasy*, see also S. Jacob, "Bro-Mante, the Movie," in *San Rocco*, no. 11, *Happy Birthday Bramante!*: 41–43.

6   Howard Roark is the protagonist of Ayn Rand's loathsome book entitled *The Fountainhead* (New York: Plume, 2005). In 1949 King Vidor made the book into an equally repugnant film in which Gary Cooper played the part of Roark.

7   G. Vasari, "Raffaello da Urbino," in *Le vite de' più eccellenti pittori scultori e architettori scritte da Giorgio Vasari pittore aretino con nuove annotazioni e commenti di Gaetano Milanesi*, vol. IV (Florence: Sansoni, 1906), 339. English ed., *The Life of Raphael*, trans. A. B. Hinds (Los Angeles: Getty Publications, 2018), 60. The episode may not be true. Charles Robertson points out that in the "Life of Michelangelo" of the 1568

edition Vasari himself says that Raphael became aware of Michelangelo's style only after the scaffolding was removed from the first half of the chapel. See C. Robertson, "Bramante, Michelangelo and the Sistine Ceiling," *Journal of the Warburg and Courtland Institutes* 49 (1986), 96, note 21.

8 Lucius Annaeus Seneca, "Epistle LXXXIV: On Gathering Ideas," in *Moral Epistles*, trans. R. M. Gummere, vol. II (Cambridge, MA: Harvard University Press, 1920), 276-283, and M. de Montaigne, "On educating children," in *Michel de Montaigne Essays*, book 1, chap. 26, trans. M. A. Screech (London: Penguin Classics, 2013), 54-69.

9 J. Swift, "The Battel of the Books," in J. Swift, *The Writings of Jonathan Swift*, ed. R. A. Greenberg and W. B. Piper (London and New York: Norton, 1973), 382-383.

10 See Robertson, "Bramante, Michelangelo and the Sistine Ceiling," 91-105. Robertson's argument, although substantially credible, is spoilt by his attribution to Bramante of the Argus in the Castello Sforzesco, now assigned to Bramantino by the majority of scholars. A summary of the story of the rediscovery of the *Argus* and the disputes over its attribution can be found in G. Agosti, J. Stroppa, and M. Tanzi, *Bramantino a Milano* (Milan: Officina Libraria, 2012), 110-121.

11 B. Cellini, "Trattato dell'Oreficeria," in *Opere di Castiglione, Della Casa, Cellini*, ed. C. Cordiè (Milan-Naples: Ricciardi, 1960), 1022. English ed., *The Treatises of Benvenuto Cellini on Goldsmithing and Sculpture*, trans. C. R. Ashbee (New York: Dover, 1967), 52. Cellini's opinion is backed by Condivi: "... he went to Rome, where Pope Julius wished to employ him, keeping still to his purpose of not going on with his tomb. It was put

into his head by Bramante and other rivals of Michael Angelo that he should make him paint the vault of the chapel of Sixtus the Fourth. ... This was done maliciously, to distract the Pope from works of sculpture." A. Condivi "Vita di Michelagnolo," in M. Buonarroti, *Le poesie e la vita* (Rome: Mancosu, 1993), 105-106. English trans. in C. Holroyd, *Michael Angelo Buonarroti* (New York: C. Scribner's Sons, 1903), 41.

12 G. Vasari, "Michelagnolo Buonarroti," in *Le vite de' più eccellenti pittori scultori e architettori*, 173. English ed., *The Life of Michelangelo*, trans. A. B. Hinds (Los Angeles: Getty Publications, 2018), 79.

13 It is worth summarizing some banal facts that convey an idea of what Julius II's papacy meant from the viewpoint of artistic production. Julius was pope for about ten years (1503-1513) and over this period commissioned the following: his unfinished sepulchral monument (of which remains, among other things, the Moses), the ceiling of the Sistine Chapel (1508-1512), Raphael's Stanze (at least the *Stanza della Segnatura* and the *Stanza di Eliodoro*, 1508-1514), the Belvedere, the Tribunali, and the new St. Peter's. There is no other example of patronage in the history of the figurative arts that—in such a short space of time and with so little money—has come anywhere near producing the results achieved by Julius.

14 The cost of the tomb was considerable. Michelangelo estimated it, with a degree of optimism, at 100,000 scudi. Condivi wrote: "The Pope asked him, 'What would be the cost of this?' Michael Angelo replied, 'One hundred thousand scudi.' 'Let it be two hundred thousand,' said Julius.'" Condivi, "Vita di Michelagnolo," 100. English trans. in Holroyd, *Michael Angelo Buonarroti*,

34. If we bear in mind that the annual expenditure on the construction of the new St. Peter's was estimated by Raphael at around 60,000 scudi, the economic impact of the tomb is clear.

15 The whole of Condivi's passage runs as follows: "When Michael Angelo had to paint the ceiling of the Sistine Chapel the Pope ordered Bramante to erect the scaffolding. For all the architect he was he did not know how to do it, but pierced the vault in many places, letting down certain ropes through these holes to sling the platform. When Michael Angelo saw it he smiled, and asked Bramante what was to be done when he came to those holes? Bramante had no defence to make, only replied that it could not be done any other way. The matter came before the Pope, and Bramante replied again to the same effect. The Pope turned to Michael Angelo and said: 'As it is not satisfactory go and do it yourself.' Michael Angelo took down the platform, and took away so much rope from it, that having given it to a poor man that assisted him, it enabled him to dower and marry two daughters. Michael Angelo erected his scaffold without ropes, so well devised and arranged that the more weight it had to bear the firmer it became. This opened Bramante's eyes, and gave him a lesson in the building of a platform, which was very useful to him in the works of St. Peter's." Condivi *Vita di Michelagnolo*, 142; English trans. in Holroyd, *Michael Angelo Buonarroti*, 82. Ackerman concluded from this and other stories that Bramante was "autocratic, self-willed, and reluctant to seek or to accept advice": J. S. Ackerman, "Notes on Bramante's Bad Reputation," in *Studi bramanteschi. Atti del Congresso internazionale. Milano-Urbino-Roma-1970* (Rome: De Luca,

1974), 349. And yet these character traits do not necessarily always go together. While undoubtedly autocratic, Bramante seems to have been decidedly capable of listening to the people around him and learning from them.

16 G. Vasari, "Bramante da Urbino," in *Le vite de' più eccellenti pittori scultori e architettori*, 162. English trans. by H. Evans.

17 The real Ronaldo, Luís Nazário de Lima.

18 Which was the period in which Vasari (1550 and then 1568) and Condivi (1553) wrote their biographies.

19 Vasari says "he told me on many occasions that he was just the executor of Bramante's design and arrangement, considering that those who first lay out a large building are its creators." Vasari, "Bramante da Urbino," 162–163. English trans. in the forthcoming *Bramante, an Introduction*. Michelangelo confirmed this judgment in his letters: "it cannot be denied that Bramante was as gifted in architecture as any other has been since antiquity. He laid the first stone of St. Peter's, not full of confusion, but clear and plain and luminous, and isolated around so that it could damage nothing of the building; and it was considered a beautiful thing as is still evident; so whoever strayed from the said order of Bramante, as Sangallo did, has strayed from the truth." Letter from Michelangelo to Bartollomeo Ferratino, late 1546 or early 1547, in *Il carteggio di Michelangelo*, vol. IV, ed. G. Poggi, P. Barocchi, R. Ristori (Florence: Sansoni, 1973), 251.

20 Bramante did not envisage facing the outer wall of St. Peter's with stone as Michelangelo would do. In Bramante's choir only the capitals and the frieze were made of travertine, while the walls and pilasters were simply made of brick, as can be seen from the view in the

Codex Coner (BAV, Coll. Ashby Nr. 329).
See P. N. Pagliara, "Una 'non imitanda
licentia' di Bramante nel dorico del coro
di S. Pietro," in *Architektur und Kunst
im Abendland*, ed. M. Jansen and K.
Winands (Rome: Herder, 1992), 83–89.
The overall effect of the mass of brick
would not have been very different from
that of Lutyens's design for the Catholic
cathedral in Liverpool (1930).

21 Michelangelo, letter to Rodolfo Pio da
Carpi (1557–1560?), in *Carteggio*, vol.
V, ed. Poggi, Barocchi, and Ristori
(Florence: Sansoni, 1983), 123.

37 Work is exhausting

22 The medal is usually attributed to
Caradosso after drawings by Bramante
and has been assigned directly to
Bramante by Luke Syson (L. Syson,
entry 33, in S. K. Scher, *The Currency of
Fame: Portrait Medals of the Renaissance*;
New York, 1994, 112–115). See too G.
F. Hill, *A Corpus of Italian Medals of
the Renaissance before Cellini*, Londra:
British Museum, 1930, p. 170; R.
Weiss, "The Medals of Pope Julius II
(1503–1513)," *Journal of the Warburg and
Courtauld Institutes* VVVIII (1965):
163–183; J. Freiberg, "Vasari's Bramante
and the Renaissance of Architecture
in Rome," in *Reading Vasari*, ed. A. B.
Barriault, A. Ladis, N. E. Land, and
J. M. Wood (Athens, GA-London: Philip
Wilson, 2005), 133–146; J. Freiberg,
"Bramante's Portrait Medal: Classical
Hero/Christian Architect," *Artibus
et Historiae*, 76 (2017): 145–155; and K.
Herrmann-Fiore, "Il tema "Labor" nella
creazione artistica del Rinascimento,"
in M. Winner, *Der Künstler über sich
in seinem Werk* (Weinheim: VCT Acta
humanoria, 1992).

23 See the entry in the catalogue compiled
by C. L. Frommel in H. Millon and V.
Magnago Lampugnani, *The Renaissance
from Brunelleschi to Michelangelo: The
Representation of Architecture* (Milan:
Bompiani, 1994), 602–603.

24 On a drawing for the exhibition *Some
Drawings for America* (Galleria AAM,
Rome, May 2–3, 1980), Aymonino had
written progettare è fatica ("designing
is hard work"), with three drops of blood
falling from the last *a* of *fatica*.

38 Public space

25 Public space is the first example
of *Öffentlichkeit* ("public sphere")
offered by Habermas in *The Structural
Transformation of the Public Sphere:
An Inquiry into a Category of Bourgeois
Society*, trans. T. Burger (Cambridge,
MA: MIT Press, 1991), 2. It is interesting
to note that, after this initial mention,
Habermas hardly speaks of it again,
as if to demonstrate how difficult it
is to comprehend public space on the
basis of the liberal assumptions that
characterize his analysis of the public
sphere. See too O. Negt and A. Kluge,
*Public Sphere of Experience: Analysis
of the Bourgeois and Proletarian Public
Sphere* (London: Verso, 2016).

26 The quote from W. R. Lethaby which
opens Lewis Mumford's *Sticks and
Stones* puts it very clearly: "Architecture,
properly understood, is civilization
itself." L. Mumford, *Sticks and Stones.
A Study of American Architecture and
Civilization* (New York: Boni and
Liveright, 1924), 5.

27 On architecture as act of
transformation see V. Gregotti, *Il
territorio dell'architettura* (Milan:
Feltrinelli, 1966).

39 Public architecture is abstract

28 *"Jà Bramante tinha observado este dualismo. Seu projeto para São Pedro, em Roma, ele o definiu a princípio como— quatro colunas—os quatros Apóstolos, que sustentavam uma cúpola—o céu. A cúpola é o projeto da comunidade (vive no céu); sustentam-na, permitam-me a imagen, não colunas mas Apóstolos. Assim, o que vem definindo a arquitectura na história—pelo menos a da civilização que nós chamamos de ocidental—é o projeto que a sociedade se impõe e que o construtor representa em um edifício."* J. B. Vilanova Artigas, *Arquitetura e comunicação* (1970), now in idem, *Caminhos da arquitetura* (São Paulo: Cosac Naify, 2004), 135. The essay is even more interesting if we consider that this reflection on the architecture of Western civilization was made in a postcolonial context and from the standpoint of a precise political commitment. It was in fact written in 1970, just after Artigas's return from exile in Uruguay. And it was on the basis of his experience as a modernist and communist architect in Brazil under the military dictatorship that Artigas proclaimed his allegiance to the project of European classicism.

29 G. Grassi, *Architectura, lingua morta / Architecture, dead language, Quaderni di Lotus* 9 (Milan: Electa/New York: Rizzoli, 1988).

30 C. Thoenes, "Vitruv, Alberti, Sangallo," in *Hülle und Fülle. Festschrift für Tilmann Buddensieg*, ed. A. Beyer, V. Lampugnani, and G. Schweikhart (Alfter: VDG, 1993), 71.

31 So it is not true that "a bicycle shed is a building; Lincoln Cathedral is a piece of architecture," as Pevsner claimed in his famous introduction to *An Outline of European Architecture* (London: Penguin, 1942), 10. The nymphaeum at Genazzano is architecture, Sant'Andrea alla via Flaminia is architecture, the flower stall in Malmo cemetery is architecture, the North Penn Visiting Nurse Association headquarters is architecture.

32 J. Stirling, "Correzioni alla pianta di Roma del Nolli (la soluzione MAF)," in G. Leonardi and G. C. Argan, *Roma Interrotta* (Rome: Officina, 1978), 83. Published in English as "Nolli Sector IV– James Stirling," *Architectural Design* 49, no. 3-4 (1979).

33 It is in this sense that we should understand Massimo Vignelli's only apparently optimistic slogan: "If you can design one thing, you can design everything."

34 On architecture's need for theory see too B. Hillier, *Space is the Machine: A Configurational Theory of Architecture* (Cambridge: Cambridge University Press, 1996), in particular 10-38.

35 English ed., Vitruvius, *Ten Books on Architecture*, trans. I. D. Rowland (Cambridge: Cambridge University Press, 1999), 21-32.

36 C. Aymonino, *Intervista sul mestiere di architetto a cura di R. Bonicalzi* (Pescara: CLUVA, 1980), 23.

37 On the distinction between environment (*Umwelt*) and world (*Welt*), see A. Gehlen, *Man: His Nature and Place in the World*, trans. C. McMillan and K. Pillemer (New York: Columbia University Press, 1987), in particular 24-31, 60-76, and 93-109.

40 Architecture as art

38 Guicciardini claims that Ludovico had poisoned his nephew Gian Galeazzo Maria. F. Guicciardini, *Storia d'Italia*, vol. I (Turin: Einaudi, 1971), ch. XIII,

92-93. On Ludovico, see too G. Benzoni, "Ludovico Sforza, detto il Moro, duca di Milano," in *Dizionario biografico degli italiani*, vol. 66 (Rome: Istituto dell'Enciclopedia Italiana, 2006). Julius II personally oversaw the siege of Mirandola (1510); on Julius, in addition to the sixth volume of von Pastor's *History of the Popes*, there is a horrible book by Ivan Cloulas, *Jules II. Le Pape Terrible* (Paris: Le Grand Livre du Mois/Fayard, 1989)—and an equally horrible one by Christine Shaw, *Julius II: The Warrior Pope* (Oxford: Oxford University Press, 1993).

39   D. Alighieri, "De vulgari eloquentia," I, VII, in idem, *Opere minori*, vol. I, *Vita nuova, De vulgari eloquentia, Rime, Ecloge* (Turin: UTET, 1983), 402. English ed., *Dante: De vulgari eloquentia*, ed. and trans. S. Botterill (Cambridge: Cambridge University Press, 1996), I, VII, 3-4.

40   Gayatri Spivak has conducted an interesting analysis of the different meanings of "representation" on the basis of the distinction between *vertreten* and *darstellen* in a passage of *The Eighteenth Brumaire* (K. Marx, *The Eighteenth Brumaire of Louis Bonaparte* [New York: International Publishers, 1963], VII, 118-137). See G. C. Spivak, "Can the Subaltern Speak?," in *Marxism and the Interpretation of Culture*, ed. C. Nelson and L. Grossberg (Chicago: University of Illinois Press, 1988), 271-313; later in G. C. Spivak, *A Critique of Post-Colonial Reason* (Cambridge, MA: Harvard University Press, 1999), 256-266.

41   As a form of institutionalization, architecture is always incredibly close to primitive accumulation. The most extraordinary expression of this relationship can perhaps be found in the relationship between Colonel Thomas Sutpen and his French architect in William Faulkner's novel *Absalom, Absalom!* (New York: Random House, 1936).

42   The phrase in reality is Samuel Johnson's. See "The Patriot. Addressed to the Electors of Great Britain," in S. Johnson, *The Major Works* (Oxford: Oxford University Press, 1984), 580-587. Kirk Douglas says it particularly well in Kubrick's *Paths of Glory* (1957).

43   A. Palladio, *I Quattro Libri dell'Architettura*, Libro IV (Venice, 1570), XVII, 64. English ed., *The Four Books of Architecture*, trans. I. Ware (New York: Dover, 1965), 276.

41 Demolishing St. Peter's

44   F. Milizia, "Bramante d'Urbino," in F. Milizia, *Vite de' più celebri Architetti d'ogni nazione e d'ogni tempo* (Rome: Paolo Giunchi Komarek, 1768), 183.

45   The history of the demolition and reconstruction of St. Peter's has been studied anew and largely redefined by Christof Thoenes. From his collaboration with Franz Wolff Metternich (F. Graf Wolff Metternich and C. Thoenes, *Die frühen St.-Peter-Entwürfe 1505-1514*, Tübingen: Wasmuth, 1987) to his latest works (C. Thoenes, "Elf Thesen zu Bramante und St. Peter," *Römisches Jahrbuch der Bibliotheca Hertziana* 41 (2013/14), 209-226) has come up with a series of hypotheses that allow to assign a precise meaning to the complex series of drawings and documents. All of my observations make reference to this extraordinary interpretative work.

46   F. Buonanni, *Numismata Summorum Pontificum Templi Vaticani Fabricam Indicantia* (Rome, 1696), 52, L. Thuasne,

Johannis Burchardi Argentinensis protonotarii capellae pontificiae sacrorum rituum magistri Diarium sive rerum urbanarum commentarium. 1483–1506, vol. III (Paris: Leroux, 1884), 422, and L. von Pastor, *The History of the Popes*, vol. VI, ed. and trans. F. I. Antrobus (London: Kegan Paul, 1901), 473–474.

47   F. Milizia, "Bramante d'Urbino," 184.

48   J. A. de Gobineau, *The Renaissance*, ed. O. Levy, trans. P. V. Cohn (London: Heinemann, 1913), 167.

49   "It is impossible to determine with certainty when Julius II adopted the plans for the new St. Peter's," declares von Pastor disconsolately in *The History of the Popes*, vol. VI, 462.

50   Vasari, "Bramante da Urbino," 161. English trans., "Bramante of Urbino," in the forthcoming *Bramante, an Introduction*.

51   "You were the trap. On your advice and through your misdeeds Julius was persuaded; on your direction and orders the workers pulled it down." A. Guarna, *Scimmia. Edizione emendata e corretta*, ed. G. Battisti (Rome: Istituto Grafico Tiberino, 1970), 104. English trans. in L. Pellecchia, "The Contested City: Urban Form in Early Sixteenth-Century Rome," in *The Cambridge Companion to Raphael*, ed. M. B. Hall (Cambridge-New York: Cambridge University Press, 2005), 63.

52   Already the fairly benign Sigismondo de' Conti could not help but observe that the building was very slow to rise and not for want of money ("*lenta enim admodum surgebat non inopia pecuniae*"). S. de' Conti da Foligno, *Le storie de' suoi tempi dal 1475 al 1510*, ed. C. Racioppi (Rome, 1883), Book XVI, vol. II, 344. For an account of the opinions of contemporaries, see H. Günther, "I progetti di ricostruzione della basilica di S. Pietro negli scritti dei contemporanei:

giustificazioni e scrupoli," in G. Spagnesi, *L'architettura della basilica di San Pietro, storia e costruzione. Atti del convegno internazionale di studi, Roma 7–10 novembre 1995*, Quaderni dell'Istituto di Storia dell'Architettura, new series, 1995–1997, nos. 25–30 (Rome: Bonsignori, 1997): 137–148.

53   Ascanio Condivi wrote that "one would sooner expect to see the end of the world than St. Peter's finished." A. Condivi, "Vita di Michelagnolo," 143. English trans. in Holroyd, *Michael Angelo Buonarroti*, 83.

54   Panvinio says that the cardinals were openly opposed to the demolition of St. Peter's: "This man [Bramante], meeting with the pope of his spontaneous initiative, gradually, with arguments that he made strongly, suggested to him that the construction of the building of the Vatican basilica should be worthy both of the magnificence of the pope's name and of the importance of such a great apostle, showing him sometimes the plans, at others drawings of that basilica, speaking often of these (the designs), and asserting that they would certainly have brought eternal glory to the Pontiff. The Pontiff, of great and noble mind, in which there was no place for minor things, always yearning after immense buildings, listened to the counsels of the excellent architect and decided to construct an exceptional new basilica, demolishing the old one. In this initiative he was opposed by almost everyone, and especially the cardinals; not because they did not wish the magnificent new basilica to be built, but because they were sorry to see the old one razed to the ground, venerated as it was all over the world, and so august in its tombs of saints, so renowned for the celebrated events that had taken place inside it. The Pontiff,

dogged in his conviction, had half of the old basilica destroyed to lay the foundations of the new construction." (O. Panvinio, *De rebus antiquis memorabilibus et praestantia basilicae Sancti Petri apostolorum principis Vaticanae*, Ms. Bibl. Vat., ca. 1563, cited in A. Mai, *Spicilegium Romanum*, vol. IX (Rome, 1839–1844), 365–366. It is interesting to note that all functionaries of the Curia extol the merits of Bramante as an architect in order to be able to assign him responsibilities that were (probably) not all his.

55 A trace of this discussion can be found in many passages of *De re aedificatoria* that advise against exaggerated undertakings and condemn the *libido aedificandi* or "lust for building": L. B. Alberti, *De re aedificatoria*, ed. G. Orlandi and P. Portoghesi (Milan: Il Polifilo, 1966), I, 9, 66; II, 2, 101; and III, 2, 66, 177.

56 C. Thoenes, "San Pietro. Storia e ricerca," in C. Thoenes, *Sostegno e adornamento. Saggi sull'architettura del Rinascimento: disegni, ordini, magnificenza* (Milan: Electa, 1998), 207.

57 G. Vasari, "Giuliano e Antonio da Sangallo," in *Le vite de' più eccellenti pittori scultori e architettori*, vol. IV, 282. English trans. by G. de Vere, "Giuliano and Antonio da Sangallo," in *Lives of the Painters, Sculptors and Architects*, vol. I (New York: Everyman Library, 1996), 704. Although the text contains considerable inaccuracies, as well as contradictions with respect to other passages by Vasari himself (Bramante was certainly in Rome prior to the election of Julius and it seems strange that his very young pupils should have been called on to guarantee the excellence of his design), this account does not seem to diverge greatly from the actual course of events, as is confirmed

by Condivi, "Vita di Michelagnolo," 100–101. English trans. in Holroyd, *Michael Angelo Buonarroti*, 34.

58 At the time the first stone was laid, Bramante was sixty-two, Julius sixty-three.

59 G. Vasari, "Bramante da Urbino, 163. English trans., "Bramante of Urbino," in the forthcoming *Bramante, an Introduction*.

60 "... In the meantime, contemplating the ruins and the buildings, which were multiplied by his [Julius II's] architect named Bramante, or rather Destroyer, as he was commonly called owing to the ruins and demolitions which had been perpetrated in Rome and everywhere because of him." The wholly incidental passage is part of a note on the visit made by Julius II to the Palazzo di Loreto. See L. Frati, *Le due spedizioni militari di Giulio II: tratte dal diario di Paride Grassi Bolognese* (Bologna: Regia Tipografia, 1886), 286.

61 H. Bredekamp, *Sankt Peter in Rom und das Prinzip der produktiven Zerstörung. Bau und Abbau von Bramante bis Bernini* (Berlin: Wagenbach, 2000), 9.

62 Size would be the principal rhetorical device of the new St. Peter's, as would emerge again from the curious book of records published in the nineteenth century by P. E. Visconti: *Metrologia Vaticana ossia ragguaglio delle dimensioni della meravigliosa Basilica di S. Pietro secondo le varie misure usate nelle diverse Città d'Italia e d'Europa* (Rome: Santarelli e Sella, 1828).

63 "Temple of the Prince of the Apostles / in the Vatican owing to age and the degraded / site from the foundations / restored by Julius from Liguria / Pontifex Maximus year 1506."

64 "[I]n cash or other things that can be converted to meet the needs of this

work." *Magnum Bullarium*, I, MDC.LV, 525, and B. J. Kidd, *Documents Illustrative of the Continental Reformation: The Bull Liquet omnibus of Julius II* (Oxford: Clarendon Press, 1911), 6.

65 "So that his [St. Peter's] basilica, which is in need of major restoration, among the other churches of the city and the world be rebuilt, constructed and enlarged with consonant and necessary structures, and once rebuilt, constructed and enlarged be preserved." *Magnum Bullarium*, I, MDC.LV, 525, and Kidd, *Documents Illustrative of the Continental Reformation*, 5. See too the letter of March 2, 1504 from the ambassador of Ferrara, Beltrando Constabili, to Cardinal Ippolito d'Este, quoted in S. B. Butters, "Figments and Fragments: Julius II's Rome," in *Rethinking the High Renaissance: The Culture of the Visual Arts in Early Sixteenth-Century Rome*, ed. J. Burke (Farnham: Ashgate, 2012), 78–80.

66 Already on January 6, 1506 the pope wrote to the English king: "Dearest King of England, God willing we have decreed that the basilica of the blessed Peter prince of the apostles in the city of Rome, extremely old and literally falling down, be rebuilt from the foundations and that it be adorned and restored with suitable works and with chapels and other necessary spaces. Since our and the Roman Church's revenues are extremely slight and meager ..." See von Pastor, *The History of the Popes*, vol. VI, app. 49a, 636–638.

67 J. W. O'Malley, "*De Aurea Aetate*. Fulfilment of the Christian Golden Age under Pope Julius II: text of a discourse of Giles of Viterbo, 1507," in *Traditio* 25 (1969): 265–338, and J. W. O'Malley, "The Discovery of America and Reform Thought at the Papal Court in the Early Cinquecento," in F. Chiappelli, *First Images of America: The Impact of the New World on the Old* (Berkeley, CA: University of California Press, 1976), 185–200.

68 See the research carried out by Ahmed Mater and published under the title *Desert of Pharan*: www.ahmedmater. com/desert-of-pharan.

69 ([T]o Pluto I will go, whom I know will do business.) Guarna, *Scimmia*, 118–121.

70 A potlatch is a ritual feast in which items of great social value are given away or destroyed in order to raise the status of those who give them up.

71 *Sometimes Making Something Leads to Nothing* was a performance carried out by Francis Alÿs in Mexico City in February 1997. The artist dragged a block of ice around the city for nine hours until it had completely melted.

72 C. Thoenes, "San Pietro come rovina. Note su alcune vedute di Maerten van Heemskerck," in idem, *Sostegno e adornamento. Saggi sull'architettura del Rinascimento: disegni, ordini, magnificenza* (Milan: Electa, 1998), 147. English trans. by H. Evans in the forthcoming *Bramante, an Introduction*. See too J. Sherman, "Il 'tiburio' di Bramante," in *Studi bramanteschi*, 567–573.

73 Desiderius Erasmus, *The Julius Exclusus*, trans. P. Pascal (Bloomington, IN: *Indiana* University Press, 1968).

74 P.: What Bramante?
A.: Our architect
P.: the destroyer of my temple?
A.: of more, of the city and of (all) the world, if he could.
(Guarna, *Scimmia*, 96)

42 Rebuilding St. Peter's

75 Sigismondo de' Conti di Foligno (1432–1512) was first "domestic" secretary (from September 1504)

and then "political" secretary (from April 1505) to Julius II (von Pastor, *The History of the Popes*, vol. VI). On his long diplomatic career and fairly lengthy literary production see the entry in the *Dizionario Biografico degli Italiani*, vol. 28 (Rome: Istituto dell'Enciclopedia Italiana, 1983).

76 At the end of the seventeenth century, Carlo Fontana calculated the costs of the church parametrically, arriving at the conclusion that it had cost 36,114,650 scudi (including Bernini's colonnade), with an additional 10,800,000 scudi for the works of art. (C. Fontana, *Templum Vaticanum et ipsius origo*; Rome: Giovanni Francesco Buagni, 1694, 432-434.) Jean Delumeau arrived at a much more moderate figure (one point five million without the colonnade): see J. Delumeau, *Vie économique et sociale de Rome dans la seconde moitié du XVIe siècle* (Paris: De Boccard, 1957-1959), vol. II, 763-768. If we consider that the annual income of the papal state (according to the Venetian ambassador cited by Delumeau) was around 400,000 scudi, the reconstruction of St. Peter's swallowed up approximately fifteen percent of the state's budget (being allocated, according to Raphael, around 60,000 scudi annually). Delumeau estimated that the total cost of rebuilding St. Peter's over the course of 120 years was more or less the same as what Clement VII spent on the siege of Florence in 1529-1530 (Delumeau, *Vita economica e sociale a Roma nel Cinquecento*, 203). See also C. Thoenes, "'Il Primo tempio del Mondo.' Raffaello, S. Pietro e il denaro," *Casabella*, no. 654 (1998): 59, notes 43-46.

77 Sigismondo's comments were made in 1512; the complete text is in Sigismondo de' Conti da Foligno, *Le storie de' suoi tempi*, book XVI, vol. II, 343-344). As already observed, St. Peter's dome is actually smaller the the Pantheon's. Anyhow, in the realized version, St. Peter's dome (diameter 42 m) would be slightly smaller than that of the Pantheon (diameter 44.3 m).

78 G. Vasari, "Bramante da Urbino," 161. English trans., "Bramante of Urbino," in the forthcoming *Bramante, an Introduction*.

79 Somehow, even Ruskin was right about this "titanic insanity": "the principal church in Italy was built with little idea of any other admirableness than that which was to result from its being huge." J. Ruskin, *The Stones of Venice*, vol. III (Boston: Aldine, 1890), 67.

80 B. Berenson, "A Word for Renaissance Churches," in idem, *The Study and Criticism of Italian Art: Second Series* (London: George Bell and Sons, 1902), 70.

81 Von Pastor, *The History of the Popes*, vol. VI, 476.

82 An attempt to come up with a theory of beauty, which might have been used to defend Julius's and Bramante's undertaking, was made by Hans Urs von Balthasar with his *The Glory of the Lord*, the monumental work of "theological aesthetics" written between 1961 and 1969 that set out to "to develop a Christian theology in the light of the third transcendental, that is to say: to contemplate the vision of the true and the good with that of the beautiful (*pulchrum*)." H. U. von Balthasar, *The Glory of the Lord: A Theological Aesthetics*, vol. 1: *Seeing the Form*, trans. E. Leiva-Merikakis (Edinburgh: T. & T. Clark, 1982), 9. Von Balthasar made beauty the foundation of his whole theory: "Beauty is the word that shall be our first" (p. 18). On the basis of this hypothesis,

Bramante's designs for St. Peter's can be seen as the investigation of a glorious form, a "luminous form of the beautiful" that is "before the sight of man" (p. 153), and triumphantly displays its "superabundant evidence" (p. 202). This is a production of form that is not carried out (as in all "modern" churches, whether Catholic or Protestant) from the viewpoint of someone seeking God, but from that of the God who has chosen to manifest himself. A God who does not remain beyond form, but has chosen to take on human form (p. 303), and who therefore also has a bodily, earthly manifestation. In this sense the *form* of the building dedicated to worship corresponds to the *form* of coexistence of the community that accepts the *form* adopted by God to manifest himself. Thus Bramante's St. Peter's would become the church of *the whole Church*, the church conceived not from the viewpoint of the individual believer, but from that of the whole community of believers seen as a totality—from "the point of view of totality," to borrow the words, marvelously out of place here, of Lukács in *History and Class Consciousness*, trans. R. Livingstone (London: Merlin Press, 1967), 27. And the fact that Julius and Bramante seem to have so little credibility as Christians, from this perspective so utterly free of any moralism, would not appear to be much of a problem, seeing that the *form* is in fact a possible, accessible, form, one that can be produced in the world, because "we should be permitted to speak of Christian beauty even here below" (von Balthasar, *Seeing the Form*, 659).

83   See for example the *Istitutiones* published by St. Charles Borromeo in 1577. See C. Borromeo, *Instructiones Fabricae et Supellectilis Ecclesiasticae*

Libri II, https://www.memofonte.it/home/files/pdf/scritti_borromeo.pdf.

84   Berenson, "A Word for Renaissance Churches," 71. However, St. Peter's is not the pope's private chapel.

85   See M. Trachtenberg, *Building-in-Time: From Giotto to Alberti and Modern Oblivion* (New Haven: Yale University Press, 2010) and H. Burns, "Building Against Time: Renaissance Strategies to Secure Large Churches Against Changes in Their Design," in J. Guillaume, *L'Église dans l'architecture de la Renaissance* (Paris: Éditions Picard, 1995).

86   On the correspondingly archaic attitude of Columbus (who wanted to reach the Orient by crossing the Atlantic in order to plunder it and use the resources to fund a new crusade), see Tzvetan Todorov's fine analysis in *The Conquest of America: The Question of the Other*, trans. R. Howard (New York: Harper & Row, 1982), in particular 14–50. On the *cosmopolitan* and *anational* (and therefore anachronistic) nature of the Italian Renaissance see too A. Gramsci, *Quaderni del carcere* (Turin: Einaudi, 1975), 401, 891–893, 1129–1130, 1293–1294, 1908–1914, 2350.

87   T. Hobbes, *Leviathan or the Matter, Forme and Power of a Commonwealth Ecclesiasticall and Civil* (Oxford: Blackwell, 1946), 458–459.

88   On the slow process that led the popes of the fifteenth and sixteenth century to turn their possessions into a true State of the Church see the important book by P. Prodi, *Il sovrano pontefice* (Bologna: Il Mulino, 1982). Prodi notes that on the eve of the Reformation this state appeared to the leaders of the Church themselves to be "a many-headed 'monster,' that neither theological nor political consideration was able to classify." Julius II seems to have been instinctively

aware of the contradictory requirements of this fatally schizophrenic political-theological creature and to have consciously kept his image politics (of which the demolition and reconstruction of St. Peter's was the principal aspect) separated from his *realpolitik*. In this, too, Julius proved to be both profoundly innovative and obstinately archaic, at once committed to the ruthless construction of a modern state (monetary and fiscal rationalization, reorganization and concentration of the law courts) and fiercely loyal to the Church as an international institution.

89 J. Burckhardt, *The Civilization of the Renaissance in Italy*, trans. S. G. C. Middlemore (New York: Macmillan, 1921), 72.

90 In *The Agony and the Ecstasy*, "Bramante" mentions two thousand men at work on the foundations. The source for this was probably von Pastor, who has Julius say—with a smile—that Bramante had told him there were two thousand five hundred (von Pastor, *The History of the Popes*, vol. VI, 475). But Bramante could only dream of two thousand workers in a Hollywood movie. In reality, even on the busiest days, there were never more than two hundred people at work on St. Peter's. See C. Thoenes, Bramante e la "bella maniera degli antichi," in C. Thoenes, *Sostegno e adornamento. Saggi sull'architettura del Rinascimento: disegni, ordini, magnificenza* (Milan: Electa, 1998), 62. Trans. into English by H. Evans in the forthcoming *Bramante, an Introduction*. On the architects of ancient Rome, see too W. L. MacDonald, "Roman Architects," in *The Architect. Chapters in the History of the Profession*, ed. S. Kostof (Oxford: Oxford University Press, 1977), 28–58.

91 Scott has stressed that Renaissance classicism could not find itself in "any rigid discipline or imposed continuity such as that which, later, in the France of Louis XIV, gave to architecture a formal and restricted aim." Renaissance classicism "needed the patronage of a large idea, but it required also space and scope, that it might attempt every mode of self-realisation yet stand committed to none." G. Scott, *The Architecture of Humanism* (New York: Norton, 1974), 30.

92 C. Schmitt, *Roman Catholicism and Political Form*, trans. G. L. Ulmen (Westport, CT: Greenwood Press, 1996), 19.

93 C. S. Singleton, "The Perspective of Art," *Kenyon Review* 15, no. 2 (1953): 169–189. See too C. Ginzburg, *Nondimanco. Machiavelli, Pascal* (Milan: Adelphi, 2018), 37.

94 M. Tafuri, "*Cives esse non licere*: La Roma di Nicolò V e Leon Battista Alberti: Elementi per una revisione storiografica," introduction to the Italian edition of C. W. Westfall's *This Most Perfect Paradise: Alberti Nicholas V and the Invention of Conscious Urban Planning in Rome, L'invenzione della città: La strategia urbana di Nicolò V e Alberti nella Roma del '400* (Rome: NIS, 1984,) 36. The essay was published in a revised version, which does not contain the cited passage, in M. Tafuri, *Ricerca del Rinascimento* (Turin: Einaudi, 1992), 33–84. English ed. *Interpreting the Renaissance: Princes, Cities, Architects* (New Haven, CN: Yale University Press, 2006), 23–58. Tafuri offers Alberti an ethical let-out from co-responsibility in Nicholas V's "plan": "the clarity of the pope's intentions" did not contaminate fully "the deeply-felt ambiguities of the man of culture." Here, as in novels written at high school, clarity is all on the

side of political power and deep feelings on the side of the man of culture.

95 Von Pastor, with perhaps even an excess of generosity, went so far as to write: "the magnificent basilica would be a glory for the whole Church. For Julius the larger aim, whether for State or for Church, was always more attractive than anything that was merely personal." Von Pastor, *The History of the Popes*, vol. VI, 464.

96 The sad fate of the Italian Renaissance is the subject of a recent book by Alberto Asor Rosa, *Machiavelli e l'Italia* (Turin: Einaudi, 2019). The book is a bit plaintive and verging on the jingoistic, but the problem that it raises is undoubtedly a decisive one. The culture of the Renaissance was not in fact a prologue that would lead smoothly to modernity (whose "ideological content" was then developed "outside Italy," in Gramsci's words). Renaissance culture was also and above all defeated before it was possible to move on to modernity. In this respect Hiram Haydn's old and perhaps crude, but unjustly discredited book on the "Counter-Renaissance" remains interesting: H. Haydn, *The Counter-Renaissance* (New York: Grove Press, 1950).

97 I do not think it possible to explain the demolition and reconstruction of St. Peter's entirely in terms of a courtly ethic of liberality and splendor in the way that Baldassarre Castiglione does in chapter 36 of the *Cortegiano*. At St. Peter's something more was afoot than the need "to give magnificent banquets, festivals, games, public shows; to have a great number of excellent horses ... to erect great buildings, both to win honour in his lifetime and to give a memorial of himself to posterity." B. Castiglione, "Il libro del cortegiano," in *Opere di Baldassare Castiglione,*

Giovanni Della Casa, Benvenuto Cellini (Naples: Ricciardi, 1960), 321–322. English ed., *The Book of the Courtier by Count Baldesar Castiglione*, trans. L. E. Opdycke (New York: Charles Scribner's Sons, 1903), 274.

98 "*Die Götter wollten nicht, dass er die Verse fertigstelle, sie wollten nicht, dass er der Verse Unstimmigkeit behebe, denn alles Menschenwerk muss aus Dämmerung und aus Blindheit entstehen, also in Unstimmigkeit verbleiben; dies ist der Götter Ratschluss. Und trotzdem, nun wusste er es: nicht nur Fluch, sondern auch Gnade ist in dieser Unstimmigkeit gegeben, nicht nur des Menschen Unzulänglichkeit, sondern auch seine Gottesnähe, nicht nur die Unfertigkeit der menschlichen Seele, sondern auch ihre Grösse, nicht nur die Blindheit des aus Blindheit geborenen Menschenwerkes, sondern auch seine Ahnungskraft, ohne deren blinde Schau es ja überhaupt nicht geschaffen worden wäre, da es—und in jedem Werk steckt der Keim hiezu—über sich selbst und den, der es geschaffen hat, weit hinausreichend, den Schaffende zum Schöpfer macht: denn all die All-Unstimmigkeit des Geschehens setzt erst ein, wenn der Mensch im All wirksam wird—weder im Geschehen des Gottes noch in dem des Tieres gibt es Unstimmigkeit—, erst in der Unstimmigkeit enthüllt sich die fruchtbare Herrlichkeit des menschlichen Loses, das ein Hinausgreifen über sich selber ist: zwischen der Stummheit des Tieres und der des Gottes steht das menschliche Wort, harrend, dass es selber in Verzückung erschweige, überstrahlt vom Auge, dessen Blindheit verzückt sehend geworden ist: verzückte Blindheit, die Nicht-Vergeblichkeit.*" H. Broch, *Der Tod des Vergils* (Frankfurt am Main: Suhrkamp, 1976), 407-408.

English ed., *The Death of Virgil*, trans.
J. S. Untermeyer (London: Routledge &
Kegan Paul, 1946), 431.

43 Ninety-five theses

99 All the "hard work of pruning the great
Oak" (G. Giovannoni, "Tra la cupola
di Bramante e quella di Michelangelo,"
in idem, *Saggi sull'architettura del
Rinascimento*; Milan: Treves, 1931, 173)
done by Michelangelo for St. Peter's
was a sort of compensation for this
unwarranted invasion. The problem
Michelangelo faced with St. Peter's
was to finish a church on which work
should never have begun. It was a
matter of finishing it quickly, of putting
right a mistake. Artistic research
was blatantly subordinated to higher
needs. Justifying his refusal to return
to Florence, Michelangelo wrote to
Lionardo Buonarroti that his position
as architect of St. Peter's was a mission
directly inspired by God: "I have always
intended ... not to leave from here
without first completing the construction
of St. Peter's so that my composition
cannot be spoilt or changed, and so as
not to give the opportunity to thieves to
return there to steal as they used and
are still waiting to do: and I have always
used and use this diligence, for many
believe—and I believe—that I have been
designated for this work by God." (Letter
from Michelangelo to Lionardo, Rome,
July 1, 1557, in *Carteggio*, vol. V, ed. Poggi,
Barocchi, and Ristori, 100–112). The
subject crops up again in many letters:
see for example the one dated September
19, 1554, to Giorgio Vasari: "But if I
left here now, I would be the cause of
the total ruin of the construction of St.
Peter's, which would be a great shame

and a very great sin." Michelangelo,
letter to Giorgio Vasari, September 19,
1554, in *Carteggio*, vol. V, 21. Translated
into English by A. Mortimer, "Letter
57," in Michelangelo, *Poems and Letters*
(London: Penguin, 2007). See too R. De
Maio, *Michelangelo e la Controriforma*
(Rome-Bari: Laterza, 1978).

100 In the incredible plate 2, added in 1813 to
the first part of his *Précis*, Jean-Nicolas-
Louis Durand read the story of St. Peter's
in this way, seeing the church as an
"example of the disastrous consequences
that stem from an ignorance of the true
principles of architecture or from the
failure to observe them" and proposing a
dramatic comparison between the plan
of St. Peter's ("Basilica of St. Peter's in
Rome. This building cost more than three
hundred and fifty million of the time")
and a counterproposal drawn up specially
for the purpose ("Plan whose adoption
would have spared three-quarters
of Europe centuries of calamities").
Without questioning the moral merits
that Durand assigns to his proposal,
it has to be said that it is a design of
exceptional ugliness. It should also be
noted that, for a reason which escapes
me, the two drawings are separated by a
diagrammatic exposition of the method
of orthogonal projection applied to the
case of a small house on a square plan.
See J. N. L. Durand, *Précis des leçons
d'architecture données à l'ècole royale
polytechnique* (Paris: Didot, 1819), Part I,
plate 2. There is an edition in English, but
it does not include the plate in question:
*Précis of the Lectures on Architecture:
With Graphic Portion of the Lectures on
Architecture*, trans. D. Britt (Los Angeles:
Getty Research Institute, 2000).

101 Berenson, "A Word for Renaissance
Churches," 74.

102 Whether Luther really did nail the

theses (*Disputatio pro declaratione virtutis indulgentiarum*, or the *Disputation on the Power and Efficacy of Indulgences*) to the door of the church is debatable. Since it is not particularly relevant to our argument, and since it is nice to think that he did, let's assume that's how it went. The text of the theses is in M. Luther, *Werke*, 73 vols. (Weimar: Weimarer Ausgabe 1883-2009), vol. I, 233-237. An English translation can be found at https://www.luther.de/en/95thesen.html.

103 Luther had probably seen St. Peter's under construction when he visited Rome in the winter of 1510-1511.

104 An attempt—highly unsuccessful and for this very reason moving—to reconcile his Lutheran faith with his boundless admiration for Bramante's architecture was made by Geymüller in the book on which he was working at the end of his life and which was published posthumously in 1911 (H. von Geymüller, *Architektur und Religion. Gedanken über religiöse Wirkung der Architektur,* Basel: Kober, 1911). In it Geymüller retraces the entire history of architecture, obsessively returning to Bramante and St. Peter's in relation to every epoch and civilization, from temples at Angkor Wat to the great mosque of Delhi.

INDEX

Axonometry, 236n12
Aymonino, Carlo, 255n24, 256n36

Bachmann, Ingeborg, 73, 229n27
Balthasar, Hans Urs von, 261n82
Bandello, Matteo, 237n19
Baroni, Constantino, 112, 131, 211n18, 240n38, 245n8
Barrel vaults, 135
Basilica of Maxentius, 14, 25-27, 65, *66*, 139, 216n62
Basilica of Saint Francis of Assisi, 82
Basilica of Sant'Ambrogio, 224n47
Battagio, Giovanni, 163
Battle between Heraclius and Khosrow (Piero della Francesca), 79
baukuh, XV, 209n18
Baxandall, Michael, 221n29, 232n23, 246n22
Beauty
    Bramante's architecture, 124, 127
    Catholic theories of, 261n82
    conquest of, 124-127
    St. Peter's demolition and reconstruction, 190-193, 196, 200, 202, 204, 261n82
Beethoven, Ludwig van, 142
Bella maniera degli antichi, 10, 60, 183, 212n26
Bellini, Giovanni, 44
Bellomo, Saverio, 233n29
Bellosi, Luciano, 101, 232n22
The Belvedere. *See* Cortile del Belvedere
Bembo, Pietro, 27, 216n63
Berenson, Bernard, 231n12, 239n29, 261n80, 262n84, 266n101
Bernini, Gian Lorenzo, 23, 64, 198, 228n20, 261n76
Bertolini, Lucia, 221n30
Bettinelli, Saverio, 87-89
Biblioteca Laurenziana, 44
Bonelli, Renato
    on Bramante
        change in style, 7
        illiterate *versus* intellectual, 221n34
        Santa Maria presso San Satiro, 147
        St. Peter's plan, 139

Da Bramante a Michelangelo, XII
    universal language, 31
Borromini, Francesco, 64, 252n4
Boullée, Etienne Louis, 155, 250n53
Bourdieu, Pierre, 238n20
Bramante, Donato. *See also* Bramante's architecture; Rome, Bramante in
    ambition, 54, 224n58
    career, 112, 118
    celebrations of, XII, 208n13
    character, 101-102, 254n15
    criticality, 101-102, 105-106, 237n17
    cultural politics, 167
    death, 223n40, 241n46
    education, 41-42, 78, 221n32, 221n34, 230n5, 239n31
    intellectualism, 101, 110, 221nn33-34, 238n20
    legacy, X
    as *ligéra* (vagabond), 97, 236n7
    name, 240n44
    portraits, 90, 235n45
    practicality, 112
    reputation, 115, 241n45
    Roman period, XII, 3-9
Bramante d'Urbino (Milizia), 184
Bramante's architecture
    arrogance and modesty, 110
    audience for, 117, 241n52
    derivative character, 20
    distance from the present, 60
    influence, 61-64
    large scale, 121, 242n59
    plans, 129, *130*, *133*, 244n1
    realist style, 14
    repertoires, 50-51
    theory, 42
    traditional knowledge, 50
Brandi, Cesare, 219n13
Bredekamp, Horst, 188
Broch, Hermann, 200-201
Brown, Denise Scott, 220n23
Brunelleschi, Filippo
    and humanism, 41
    impact, 117

Dolcebuono, Gian Giacomo, 163
Donatello, 41
Doni, Anton Francesco, 250n49
Don Quixote, X, 65, 227n13
Doric order, 16–17, 32, 35, 48, 56, 107, 117, 181, 223n46, 241n57
Duck, 36–38, 220n23
Durand, Jean-Nicols-Louis, 265n100
Duration, 62, 67–68

Eclecticism, 52–53, 224n56
Eco, Umberto, 217n6, 250n54
Eliot, Thomas Stearns, 49, 208n10
Environment *versus* world (as in Gehlen), 179–180
Epistle to Cangrande, 88, 233n29
Erasmus, 216n64
The Erechtheion, 33
Eyck, Jan van, 83

Fabian, Johannes, 225n62
Faulkner, William, 257n41
Fear and intimidation, 125, 244n73
Fedeli, Matteo, 238n25
Figure, regularity and improbability, 151
Fischli, Peter, *164*
Flagellation (Bramante), 101, 237n18
Fontana, Carlo, 261n76
Fontana, Domenico, 240n40
Foppa, Cristoforo Caradosso. *See* Caradosso's medal
Form
    as compromise, 70
    content, 17
    and function, 71–72
    geometric, 151, 153–154
    historical contexts, 111
    immediacy, 153, 155, 250n51
    and life, 181
    logical equivalency, 16, 50
    regular, 151, 153, 250n50
    risk, 61, 227n7
    Roman, 8–12, 212n20
    systematization, 31

universalism, 48–49
    Wittgenstein's definition, 69, 229n21
Formalism, 22
Förster, Otto, *152*
Fortuna, 172
Forty, Adrian, 218n9
Foscolo, Ugo, 125
Foucault, Michel, 244n73
Fra Carnevale, 78, 221n32, 230n5
Fregoso, Antonio, 234n42
Frommel, Christoph Luitpold, 172, 211n15, 242n61
Fubini, Riccardo, 210n6
Functionalism, 71–72, 229n25

Geers, Kersten, XIV
Gehlen, Arnold, 151, 250n50
Genazzano, 112, 256n31
Geymüller, Heinrich von
    Architektur und Religion, 266n104
    Bramante's importance, 224n58
    Bramante studies, XII
    Prevedari Engraving, 239n28
    St. Peter's, *141*, 201
    on Vasari's "Life of Bramante," 236n1
    voids, 207n7
Giedion, Siegfried, 228n19
Gilbert, Creighton, 209n3, 216n61, 243n65
Giles of Viterbo, 54, 189, 225nn60–61, 260n67
Ginzburg, Carlo, 233n29, 263n93
Giontella, Massimo, 210n6
Giotto di Bondone
    Annunciation to Saint Anne, 83–85
    and Dante, 85–86, 232nn20–21
    gesture painting, 82–83, 231n14
    influence, 80
    Legend of Saint Francis, 82, 232n16
    political mode, 87
    Scenes from the Story of Isaac, 232n19
    Scrovegni Chapel *cubicles*, 148–150
    spatial research, 82–83
Giovannoni, Gustavo, 230n4, 252n2
Giuliano da Sangallo, 213n31
    architectural attitude, 42, 132

Acknowledgments

Renzo, Silvana, and Alberto; Franco; George; Victoria, Delfina, and Antonio.

Jason Begy, Huw Evans, Pamela Johnston, Francesca Pellicciari, Ilaria Pittassi, Bas Princen, Thomas Weaver.

Marta Allegrina, Stanley T. Allen, Paul Andersen, Matteo Ardente, Pier Vittorio Aureli, Ido Avissar, Fabrizio Ballabio, Francesca Benedetto, Fabrizia Berlingieri, Marco Biraghi, Stefano Boeri, Gianfranco Bombaci, Michele Bonino, Massimo Bricocoli, Antonio Buonsante, Massimiliano Bussetti, Chiara Carpenter, Paolo Carpi, Matilde Cassani, Filippo Cattapan, Ludovico Centis, Joachim Declerck, Giacomo Donati, Emanuel Christ, Asli Cicek, Jean-Louis Cohen, Matteo Costanzo, Cynthia Davidson, Massimo De Carlo, Marco De Michelis, Ambra Fabi, Fredi Fischli, Peter Fischli, Giancarlo Floridi, Léa Fluck, Salomon Frausto, Gabinetto Disegni e Stampe - Gallerie degli Uffizi, Giulio Galasso, Fabrizio Gallanti, Christoph Gantenbein, Roberto Gargiani, Cloé Gattigo, Chris Garofalo, Douglas A. Garofalo Fellowship, Francesco Garofalo, Kersten Geers, Grant Gibson, Hannes Grassegger, Stefano Graziani, K. Michael Hays, Raphael Hefti, Sarah Herda, Sam Jacob, Sharon Johnston, Thomas Kelley, Djamel Klouche, Wilfried Kuehn, Eric Lapierre, Quinn Latimer, Lorenzo Laura, Mark Lee, Alexander Lehnerer, Francesco Librizzi, Angelo Lunati, Silvia Lupi, Oliver Lütjens, Vittorio Magnago Lampugnani, Camillo Magni, Simona Malvezzi, Michele Marchetti, Federico Masin, Michael Meredith, Agata Mierzwa, Vedran Mimica, Carles Muro, Alexa Nürnberger, Carlo Olmo, Manuel Orazi, Nicolò Ornaghi, Lluis Ortega, Thomas Padmanabahn, Gabriele Pasqui, Maria Chiara Pastore, Silvia Piombo, Giovanni Piovene, Daniele Pisani, Eleonora Pistis, Vittorio Pizzigoni, Josef Ploder, Paolo Portoghesi, Caroline Poulin, Paul Preissner, Giacomo Raffo, Pietro Salamone, Irénée Scalbert, Paola Scaramuzza, Valter Scelsi, Adam Sherman, Giovanna Silva, Jorge Silvetti, Martin Sobota, Robert E. Somol, Martino Stierli, Giacomo Summa, Martino Tattara, Guido Tesio, Oliver Thill, Jacopo Tondelli, Milica Topalovic, Francesca Torzo, Ilaria Valente, David van Severen, Federica Verona, Stanislaus von Moos, Sarah M. Whiting, Ellis Woodman, Guillaume Yersin, Vitale Zanchettin, Andrea Zanderigo, Elia Zenghelis, Francesco Zorzi, Cino Zucchi.

This book was set in Lyon Typeface (Kai Bernau)
Designed by pupilla grafik
Printed and bound in Italy by Longo (Bolzano)

Library of Congress Cataloging-in-Publication Data
Names: Tamburelli, Pier Paolo, author. | Princen,
Bas, photographer (expression)
Title: On Bramante / Pier Paolo Tamburelli;
with photographs by Bas Princen.
Translated by Huw Evans
Description: [Cambridge]: Massachusetts Institute
of Technology, [2022] | Includes bibliographical
references and index.
Identifiers: LCCN 2021010582 |
ISBN 9780262543422 (hardcover)
Subjects: LCSH: Bramante, Donato,
1444?–1514—Criticism and interpretation.
Classification: LCC NA1123.B7 T36 2022 |
DDC 720.92—dc23
LC record available at https://lccn.loc
.gov/2021010582

10 9 8 7 6 5 4 3 2 1

Basilica of Maxentius, Rome,
308–312 CE, exterior from via dei Fori Imperiali.

Sanctuary of Fortuna, Palestrina,
second century BCE, intermediate ramps.

Donato Bramante,
Tempietto of San Pietro in Montorio, Rome,
ca. 1502–1508, exterior and courtyard.

Donato Bramante,
Tempietto of San Pietro in Montorio, Rome,
ca. 1502–1508, exterior detail.

Donato Bramante,
Tempietto of San Pietro in Montorio, Rome,
ca. 1502–1508, interior detail.

Donato Bramante,
Cloister of Santa Maria della Pace, Rome,
ca. 1500–1504, detail of the upper order.

Donato Bramante, Giovanni Antonio Amadeo,
Santa Maria delle Grazie, Milan,
ca. 1492–1499, detail of the crossing.

Donato Bramante, Giovanni Antonio Amadeo,
Santa Maria delle Grazie, Milan,
ca. 1492–1499, south apse.

Donato Bramante, Giovanni Antonio Amadeo,
Santa Maria delle Grazie, Milan,
ca. 1492–1499, north apse.

Donato Bramante,
Piazza Ducale, Vigevano,
ca. 1492–1494, western gate from via del Popolo.

Donato Bramante,
Piazza Ducale, Vigevano,
ca. 1492–1494, western gate from the square.

Perin del Vaga,
Belvedere Courtyard with Naumachia,
Castel Sant'Angelo, Rome,
ca. 1545–1547

Donato Bramante,
Belvedere courtyard, Rome,
ca. 1504–1508, view from St. Peter's dome.

Donato Bramante, Raphael, Fra Giocondo, Antonio da Sangallo,
Baldassarre Peruzzi, Michelangelo, Carlo Maderno, Gian
Lorenzo Bernini and others,
St. Peter's, Rome,
1506–1626, interior view with main crossing and baldachin.

Donato Bramante, Raphael, Fra Giocondo, Antonio da Sangallo,
Baldassarre Peruzzi, Michelangelo, Carlo Maderno, Gian
Lorenzo Bernini and others,
St. Peter's, Rome,
1506–1626, interior view with main crossing and baldachin.

Donato Bramante, Raphael, Fra Giocondo, Antonio da Sangallo,
Baldassarre Peruzzi, Michelangelo, Giacomo della Porta, Carlo
Maderno and others,
St. Peter's, Rome,
1506–1626, view from via Piccolomini.